WORLD ENOUGH AND TIME

THE LIFE OF ANDREW MARVELL

By the same author

BRUCE CHATWIN
PLAUSIBLE FICTIONS (poetry)
A LIFE OF MATTHEW ARNOLD
AFTER ARNOLD: CULTURE AND ACCESSIBILITY

WORLD ENOUGH AND TIME

THE LIFE OF ANDREW MARVELL

Nicholas Murray

LITTLE, BROWN AND COMPANY

A *Little, Brown* Book

First published in Great Britain in 1999
by Little, Brown and Company

A CIP catalogue record for this book
is available from the British Library.

ISBN 0 316 64863 9

Typeset by Palimpsest Book Production Limited,
Polmont, Stirlingshire
Printed and bound in Great Britain by
Clays Ltd, St Ives plc

Little, Brown and Company (UK)
Brettenham House
Lancaster Place
London WC2E 7EN

For S.

My vegetable Love should grow
Vaster then Empires, and more slow.

Marvell, therefore, more a man of the century than a Puritan, speaks more clearly and unequivocally with the voice of his literary age than does Milton.

T.S. Eliot

Contents

Prologue

He walked in the funeral procession of Oliver Cromwell, guiding the steps of the blind poet, Milton, along the Strand, yet he would later sit in the Restoration Parliament and declare of the English Civil War: 'The Cause was too good to have been fought for.' He wrote one of the finest and most subtle political poems in the English language, ostensibly in praise of Cromwell the political strongman, but most memorable for its compassionate gesture towards the executed King Charles I. He worked as a civil servant for the English Republic, and was friendly with the leading revolutionary Puritans of his time, yet he wrote pamphlets at the Restoration, at least one of which gave pleasure to King Charles II.

For some, there is too much smoothness in these transitions. They seem to hint at opportunism. The truth, perhaps, is that he was, in T.S. Eliot's phrase, 'a lukewarm partisan', consistent in his support for the Good Old Cause, but not as committed a fundamentalist as his friend John Milton. He was something of a fatalist who wrote: ''Tis Madness to resist or blame/The force of angry Heavens flame.' His early lyric poems – in their obliquity, their vulnerable tenderness, their search for some sense of balance or perspective – to some degree embody the fractured consciousness of his time, a revolutionary period in English history that saw another of those decisive moments in the transition from feudalism to modern bourgeois democracy. Drawn towards solitude and the reflective life, he could not ignore the divided society around him, its tensions and conflicts, its calls to public duty. His strangely complex poetic conceits make him one of the more politically interesting, edgy and wholly distinctive poets of the seventeenth-century school labelled the Metaphysicals. The poet Gerard Manley Hopkins called him 'a most rich and nervous poet'. It was Marvell's gift to find an aesthetic counterpoint to the troubled society history had placed him in.

And yet he was so often absent. During the great upheaval of the Civil

War he was abroad on a Grand Tour. His life contains many passages of enigma. There are occasional periods of darkness in the record. There is the hint of mystery and intrigue. He remains always a contradiction. He was a Puritan and a sensualist, a private and a public man, a cool and detached lover of solitude and reserve yet passionate in religious and political polemic, an apparent treader of the *via media* who could be quick-tempered and angry on the floor of the House of Commons. He was a champion of political liberty and religious toleration who was in the grip of a virulent anti-Catholicism. He was a love poet of great tenderness and delicacy yet, in the words of one of his early biographers: 'He had no wife, and his gallantries are not known.' He was a celebrant of childhood innocence who was himself childless. He wrote some of the most exquisitely crafted and formally perfect poems in English yet penned many coarse satires that occasionally descend to the level of slapstick.

The only reliable portrait we possess of Andrew Marvell turns out to be a disappointment. This graceful, witty, complex artist looks out from the heavy frame in the National Portrait Gallery with the plump cheeks and cold demeanour of a discountenanced pork butcher. Scholars have doubted whether even this painting, by an anonymous artist, is genuine. At all points Marvell resists attempts to pin him down.

Marvell's current reputation was largely formed in the twentieth century. None of the poems for which he is best known was published in his lifetime. None survives in his own manuscript. In his day he was known as a satirist and a pamphleteer, a champion of political liberty and religious toleration, an incorruptible patriot. This image persisted (with embellishments) throughout the eighteenth century, which had little taste for the Metaphysical style, considering it fantastic and lacking in true poetic decorum. Slowly, the lyric poetry of Marvell made headway in the nineteenth century. A few poems (but not 'To his Coy Mistress') found their way into that defining anthology of Victorian taste, Palgrave's *Golden Treasury*, in 1861. Tennyson was said to have walked up and down declaiming: 'But at my back I alwaies hear/Time's winged Charriot hurrying near.' Charles Lamb praised Marvell's 'witty delicacy'. But it was not until the early twentieth century that Marvell was finally launched into his current eminence.

In 1921, a seminal essay by T.S. Eliot – then enjoying an almost papal critical authority – declared that Marvell speaks in his poetry 'more clearly and unequivocally with the voice of his literary age than does Milton'. He praised Marvell's distinctive quality of Metaphysical wit: 'a tough reasonableness beneath the slight lyric grace'. In the same year he published his essay on 'The Metaphysical Poets' with its famous (though not unchallenged) theory, possibly purloined from William Hazlitt,[1] of 'the dissociation of sensibility', that fatal separation of thought and feeling whose origins Eliot traced to the seventeenth century in the wake of John Donne, for whom a thought 'was an experience; it modified his sensibility'. A revolution in poetic taste was complete. Perhaps a generation recovering from the profound national trauma of the Great War could finally warm to a poetic sensibility forged out of a similar collective psychic upheaval where fracture and conflict could be explored, if not resolved, aesthetically. After this, it was left to the burghers of Hull, Marvell's native town, to celebrate his tercentenary the same year with a fleet of municipal trams decorated with Marvellian livery.

If criticism has taken to Marvell with great energy, biography has lagged behind. Apart from a few brief passages by his contemporaries, the first lives were those of his early editors in the eighteenth and nineteenth centuries. The first – and, astonishingly, the last – fully comprehensive modern biography of Marvell was written in French by Pierre Legouis and published in an edition of only 500 copies in 1928. This appeared again, in English, abridged and shorn of its valuable footnotes, in 1965. At the tercentenary of Marvell's death in 1978 the British Library mounted an exhibition of Marvell's life and work that incorporated the findings of recent research. The catalogue of that landmark exhibition was published in 1978, a year that also saw a new study of Marvell's life and writings by John Dixon Hunt. But in spite of the extraordinary volume of twentieth-century Marvell criticism, no major biography has appeared since Legouis and no life of Marvell is currently in print. For too long scholars have insisted that not enough is known about Marvell's life, but that view is now unsustainable, largely as a result of the quiet and diligent efforts of a small cluster of Marvell scholars whose work I acknowledge at the end of this book and without whose findings I could not have attempted this life.

Marvell is not an easy man to know, but the attempt to find him is deeply rewarding. 'He was of middling stature,' wrote John Aubrey, 'pretty strong sett, roundish faced, cherry cheek't, hazell eie, browne haire. He was in his conversation very modest, and of few words . . . He had not a generall acquaintance.' The personality behind the poems is as elusive as the man was to his contemporaries, and it cannot be said that this teasing obliquity is without its own appeal. Marvell remains one of the most fascinating figures in seventeenth-century poetry. Yet his life was not lived in total obscurity. For nearly twenty years he was a member of the House of Commons. His speeches and his letters to constituents are on record, and he was witness to some of the most important political events of the century. This makes the life of Marvell of interest not just to the lovers of seventeenth-century poetry but to all with an interest in English history and the shaping of the modern political outlook. Marvell's intimate yet oblique insight into the contemporary political universe has long been recognised by the more discerning historians who have seen him as a witness of incalculable value. There has long been a need for a biography of Marvell that seeks to integrate the various elements of his life, to regard his Cromwellian period and his long Parliamentary career after the Restoration not as a sad falling off from his exclusive role as a lyric poet but as a dedicated avocation, drawing on his energy, imagination, moral commitment and literary skill in such a way that requires the modern reader to apply the same kind of attention that has been paid to the poetry during the twentieth century. If the aim of biography is to render a life in the most complete way, we do Marvell little service by cordoning off the poet from the politician, the actor in history. To do so would be to isolate and misrepresent something which is actually intrinsic to Marvell's peculiar genius.

Marvell's finest poetry, that which is so immensely popular today, needs no special advocacy. What Eliot wrote in 1921 is still true today: 'His grave needs neither rose nor rue nor laurel; there is no imaginary justice to be done.' Profoundly rooted in the circumstances of its time and indelibly marked by one of the crucial passages in English history, Marvell's poetry can, it hardly needs emphasising, more deeply be understood by a knowledge both of the poet who created it and of his time. But in spite of advances in biographical knowledge, intriguing areas of mystery remain, and his best poetry – which a narrative of the life must sometimes seem to pass by with too little commentary for this very reason – often enjoys a vestigial connection with the definite historical personality. The poems are what bring us back to Marvell; his prose works are now little read. But the clearer picture that we now have of his life, both in poetry and out of it, sheds, I believe, a brighter light on him and deepens his enduring appeal.

1

By the Tide of Humber

. . . a certain Jack Gentleman that was born of pure parents, and bred among Cabin-boys . . .

Samuel Parker[1]

In the early part of the seventeenth century the flat peninsula of Holderness in the East Riding of Yorkshire, which extends south-eastwards between the Humber estuary and the North Sea and ends in the wispy curlicue of land known as Spurn Head, might have looked much as it does today. Changes in agricultural practice combined with the ravages of Dutch elm disease have perhaps left it a little more bare and unwooded, but it is still the peculiarly exposed and low-lying tract of country alluded to in the opening couplet of Chaucer's *Somnour's Tale*:

Lordinges, ther is in Yorkshire, as I gesse,
A mersshy contree called Holdernesse.

A later Elizabethan satirist, Joseph Hall, referred in his *Virgidemiarum*, to 'the wastes of Holderness'[2] and Marvell's first modern biographer, Pierre Legouis, would find the landscape, in the 1920s, '*plate et triste*'. It is also the landscape of Philip Larkin's poem, 'Here', from *The Whitsun Weddings*. A saying can still be heard on the lips of local farmers today: 'The plains of Holderness, where the winds whistle.'

It was to this bleak spot that the Reverend Andrew Marvell, father of the poet, came on 23 April 1614 to receive, from Sir Christopher Hildyard, the head of the local landed family, the living of the Church of St Germain, Winestead-in-Holderness. It is a small, dumpy church, twelfth-century in origin, half-hidden behind trees, and it was in the rectory, long since demolished, that Andrew Marvell was born on Easter Eve, 1621. His father had previously held the post of minister at Flamborough, where he had arrived from Cambridgeshire in 1610.

Although the Reverend Andrew Marvell had been born in the Cambridgeshire village of Meldreth, where a half-timbered house called 'The Marvells' (later Meldreth Court) was still standing at the end of the nineteenth century, his ancestors came from the nearby village of Shepreth. In the first of many variations of the family's name, in the sixteenth century 'Merwell' was possibly derived, in that country of meers and fens, from 'meer-well'. In October 1528 a John Marwell left a will that included, for the high altar of All Saints Church, Shepreth, '2 bushells of Barley for tythes forgotten' and also 'a cowe for my yearly memory'. In October 1531 another equally pious provision to the church was made by a John Marvell, together with four sheep for each of his daughters. And Thomas Mervell in February 1543 continued this tradition of family piety with similar bequests.[3] Although these wills appear to indicate a traditional religiosity and Mariolatry, a marked Puritan strain would soon emerge in the Marvells.

The Reverend Andrew Marvell was sent to the most Puritan of Cambridge colleges at that time, Emmanuel, where he took his MA degree in 1608. It seems likely that the clergyman's father was one of a group of local residents who refused to pay a forced loan levied by Charles I without Parliamentary authority in 1627. A list of local defaulters, sent to London on 13 October of that year by one of the county Commissioners for the loan, contains the name of an Andrew Marvell, assessed to pay £2. Written against his name are the words 'Removed into Yorkshire'. This is almost certainly the 'Andrew Marvell, yeoman' whose name is in the burial register at Holy Trinity, Hull for 13 April 1628. The poet's grandfather, who thus died a year after the family moved from Meldreth to Humberside, was patently no Royalist.[4] His grandson would later call that loan, and the ecclesiastical backing for it, one of the major causes of the Civil War.[5]

Marvell later wrote, in the second part of his prose polemic against the Bishop of Oxford, Samuel Parker, *The Rehearsal Transpros'd* (1673):

> *But as to my Father, he dyed before ever the War broke out, having lived with some measure of reputation, both for Piety and Learning: and he was moreover a Conformist to the established Rites of the Church of* England, *though I confess none of the most over-running or eager in them.*[6]

Thomas Fuller, author of *The Worthies of England* (1622), wrote of the Reverend Andrew Marvell, as a clergyman, 'for his lifetime he was well beloved. Most *facetious* in his *discourse*, yet *grave* in his *carriage*, a most excellent preacher, who like a good husband never *broached* what he had new *brewed*, but preached what he had pre-studied some competent time before. Insomuch that he was wont to say that he would cross the common proverb which called *Saturday the working day, and Munday the holy day of preachers.*'[7] Abraham de la Prynne called the poet's father: 'a Verry Learned, Ingenious & Florid Man'.[8] All these comments suggest that the liveliness of humour and anti-Establishment temper, coupled to an underlying seriousness, that characterised the son were qualities also present in the father.

On 22 October 1612, the Reverend Andrew Marvell married Anne Pease at Cherry Burton, near Flamborough. Their first daughter, Anne, was born in 1615, the year after the move to Winestead. Mary was born in 1616, and Elizabeth in 1618. The two elder sisters would later marry into the Hull merchant aristocracy, ensuring good business and parliamentary contacts for their younger brother when he became an MP for the town.

Andrew was born on 31 March 1621, on Holy Saturday, and he was baptised by his father in the thirteenth-century Winestead font on 5 April. His antagonist of adult years, Bishop Samuel Parker, the source of the more vividly disparaging comments we have about Marvell, would call him 'an hunger-starved whelp of a country vicar'[9] (the charitable epithet emerging from the comfort of a well-endowed Kentish rectory) but there is no evidence of any poverty in the family or meagreness in the living. The boy's godfather was John Duncalfe of adjoining Patrington, who later left the sixteen-year-old poet ten shillings in his will.[10] The parson entered his son's name in the church register with the words: 'Andrewe the sonne of Andrew Marvell borne Martij ultimo, being Easter-even, was baptized Apr: 5to.' Although a respected minister to the small flock of thirty families, the Reverend Andrew Marvell had been summoned by the Archbishop in 1619 'for suffering the Winestead chancell to be in ruine, being parson there'.[11] He appeared in person but the case was dismissed when it was stated that he had already made the necessary repairs.

In 1623 a younger brother, John, was born, but he died the following year aged one, ten days before the Reverend Andrew Marvell was appointed to the post of 'lecturer' or assistant preacher at Holy Trinity Church in the centre of Hull. After three years spent in the rectory garden of Winestead, Andrew and his family moved to the city with which he would be associated throughout his life.

In addition to his post as lecturer at Holy Trinity, the Reverend Andrew Marvell was made Master of the Charterhouse charitable foundation, known also as God's House, where his official presentation was sealed on 2 October 1624. The Marvells lived just outside the city walls in the Master's lodgings, an obligation of the Reverend Andrew Marvell's appointment and from where he was not allowed to be absent without first obtaining the permission of the Corporation. Wenceslaus Hollar's engraving of Hull, done in about 1640, shows the Charterhouse as a cluster of buildings with three walled gardens. The site extended to about one and a half acres on the banks of the River Hull, and was once part of a neighbouring Carthusian priory, dissolved in 1539. It was inhabited during the early part of the century by the Alured family. Andrew Marvell would thus live for his first twelve years surrounded by gardens, among 'a prospect of flowers', commuting daily into town to attend lessons at Hull Grammar School. Both the priory and the Charterhouse were demolished in September 1643 by order of Ferdinando, Lord Fairfax, the Governor of the Hull garrison, who feared that the Royalist forces might use them as a siege-point.

That Andrew attended Hull Grammar School seems certain, though no actual record of his attendance exists, the admissions register not having been started until 1635. The school's historian, John Lawson, suggests that 'Andrew Marvell's connection with the school is as probable and as unprovable as Shakespeare's with that at Stratford-on-Avon.'[12] He probably attended the school between 1629 and 1633, and an early legend that his father – in spite of his crowded life as a preacher, charity administrator and performer of good works – was his teacher at the grammar school is clearly unfounded. Marvell himself, in later life, referred in print to his having scanned Latin verses 'at Grammar School'[13] and there was only one grammar school in Hull. In the seventeenth century, about forty or fifty boys attended Hull Grammar School, most of whom lived within walking distance and who were aged from seven or eight years old to fourteen or sixteen. Samuel Parker's later gibes at Marvell's 'first unhappy Education among Boatswains and Cabin-Boys'[14] would seem a little wide of the mark for the curriculum was, as John Lawson describes it, formidable: 'The aim was a simple one: to teach boys to write and speak the best Latin, to read and write Greek, and to a less extent Hebrew, and to season them in the Bible and the doctrines of the Church of England.' The boys read Cicero, Aesop, Ovid's *Metamorphoses,* Erasmus, Terence, Virgil, Horace, Homer, Hesiod, Aristophanes, Plutarch, and many more. Marvell's wide and easy command of Latin and the classical authors, evident in both poetry and prose, plainly had its origins here, though he conceded that the 'liberal Art' of scanning Latin verses was practised 'before we did, or were oblidged to understand them'.

No doubt the regime was strict, but Marvell cannot have harboured any resentments against his first schooling for he would come to censure those who spent the rest of their lives replaying grievances against their teachers: 'I never remarked so irreconcilable and implacable a spirit as that of Boyes against their Schoolmasters or Tutors,' he wrote in 1672. 'The quarrels of their Education have an influence upon their Memories and Understandings for ever after. They cannot speak of their Teachers with any patience or civility: and their discourse is never so flippant, nor their Wits so fluent, as when you put them upon that *Theme.*'[15] Instead, games were played in the school garden or along the riverside wharves. He must also have seen the Artillery Yard which he later recalled in a letter to the Hull Corporation: 'I cannot but remember, though then a child, those blessed days, when the youth of our town were trained for your militia.'[16]

Andrew's father seems to have been an efficient and enterprising administrator of the hospital, which was designed to support thirteen men and thirteen women. His duties as lecturer were to preach in the church on the afternoons of alternate Sundays and Wednesdays. Anthony Wood called the preacher 'the facetious, yet Calvinistical, minister of Kingston upon Hull in Yorkshire'[17] and it is clear that, in the religious climate of the day, when attempts were being made to enforce religious conformity against the tendency of 'Calvinistical' preaching, the Reverend Andrew Marvell, though popular with the Hull burgesses who appointed him, was likely to clash with the Church hierarchy eventually. In 1639 he was disciplined by officials of the York diocese for not giving sufficient prominence before his weekly lecture to readings from the Prayer Book, an instrument then being used to curb the perceived excesses of the Puritan party. Shortly before this, however, he had consolidated his reputation by preaching at the funeral of the Mayor of Hull, John Ramsden, who in 1637 had died in the terrible plague that killed nearly half the population of Hull as it raged between 1635 and 1638, with an estimated 2,000 'reduced to beggary'.[18] In addition to performing his duties fearlessly during the plague, the preacher, according to the eighteenth-century Hull historian Thomas Gent, on this occasion 'deliver'd to the mournful weeping congregation a most excellent Funeral Sermon (afterwards printed) in such pathetick moving oratory, that both prepar'd and comforted their hearts chearfully to bear whatever might happen to them in their lamentable condition'.[19] Alexander Grosart, an early biographer and editor of Marvell's works, wrote in 1872, on the basis of some manuscript sermons of the Reverend Andrew Marvell that he claimed to have seen, a vignette of the preacher: 'A fiery-souled, audacious, intense nature, impatient of stupidity, plain-spoken to complacent ignorance and prejudice, wrathful to high-seated "bad" livers, yet withal pitiful and gracious and sparkling with wit'.[20]

As early as 1625 the Reverend Andrew Marvell had clashed with the vicar of Holy Trinity, Richard Perrott, a High Church Anglican whose attempts to repair and revive the use of the church organ were not encouraged by his largely Puritan flock. Evidence of his willingness to engage in an argument – a characteristic his son would learn to share – also comes in letters he exchanged with a local man, Richard Harrington. The source of their quarrel is now obscure but Harrington wrote a splendidly choleric letter to the preacher on 17 April 1632: 'Your later letters are full stufte wth swellinge, (I may justly retorte), snarlinge, bitinge belching termes of disparadginge, false accusinge, rash censuringe, challengeinge, and threatinnge, all of which smell ranklie of a proud (to say noe worse) and hautie spiritt'. The Reverend

Andrew Marvell replied laconically: 'Mr Harrington, You teach me to write shorter.'[21]

The Reverend Andrew Marvell was a busy man, with plans for the improvement and development of the Charterhouse. In particular he planned to institute a library for the use of the Master, 'as an incouragement unto me in mine imployments', and for any other approved scholars in the town. 'Scholers,' he wrote to the Corporation, in a conceit worthy of his son, 'are like other tradesmen, they cannot worke w'thout tooles, nor, spider like, weave their web out of their own bellyes.'[22] He offered to donate £35 worth of his own books to start the library off. In his dealings we can see the liberal outlook and shrewd practical spirit, the sheer competence in the administration of affairs that would be passed on to his son. Unfortunately, his life was cut short before his plans could be realised.

The account of the death of the Reverend Andrew Marvell has been improved in the telling and has no independent verification. Fuller's account was the first:

> *It happened that,* Anno Dom. *1640 [1641 in the modern calendar] Jan 23, crossing* Humber *in a* Barrow-boat, *the same was* sand-warpt, *and he (with Mrs.* Skinner *(daughter to Sir* Ed. Coke*) a very religious Gentle-woman) drowned therein, by the* carelessness *(not to say* drunkenness*) of the boat-men, to the great grief of all good men.*

Thomas Gent, in his *History of Hull*, adds a further detail about 'a violent storm' that upset the boat and swept away all remains of the preacher and Mrs Skinner. He also introduces into the account, and the boat, 'a young beautiful couple who were going to be wedded'.[23] A later biographer, Hartley Coleridge, attempting to deal with the historical fact that Mrs Skinner did not die in this incident, suggests that it was her daughter who did so. He writes that Mrs Skinner was 'a lady whose virtue and good sense recommended her to the esteem of Mr Marvell' with a dutiful daughter to whom she was so attached that she could not bear to be parted from her. Nonetheless, she agreed to allow her daughter to cross the Humber with the preacher so she could stand godmother to one of his children, an implausible detail since his last living child, Andrew, had been baptised on 5 April 1621, nineteen years previously. On her return the boatmen advised that the weather would make a crossing dangerous, but the young woman, thinking of how anxious her mother would be, insisted. The Reverend Andrew Marvell felt bound to accompany her and, before entering the boat, threw his gold-headed cane ashore with the cry: 'Ho for Heaven!' and, scenting the danger, asked his friends who had come to see him off to ensure that if anything happened to him his son would receive the cane in memory of his father.[24] There is no mention in this account of 'the beautiful couple', unless Mrs Skinner's daughter was accompanied by her betrothed. The only certain fact is that the Reverend Andrew Marvell died, leaving his nineteen-year-old son, then in his last year at Cambridge, fatherless.

2

Cringes and Genuflexions

Mr Marvell at this excentrick period was not exempt from imprudence . . .[1]
Edward Thompson

Andrew Marvell entered the University of Cambridge in December 1633 at the age of only twelve. The Praelector's record in the Cambridge University Archive shows that he matriculated at Trinity College on 14 December, one of five new admissions, described as subsizatores, each of whom paid 4d for the privilege. Marvell has traditionally, but inaccurately, been described as a sizar (one of three categories of student, the other two being fellow commoners and pensioners). The sixty sizars allowed for by College Statutes paid for their board and education partly by carrying out menial tasks for their wealthier fellow students for which they received an allowance of 6s 8d every year, called liberatura, plus a further 4d a week for food and other necessities. The subsizars, as the name suggests, were an even more inferior form of undergraduate life, unspecified in numbers, who had no allowance for food but who were required to pay only a minimal fee to receive instruction from a tutor known as the Lector Primarius.[2]

Five days after Marvell's matriculation, on 19 December, his eldest sister, Anne, married James Blaydes, the son of a Yorkshire JP, in the chapel of Charterhouse in Hull. Their son Joseph Blaydes would later become Mayor of Hull, as would their son-in-law, Robert Nettleton, whose own son, also called Robert, would present to the nation the portrait of Marvell that now hangs in the National Portrait Gallery.

More significant for Cambridge and for the religious life of England at the time had been the appointment that year of William Laud as Archbishop of Canterbury. Laud would eventually die on the scaffold in 1645, but in 1633 he was starting to engage on a policy of enforcing conformity in the Church of England. 'Happy had it been for the King, happy for the Nation, and happy for himself, had he never climbed that Pinacle,' Marvell later wrote, adding: 'Though so learned, so pious, so wise a Man, he seem'd to know nothing beyond *Ceremonies, Arminianism,* and *Manwaring.*'[3] Marvell felt that Laud's authoritarian and intolerant style of ecclesiastical government had helped to provoke the conflict. During the Civil War the town of Cambridge would embrace the Parliamentary cause but the University in the 1630s, although more resistant than Oxford to Laud's reforms, was not uniform in its religious politics. The Cambridge Platonists – preachers like Benjamin Whichcote and John Sherman, the latter preaching in Marvell's own college chapel during his years as an undergraduate – probably won Marvell's allegiance. Together with the Latitudinarians, they were probably nearer to the family Puritan tradition. His father, however, in selecting Trinity in preference to either his old college of Emmanuel, 'the seminary of Puritans', or the Ritualist stronghold of Peterhouse, was perhaps deliberately choosing a halfway house, though how much even a precocious twelve-year-old boy would make of all this ecclesiastical fine distinction is moot.

In the years immediately preceding Marvell's matriculation, the contemporary historian Thomas Fuller, in his *History of the University of Cambridge,* reported: 'it now began to be the general complaint of most moderate men, that many in the University, both in the schools and pulpits, approached the opinions of the Church of Rome nearer than ever before'. This was accompanied by a rebirth of church architecture and ritual which aroused the suspicions of the Puritan temperament:

> *Now began the University to be much beautified in buildings, every college either casting its skin with the snake, or renewing its bill with the eagle, having their courts, or at leastwise their fronts and gatehouses repaired and adorned. But the greatest alteration was in their chapels, most of them being graced with the accession of organs . . . Yet some took great distaste thereat as attendency to superstition.*[4]

Marvell left no record of his undergraduate regime but it is likely that it did not differ greatly from the account of Milton's student days at Christ's College, Cambridge only a few years earlier, given by David Masson in his nineteenth-century life of the poet. There were three terms: Michaelmas from 10 October to 16 December; Lent from 13 January to the second Friday before Easter; and Easter or Midsummer Term from eleven days after Easter to the Friday after Commencement Day in July. Students would probably remain in college during the Christmas and Easter vacations. The day began at Christ's with a 5 a.m. assembly in the college chapel – an hour-long morning service – then breakfast, followed by college studies in Latin, Greek, logic, mathematics and philosophy, then University Exercises at the 'public schools' to hear the University professors. These lasted four hours and were followed by lunch in hall at noon, then an hour or two of listening to 'the declamations and disputations of contending graduates'. The rest of the day was free except for evening service in chapel and supper in hall at 7 p.m. Undergraduates were not allowed out of college after 9 p.m. without special permission and except in hours of official relaxation were required to speak to each other in Latin, Greek or Hebrew. Taverns were forbidden, as were 'boxing-matches, skittle-playing, dancings, bear-fights, cock-fights and the like; or frequenting Sturbridge Fair'. Dogs and 'fierce birds' were not allowed in undergraduate rooms and cards and dice were also banned. Marvell's college, Trinity, held a regular service of corporal punishment in the hall every Thursday at 7 p.m. in order to deal with those who had infringed such statutes. In practice these rules, derived from Elizabethan statutes, were regularly broken and bathing in the Cam or frequenting taverns like the Dolphin, Rose or Mitre was common. It is probably safe to assume that the tavern-banter was not conducted in Greek or Hebrew.[5]

Marvell's seven-year undergraduate career – an initial four-year quadriennium leading to the degree of BA, followed by a three-year period leading to MA – was not unusual, though some students left earlier to pursue studies elsewhere, for example, at the Inns of Court. Oliver Cromwell left Sidney Sussex College to do this after only a year.

On 18 August 1636, during the summer vacation, Marvell probably attended the wedding of his second oldest sister, Mary, again at the Charterhouse Chapel. She married a local man, Edmund Popple, described in the marriage register of Holy Trinity as '*nautam*'. He would become one of the Wardens of Trinity House, Hull, and a Sheriff, in which capacity he would ensure that his brother-in-law was made a 'free Burgesse' of the Corporation of Hull. He also acted as Marvell's banker and business adviser.[6] The couple's only son, William, born two years later, would become Marvell's favourite nephew and the recipient of some of his more relaxed and personal letters, as well as being himself a poet whose verses are preserved in manuscript in the British Library.

The following year, Marvell wrote his first published verses. King Charles I's fifth child, Anne, was born on 17 March 1637 and the University assembled a collection of verses in Latin and Greek to celebrate the event. Preparation began early, which might explain Marvell's failure to refer to the sex of the royal offspring. These compilations were customary and gave clever young undergraduates and dons the opportunity to display both their skill and their loyalty. During the decade many well-known Cambridge poets contributed to such collections, celebrating royal births or public events such as the King's return from Scotland. In 1632 even the King's recovery from an outbreak of pustules prompted the *Anthologia in Regis Exanthemata.* Cambridge at this time was extraordinarily rich in poetic talent. Poets, some now less well remembered than others, included Richard Crashaw, Francis Beaumont, John Cleveland, Robert Wild, John Saltmarsh, Clement Paman, William Hammond, Thomas Stanley, Nathaniel Whiting, Francis Kynaston, Edward King and Abraham Cowley. Much of this work circulated in manuscript, although many important collections of seventeenth-century poetry were published around this time. Marvell's contribution to the 1637 volume, presented to the King in a specially bound copy, consists of the Latin verses '*Ad Regem Carolum Parodia*' and the Greek Συνωδια. The term 'parodia' in the title has a more neutral connotation than 'parody', suggesting imitation (in this case of Horace, *Odes* I.2), but the verses, which contain an allusion to the recent plague in Cambridge, are, as might be expected from such an exercise, of little poetic interest. The Greek verses contain an elaborate play on the word five (Anne would be the King's fifth child) with allusions to two plots against the life of James I on 5 August 1600 and 5 November 1605.

On 13 April the following year, on the same day that Marvell was admitted to a scholarship at Trinity, his mother, Anne Pease, died in

Hull. She was buried on 28 April at Holy Trinity Church. Unfortunately, nothing is known of her, and seven months later the Reverend Andrew Marvell remarried. His new bride was Lucy Harris, whose third marriage this was and who came from Derbyshire, where the couple were married on 27 November in the parish church of Norton. Lucy had long been known to her new husband because she was the daughter of John Alured, whose family lived in the old Carthusian priory in Hull, next door to the Charterhouse where the Reverend Andrew Marvell was Master. When the Marvell family arrived in Hull from Winestead in 1624, Lucy's brother Henry Alured was the squire. They were minor gentry and John Alured had been twice MP for Hull. Pauline Burdon, who has written extensively about the Marvell kindred,[7] suggests that the two families were brought close through common experiences of bereavement and the similar ages of their children. This could have resulted in shared lessons. It has been suggested that a woman twice widowed might bring a useful dowry to enable the Reverend Andrew Marvell to support his son at Cambridge and his unmarried daughter, the twenty-year-old Elizabeth, at home.[8] But Burdon's picture of her as 'a courageous and intelligent woman' suggests a more natural foundation for the relationship. Less than two years later she would be widowed again. She lived on as Marvell's stepmother until 1664, though she would have seen little of him in the years after Cambridge, when he was travelling abroad.

The Admission Book of Trinity College, Cambridge records Marvell's signature among the names of thirty-nine scholars on 13 April 1638 after the annual Easter Term elections: *Andreas Marvell discipulus.* The scholarship entitled him to draw an annual stipendium of 13s 4d, with a further shilling each week for food. When he graduated as a BA in the Lent Term of 1639, the latter sum would be raised by 2d a week.[9] Another signature, now in the Cambridge University Archives, dated 27 February 1639 records the occasion when, according to a statute of 1613, Marvell had to sign articles promising to recognise the royal supremacy in ecclesiastical and temporal matters and give unqualified acceptance to the Book of Common Prayer and the Thirty-Nine Articles before he could 'supplicate' for the degree. He was already a year late in doing so for usually only four not five years elapsed before supplicating. Marvell had perhaps been considered too young the previous year, or had been absent from the University for some reason. The most obvious explanation was the strange episode of his seduction by Jesuits.

Marvell's eighteenth-century editor, Edward Thompson, whose edition of Marvell's works and the appended life *Of That Most Excellent Citizen and Uncorrupted Member of Parliament Andrew Marvell* appeared in 1776, was at pains to construct a legend of Marvell the incorruptible patriot and stout Protestant Englishman. The Jesuit episode caused him obvious embarrassment. He conceded stiffly that: 'Mr Marvell at this excentrick period was not exempt from imprudence: the Jesuits at that time were sedulous everywhere to make proselytes.'[10] Marvell's lifelong phobia in relation to Catholicism, which he called 'the Romish yoak' oppressing so many other nations, makes the episode even more piquant.

It has been suggested that the Jesuits at this time had targeted the Universities for recruitment. The story of Marvell's being led away by their Romish wiles first appeared in the *Life* of the poet written in 1726 by Thomas Cooke, Marvell's first editor. Cooke claimed to have derived some of his information from conversations with Marvell's family but, as with several other vivid anecdotes about Marvell, there is no supporting evidence other than tradition. In Cooke's words: 'They used all the arguments they could to seduce him away, which at last they did. After some months his father found him in a Bookseller's shop in London, and prevailed with him to return to the College.'[11] In 1872, Alexander Grosart unearthed a rather more substantial piece of evidence in the archives at Hull. It was a letter, unsigned and undated, though now identified as being from a local clergyman, the Reverend John Norton of the parish of Welton, close to Hull.[12] Written about January 1640, the letter is addressed to his fellow clergyman, the Reverend Andrew Marvell, and relates a similar experience that befell his own son, then studying at Catherine Hall, Cambridge, at the hands of Jesuits. Norton's son was apparently invited to supper by some proselytisers at the University, offered accommodation, and exposed to various 'popish arguments' of a 'rotten and unsavory' kind. He was also invited to Somerset House, then the location of Queen Henrietta's chapel and an obvious centre of 'Popish' influence and intrigue if any existed. 'I perceive by Mr Breercliffe [presumably some common acquaintance of the two clergymen] some such prank used towards your sonne: I desire to know what you did therin,' Norton wrote. He added that the evidence should be used to persuade the government to take action 'for if such fearfull practises may goe unpunished I take care whether I may send a child [words missing but probably something like "with confidence to any University"]'. The letter could not have been written earlier than November 1639 because it mentions the name of the Vice-Chancellor, Dr Cosens, who was not appointed until that date.

There is no concrete evidence for the length of time Marvell's dalliance lasted. College bursars' records show that he received his quarterly stipendium of 3s 4d throughout 1639 and 1640, so the date of the incident could have been a little earlier, perhaps in 1638, the absence for 'some Months' explaining his late subscription for his BA in February 1639. Whatever the truth of the episode and its exact dating, Marvell's early biographers were in no doubt that the experience stiffened the poet's resolve throughout the rest of his life to adhere to the cause of anti-Popery. In the *Rehearsal Transpros'd* he wrote with disdain even of the High Church ceremonies within the Church of England advocated by Archbishop Laud involving 'so many several Cringes & Genuflexions, that a man unpractised stood in need to entertain both a Danceing Master and a Remembrancer', a state of popish-inclined affairs 'very uncouth to *English* Protestants, who naturally affect a plainness of fashion'.[13]

Andrew Marvell continued to work for his MA throughout 1640, but the following year, whether or not in consequence of the trauma of his father's drowning on 23 January, he seems to have abandoned his studies. Towards the end of the long vacation of 1641 an entry in a Trinity College register known as the 'Conclusion Book' shows Marvell's name among a list of scholars who had failed to make even the minimal attendances required for MA candidates. 'It is agreed by the Master and 8 seniors,' ran the entry for 24 September 1641, 'that Mr Carter and Ds Wakefield, Ds Marvell, Ds Waterhouse, and Ds Maye, in regard that some of them are reported to be maryed and the others looke not after their dayes nor Acts, shall receave no more benefitt of the College, and shalbe out of their places unles they shew just cause to the College for the Contrary in 3 months'.[14]

No later than the summer of 1641, therefore, Andrew Marvell left Cambridge for good without obtaining his MA degree. A new phase in his life would open, of freedom from the schoolroom-like constraints of seventeenth-century undergraduate life that had been his lot for seven years. He had entered the University as a twelve-year-old boy from the provinces, but now, like any other bright, talented twenty-year-old, he would be preparing to face the challenge of making his way in adult life. The first thing that appears to have attracted him was the prospect of travel.

3

At the Sign of the Pelican

... he was sent abroad to gain Cunning and Experience, and beyond Sea saw the Bears of Bern, *and the large race of Capons at* Geneva, *and a great many fine sights beside, and so return'd home as accomplish'd as he went out ...*

Samuel Parker[1]

The years between Marvell's final departure from Cambridge in September 1641 and his certain presence in England again six years later, when he witnessed a deed at Meldreth on 12 November 1647, present biography with its greatest challenge. There is certain evidence of his presence in London at the end of February 1642 but for the four to five years subsequent to this, during the most turbulent period of the English Civil War, Marvell appears to have been absent from England.

Speculation about his whereabouts has included the suggestion that he could have studied briefly at the Inns of Court or returned to Hull to work in business with his brothers-in-law. It is possible also that he could have gone to Hull to receive either a legacy from his father or the compassionate support of the woman with whose daughter, allegedly, his father was drowned while crossing the Humber. But the most compelling evidence is that he spent most if not all of this period abroad, either funded by these same means or, what is more likely, working, as his step-uncle, Thomas Alured, had done, as tutor and companion to a young man of means. Certainly, the profession of personal tutor was to be Marvell's for the whole of the 1650s.

Milton's famous letter of 21 February 1653, recommending Marvell for the vacant post of assistant Latin Secretary under him, would refer to the fact that 'he hath spent foure yeares abroad in Holland, France, Italy, & Spaine, to very good purpose, as I beleeve, & the gaineing of those 4 languages'.[2] Scattered through Marvell's later writings, in poetry and prose, are references to having been in these European countries and a mention of 'My Fencing-master in *Spain*'[3] suggests that he was not a penniless wanderer but someone engaged in the traditional gentlemanly pursuits of the Grand Tour.

During Marvell's years at Cambridge, and throughout the 1630s, Charles I had ruled without Parliament. On 13 April 1640, desperate for funds to sustain his war with the Scots, he had summoned Parliament for the first time since May 1629, in the hope that it would grant him the funds he needed, but it was not so accommodating, presenting demands for its own liberty, for something to be done about the growth of 'popery', and for a lessening of taxation. The King was infuriated, causing him to dissolve it on 5 May. The collapse of this so-called Short Parliament was setting the King on a collision course that could end only in war. By the time the King raised his standard in defiance of the Parliamentary forces at Nottingham on 21 August 1642, however, Marvell was almost certainly abroad.

The alternative to the Grand Tour theory – which may point only to a delay, rather than constituting an argument that he did not travel at all (which appears unsustainable) – is that Marvell returned from Cambridge to Hull during 1641, possibly entering the trading-house of his brother-in-law Edmund Popple, ship-builder, master mariner and merchant. In his later years as an MP, Marvell would evince a shrewd knowledge of business and maritime affairs that could have been derived from an early experience of this kind. In Hull there has long been a tradition that Marvell was employed in this way. The city's Wilberforce Museum has a small circular box said to have been made from oak taken from the building in the High Street in which Marvell served his clerkship. In the nineteenth century local historians described an armchair in an inn known as the White Hart made from oak of the same source. Others located his apprenticeship at a house on the corner of Rottenherring Street.[4] William Empson, who has speculated liberally on various aspects of Marvell's life in addition to his more famous analysis of the poems, endorses this tradition. He puts the following words into the mouth of Edmund Popple, making him argue that he supported Marvell's decision to abandon an MA that would have been the passport to a career like his father's as a parson: 'What do you want an MA for? You ought to be joining us. First you must spend about a year in the office in Hull, learning the ropes; then you can go abroad. I will see you don't starve.'[5] Empson goes on to suggest that Marvell would have been used by Popple as a temporary employee in Europe with the job of reassuring the European shipping trade that Hull was open for business, in spite of the recent plague and the political uncertainty of the Civil War. Marvell's lack of money at this time – the general condition of recent graduates in any epoch – may have been compounded by the fact that any money accruing through his father from the inherited wealth or property of the Cambridgeshire ancestors would have been used up in providing the dowries for his three daughters, all of whom married well, into prosperous families that would expect such generosity from the bride's father.[6]

Another tradition holds that the Mrs Skinner whose daughter was drowned with the Reverend Andrew Marvell provided the young man with a bequest. The unreliable accounts of the drowning incident have contributed to this legend but it is now considered unlikely that Mrs Skinner's daughter Bridget – the only possible candidate – was even in the boat that sank.[7] There is a faint possibility that she offered some financial support out of compassion for the fatherless young man because she was a friend of the family. The Marvells and the Skinners certainly knew each other well as is evidenced by letters showing that Marvell was acquainted with Cyriack Skinner, another child of Mrs Skinner.[8] Cyriack's sister, Theophila, later married a Humphry Cornewall, becoming therefore the 'T.C.' in Marvell's poem 'The Picture of little T.C. in a Prospect of Flowers'. There is also a very tentative speculation, discussed below, that Marvell's young charge as tutor on the European tour was Edward Skinner, Mrs Skinner's eldest son. The last piece of evidence is the fact that Marvell's father dedicated a sermon to Mrs Anne Sadleir, sister of Mrs Skinner, describing her as 'a Constant benefactress to me & to my family'.[9]

That Marvell was in London rather than Hull immediately before setting off on his European tour is confirmed by his signature, as a resident of Cowcross in Clerkenwell, to a 'protestation' of loyalty to the Protestant religion on 17 February 1642. The protestation had been ordered by the Long Parliament on 3 May 1641, against the background of an army plot against Parliament in which the King may have been partly implicated. MPs were obliged to sign a loyalty oath promising to uphold 'the true reformed Protestant religion ... against all Popery, and Popish innovation within this Realm' and to defend the 'Power and Priviledge of Parliaments, the Lawful Rights and Liberties of the Subjects' and to 'endeavour to preserve the Union and Peace betwixt the three Kingdoms of England, Scotland, and Ireland'. Initially imposed on MPs, the Protestation was printed in January 1641 and circulated around the country for signature by ordinary citizens, who responded with enthusiasm. Marvell's name appears as one of 'severall persons which dwell within the said Liberty' of Cowcross returned by a constable, Robert List.[10] The relative proximity of Cowcross to the Inns of Court has encouraged the speculation – though there is no evidence in enrolment records – that Marvell may have been a student of law at one of the Inns at this time.

In the same month, on 8, 10 and 21 February, Marvell's signature occurs again on three legal documents witnessing a lease, release and mortgage of a Yorkshire property owned by Sir William Savile of Thornhill and acquired by his distant relative, another rich West Riding landowner, Thomas, Viscount Savile. Lord Savile was the King's Treasurer of the Household; Sir William Savile was nephew of the Earl of Strafford, Thomas Wentworth. One of the other witnesses to this property transaction was Sir Robert Lewys, a barrister of Gray's Inn. This fact, combined with the evidence of the Protestation, implies that the deed was witnessed in London, probably at one of the Inns, not Yorkshire. Marvell, it has been suggested, could even have been in the service – possibly as a tutor – of one or other of these rich fellow Yorkshiremen, either before the signing or as a result of forging the contact at the signing, but there is no concrete evidence of his employment or the possible role of either in financing his subsequent foreign travel.[11] Marvell's fondness for these teeming London districts and the busy life of the capital – a preference that stayed with him throughout his life, in spite of his constant pull towards rural solitude and apartness – evidently began early.

Marvell probably began his European trip in the spring or summer of 1642 with a visit to Holland, a country he was later to satirise as 'This indigested vomit of the Sea' in the poem 'The Character of Holland'. He was possibly in France in 1643, when the poet Antoine Girard Saint-Amant, author of a poem called '*La Solitude*', which has been seen as an important influence on Marvell's treatment of the theme, was at the height of his fame. According to Marvell's detractors like Samuel Parker, who were keen to portray him as a vexatious Calvinist, he visited Geneva; Parker referred to him crossing the Alps and visiting Berne and Lyons. The nearest we come to a reliable sighting of Marvell, however, is in 1645 or 1646, when he visited the English poet Richard Flecknoe in Rome. Italy was an important stop on the English grand tour and Parker paints a vivid portrait of Marvell as one who has 'seen all the *Tredesian* rarities and old stones of Italy, that has sat in the Porphyrie Chair at *Rome*, that can describe the method of the Election of Popes, and tell stories of the tricks of Cardinals . . .'[12] There is a traditional, though once again unsubstantiated, story of Marvell meeting Milton in Rome and the two discoursing on the iniquities of popery in the vicinity of St Peter's itself. In his Latin verses on the Louvre, '*Inscribenda Luparae*', there is an allusion to a Latin inscription in the church of St John Lateran at Rome which he may have seen[13] and in 'The Garden' his reference to a floral clock has led some scholars to surmise that he may have seen the famous example by Famianus Strada in the garden of Aldobrandini's villa in Rome.[14] As well as the reference to his Spanish fencing master he seems to have attended at least one bull-fight while in Spain, if we take as a literal report on experience his comparison, in 'Upon Appleton House' of the newly mown meadows to the '*Toril*/Ere the Bulls enter at Madril'.

Despite his views on Catholicism, and the seminary's reputation among hostile witnesses from the previous century as a place where treason was spoken (see, for example, Anthony Munday's *The English Roman Life* of 1582), Marvell may in 1645 have visited the English College at Rome, as Milton certainly did before him in October 1638. The College was on the itinerary of English visitors to Rome, regardless of their religious affiliation, the feast of St Thomas of Canterbury being a particularly popular day for the English to call.

Marvell's putative visit depends on a theory that he was a tutor to Edward Skinner. The College's 'Pilgrims' Book' contains an entry for 18 December 1645, mentioning a 'N. Skinner' having dined there with the seventeen-year-old Henry Howard (later the sixth Duke of Norfolk) and another young man, the son of the author and naval commander Sir Kenelm Digby. Skinner is said to have been there '*cum suo tutore*' (with his tutor), which could be a reference to Marvell. Reserved and unobtrusive as ever, Marvell may not have pressed forward any other identity than '*tutore*'. The difficulty with this theory lies in that initial 'N'. It could be an abbreviation of the familiar 'Ned', or it could simply be the customary initial used to indicate the place where a name was to be inserted. The College Rector, who would have made the entry, did not record young Digby's first name either. Skinner's two companions, however, were recorded seven weeks earlier in a register of British visitors kept at the University of Padua. On 31 October 1645 a Stephen Skinner – no relation to the family whose mother was not drowned in the Humber – was entered in the Padua record, making him a more likely candidate for attendance at the Roman lunch.[15] Another name which appears several times in the Pilgrims' Book of the English College in 1645 and 1646 is the much more interesting one of Richard Fleckno or Flecknoe, whose connection with Marvell is quite beyond doubt.

Posterity has dealt harshly with Richard Flecknoe, the protagonist of Marvell's poem 'Fleckno, an English Priest at Rome'. John Dryden – prompted in part by Flecknoe's fierce attacks on the obscenity of the London stage – would in 1682 make him the eponymous subject of his poem 'Macflecknoe or a Satyr upon the True-Blew-Protestant Poet, TS.', an attack on the poet Thomas Shadwell. In Dryden's poem, Flecknoe is presented as the epitome of dullness and one who 'In Prose and Verse was own'd, without dispute/Through all the realms of Non-sense, absolute'. Although Marvell's poem is scarcely more respectful, there is evidence in Flecknoe's writing that he may have enjoyed occasional remissions from tediousness. His statement that 'I write chiefly to avoid idleness, and print to avoid the imputation (of idleness), and as others do it to live after they are dead, I do it only not to be thought dead whilst I am alive'[16] is not wholly devoid of wit.

Richard Flecknoe, described in Gillow's *Dictionary of the English Catholics* as 'priest, poet and dramatist', was born in Oxford (date unknown) and was the nephew of the Jesuit, Father William Flecknoe SJ. He was sent abroad to be educated at one of the Jesuit colleges where he was said to have entered the Society of Jesus and been ordained priest. According to

Gillow: 'Naturally of an easy-going disposition, with a strong objection to the trammels of discipline, it was no wonder that he soon left the Society. His weakness was vanity and conceit, and fondness for society in which he was ambitious to shine as a polite English scholar.'[17] It is not difficult to see why satirists were attracted to the pompous, social-climbing author of *A Treatise of the Sports of Wit* (1675) as an easy target, though his poems would earn passing praise from Robert Southey and Charles Lamb in the nineteenth century.

In 1640 Flecknoe left an England drifting towards a civil war in which Catholics might not prosper (though he would later write a worthless eulogy of Oliver Cromwell in 1659 which praised the Lord Protector, opining that 'a Greater and more Excellent personage has no where been produc'd by this latter Age').[18] His travels began in the Low Countries and would later take him to Constantinople, Portugal and Brazil, as described in his *A Relation of Ten Years Travells in Europe, Asia, Affrique, and America* (1656). In the opening pages of this work he announces breezily his reasons for leaving a conflict-ridden country: 'I'm too weak and slight-built a Vessel for Tempestuous Seas . . . England is no place for me and for Poets . . . I, like one who flies an *Incendium*, wholly indifferent whither I went, so I sav'd myself.' We laugh, and Marvell laughed, but might his own motives have been similar?

Flecknoe enjoyed his exile amongst English titled expatriates, until, that is, their complaints about their losses at home began to bother him, at which point he moved on: 'I, by relating all to the narrow compass of one *Portmanteau*, travel lightly up and down, injoying that Liberty, *Fortune* has bestow'd on me,' he declares. In Brussels, he flattered various titled ladies: 'amongst Men (such is the corruption of the Times) one learns nothing but *Libertinage*, Vice and *Deboisherie*'. He passed through France, then to Monaco, where he was lodged in the Palace of the Prince, and then into Italy, always on the run from political conflict. No sooner had he arrived in Genoa than the Marquis Philippo Palavicino despatched a carriage to fetch him from his inn to the Palace. By 1645 he had arrived in Rome where something clearly went wrong. 'I swear I like it not,' he writes. 'Give me good Company, good Natures, & good Mirth, & the Devil of any such thing they have here.' He was impressed by the ruins and the antiquities, but did not care for the living inhabitants of the city. He wrote to his noble friends in Flanders: 'I converse more with the dead than the living here (their antient *Statua's* and *Pictures,* I mean) . . . how melancolly a Creature I am.' This was the condition in which Marvell found him, explaining in the poem's opening lines that he called at the poet-priest's lodgings because he was 'Oblig'd by frequent visits' from Flecknoe to do so, which suggests that Marvell had for some time been well-integrated into English expatriate life in Rome.

'Flecknoe, an English Priest at Rome', which is formally reminiscent of the satires of Donne and Horace, is hardly a charitable poem, making fun of Flecknoe's poverty and pinched surroundings, from which, on this occasion, no aristocratic patron had been able to rescue him. The poet mockingly recounts a visit to Flecknoe's lodgings 'at the Sign/Of the sad *Pelican*'. Once there, he is required to climb three flights of stairs, at the top of which he finds a garret which was so small, three feet by seven, it 'seem'd a Coffin set on the Stairs head'. The act of opening the door blocked half the room, making it a 'Wainscot'. In contrast to its tight dimensions, however, the room contains poetic stanzas in abundance and no sooner does Marvell squeeze himself in than the awful poet begins in 'a dismal tone' to read his 'hideous verse'. He resigns himself to this 'Martyrdom', which is rapidly followed by a performance on the lute, over whose frets the poetaster's 'gouty Fingers' move, the rumblings of his empty stomach making a sympathetic music with the strings. Marvell's language in the poem is wittily blasphemous about the Catholicism of Flecknoe, who is pitiably thin from starvation 'as if he only fed had been/With consecrated Wafers', and who is fattened only by wads of his terrible rhymes. He watches the scarecrow dress and, after a farcical encounter with another caller while trying to get down the narrow stairs, all three go out for a meal where, replenished, the poems start again, read this time by the third party, probably an Italian because he is said to appreciate the poems 'because he understood/Not one Word'. This local youth may also be hiring the poet to write hack verses addressed to his *inamorata.* Hearing his poems inadequately rendered, the 'disdainful Poet' stamps off in high dudgeon. Marvell, finding himself free at last, pretends mockingly that he will go off to St Peter's to hang a votive offering there in gratitude for his release.

Such a bald summary, of course, does scant justice to the allusive wit and word play of the poem, which cleverly satirises such theological concepts as transubstantiation as well as Catholic practices such as the Lenten fast. Moreover, like every poem of Marvell's, it is instinct with classical allusion and lightly worn learning. Such a wit implies an appreciative audience so perhaps the author, who on internal evidence had a long acquaintance with the city prior to the visit, had some learned friends among the English in Rome who would enjoy both the manuscript verse – it was not published until after his death in the 1681 edition of his poems – and the mockery of Flecknoe, who might have been a standing joke among them. Pauline Burdon speculates that the readership could have included the second Duke of Buckingham, who had been in Rome since late 1645 and would stay until May 1646. Flecknoe later addressed some verses to him and one reason for cultivating Marvell might have been the hope that the latter's contacts might bring him together with a much needed potential patron.[19]

It is probable that the encounter between the two poets took place in March 1646 during Lent. Flecknoe seems to have arrived in Rome at least as early as January 1645, according to the English College records, to perform a mission for one of his patronesses, the Duchess of Lorraine. Once that mission was completed he seems to have slid gently, during late 1645 and 1646, into the poverty in which Marvell found him, having no other means of support.[20] His visits to the English College may have occurred during this period of hardship when he would appreciate the opportunity to dine.

Another of Marvell's poems can possibly be dated to this time. 'A Dialogue between Thyrsis and Dorinda' was set to music by the English composer William Lawes, the setting having survived in Lawes's own hand in a manuscript now in the British Library. Since Lawes was killed fighting for the Royalist side at the siege of Chester in September 1645 the poem must have been written in the first years of the decade, though the version that appears in the 1681 edition of Marvell's poems appears to have been revised later. It shows that the delicate pastoral verses, such as those that appear in the early pages of the *Miscellaneous Poems,* began early.

The final stage of Marvell's tour was Spain. He would have set off from Italy no sooner than the spring of 1646, it being the habit of travellers to winter in cities. The next certain sighting we have of him is in Cambridgeshire, in the autumn of 1647. He would travel again, on official missions, some more clandestine than others, but this period of four to five years was the most extended and probably most relaxed of his periods abroad. His mockery of Flecknoe's poverty suggests that this was not his own condition. To have sustained himself for such a long period implies some form of financial support, either from a patron at home or from the income derived from working as a tutor to a young man of wealthy family.

He would, however, return – with skills newly acquired from a Spanish fencing-master – to an England engaged in an altogether less frivolous and foppish presentation of arms.

4

The World's Disjointed Axle

Then is the Poets time, 'tis then he drawes,
And single fights forsaken Vertues cause.[1]

Arriving back in England, perhaps in the summer or early autumn of 1647 at the port of Hull, after four or five years of relaxed foreign travel, the twenty-six-year-old poet, who would not find a permanent job until at least the middle of 1650 or the beginning of 1651, found himself in the middle of a still raging conflict. In November 1647, the King, who had been taken into Army custody earlier in the year, escaped from Hampton Court and fled to Carisbrooke Castle on the Isle of Wight. The Second Civil War was just about to start.

Marvell's mind would naturally turn to how he could earn his living. He was unmarried, apparently without a settled profession, and with no obvious means of support. He was probably starting to write the lyric poetry that is the basis of his current reputation, but it would have been invisible to most of his contemporaries, with the exception of those lucky enough to be given it to read in manuscript. The notion of a career as a professional writer would not even have occurred to a poet of his epoch.

Marvell had, however, identified a possible source of funds. In November he set off for Meldreth in Cambridgeshire, the village where his father was born, to arrange the sale of some family property he had inherited several years earlier. His signature appears on a deed of 12 November 1647 where he is described as 'Andrew Marvell of Kingston super Hull

Gentleman'.[2] An accompanying document is also signed by Marvell, who promises, in Latin, that he will keep the bargain at a penalty of £80. The fact that two local men, Mathew East and Henry Gosling, were present as witnesses proves that Marvell was in Meldreth in person for the signing. A further note on the back of the main deed, dated 23 December, shows that Marvell was also present on that date.

Marvell may have inherited the property at Meldreth when his father was drowned on 23 January 1641. Had there been any doubt, or intestacy in his father's will, he would in any case have come of age in March 1642, shortly before he departed for Europe. The deeds also show that this was not the first such transaction for Marvell, for the Meldreth property in this instance is described as being situated 'betweene the lands late of the sayde Andrewe Marvell now John Staceys on both sides', suggesting that Marvell had sold part of the property in 1642 just before going on his travels, which raises the possibility that his trip could have been financed by this means. In 1647 he was selling the remainder of his inheritance – his grandfather's house and three and a half acres of land – to John Stacey. The fact that his bond was for £80 suggests that the income from the sale was £40 (a bond generally being set at twice the value of the transaction), a considerable sum in 1647 and easily enough to have supported Marvell for the next couple of years in London. In 1624 his father had supported a wife and five children on an annual income of £12.

Although he was described as a gentleman of Hull, Marvell is more likely to have been establishing himself in London at this time, a city to which he was clearly attracted and where his career was most satisfactorily to be forged. Until his employment, in late 1649 or 1650, as tutor to the daughter of the famous Parliamentary general, Lord Fairfax, Marvell seems to have been not just his usual moderate self in politics but apparently to have leant towards the Royalist tendency. The historian Christopher Hill suggests that, taking the period of the European tour and the pre-Fairfax period together: 'Most of Marvell's friends at this time seem to have been aristocratic young cavaliers of the type he was likely to meet in continental salons; and when he returned to England his own sympathies were apparently Royalist.'[3]

Marvell's witty and graceful manner in poetry would have endeared him to the Cavaliers, such as the poet Richard Lovelace (though Marvell's wit was of a more robust and intellectual kind). Lovelace was a wealthy and stylish courtier who was thrown into prison in 1642 for presenting a 'Kentish Petition' on behalf of the King (a previous such petition having been ordered to be burnt by the public hangman). He and Marvell may have met at Cambridge in the 1630s, when the youthful Lovelace as described by Anthony Wood was 'then accounted the most amiable and beautiful person that ever eye beheld . . . much admired and adored by the female sex'.[4] After his release from the Gatehouse Prison in June, Lovelace set off, like Marvell, for Europe, where the two could have met again. The Parliamentarians had imposed censorship under a Printing Ordinance of June 1643 which was still in force in spite of such high-toned defences of freedom of speech as Milton's *Areopagitica* in November 1644. Lovelace was imprisoned for a second time in 1648, where he prepared for the press his volume *Lucasta*. The censors gave it a licence on 4 February 1648 and a series of 'commendatory verses' was attached to the volume when it appeared in May 1649. Among the Royalist poets who offered their tributes were John Harmar and John Hull, Cambridge contemporaries of Marvell, who himself contributed a short verse commendation to this unimpeachably Royalist exercise.

Marvell's poem 'To his Noble Friend Mr Richard Lovelace, upon his Poems' was probaby written at some time after the second Petition of Lovelace on 2 May 1648 (because he refers to the 'first Petition by the Author sent'). It shows little patience for the contemporary political climate and its vengeful temper: 'Our Civill Wars have lost the Civicke crowne, [a bitter reference to the oak leaves bestowed on someone who saved the life of a fellow citizen in war in ancient times]/He highest builds, who with most Art destroys.' Marvell paints a portrait of petty literary rivalry and politically inspired abuse cast by self-righteous Puritans at the imprisoned writer:

The Ayre's already tainted with the swarms
Of Insects which against you rise in arms.
Word-peckers, Paper-rats, Book-scorpions,
Of wit corrupted, the unfashion'd Sons.
The barbed Censurers begin to looke
Like the grim consistory on thy Booke;
And on each line cast a reforming eye,
Severer then the yong Presbytery.

Another poem sometimes attributed to Marvell and written at about the same time is 'An Elegy upon the Death of my Lord Francis Villiers'. Francis Villiers, another Grand Tourist at the time Marvell was in France and Italy and whom Flecknoe, as suggested above, may have tried to solicit as a patron, was killed on 7 July 1648 in a skirmish with Parliamentary forces in Surrey. The only surviving copy of the poem is in the library of Worcester College, Oxford, but it cannot be proved to be from Marvell's hand. The strongest argument against its being a product of the future servant of the English Republic is its too stridently Royalist tone and the declaration in the closing lines of determination to renew the civil slaughter. Such passion ('Not write so many, but so many kill') is uncharacteristic of Marvell's political temper.

A further, this time undisputed, poem from this period is Marvell's contribution to some verses published in 1649 to mourn the death on 24 June from smallpox of the twenty-year-old Henry, Lord Hastings, son of the Earl of Huntingdon. Among the contributors to this *Lachrymae Musarum* were Robert Herrick, Sir John Denham and John Dryden, a demonstration as much that Marvell was now naturally consorting with his poetic peers, his talent and stature fully acknowledged, as that he was in Royalist company.

The contrast between the composition of these elegant verses and the brutal reality of the times could not be more pointed. For at the start of the same year that *Lucasta* and *Lachrymae Musarum* were published, King Charles I was beheaded in Whitehall, while Oliver Cromwell moved to suppress both the Levellers at home and the rebellious Catholics in Ireland. There is also a powerful aesthetic contrast between the achieved but not greatly distinguished occasional verses written by Marvell after his return to England and the triumphant artistic maturity of his 'An Horatian Ode upon Cromwell's Return from Ireland' written probably in June or July 1650 when Marvell was twenty-nine years old, though caution must be expressed about the pastoral lyrics, which cannot be dated exactly. They were probably written during his period with Fairfax in Yorkshire.

Cromwell returned from his brutal mission in Ireland in May 1650, his hands dripping with blood. Even sympathetic biographers of Cromwell such as Christopher Hill make no attempt to whitewash this episode or minimise the truth of 'Cromwell's racial contempt for the Irish'.[5] As

Hill points out, this hatred of the Irish was not unique to Cromwell but common to most propertied Englishmen at the time. Even articulate exponents of political liberty like Milton 'shared the view that the Irish were culturally so inferior that their subordination was natural and necessary'. Cromwell arrived in Ireland in August 1649 and on 11 September he sacked the town of Drogheda, slaughtering virtually the whole garrison and all priests that were captured. This was closely followed by another massacre at Wexford where, after an eight-day siege, the town was sacked and up to 2,000 troops, priests and civilians were butchered. The remainder of the town's population fled, leading Cromwell to report to Parliament that it would now be a good place for English colonists to settle. Cromwell was untroubled by doubt and declared: 'We come (by the assistance of God) to hold forth and maintain the lustre and glory of English liberty in a nation where we have an undoubted right to do it.'[6] Cromwell's conviction – shared by Marvell and other Puritans – that liberty and religious freedom did not apply to Catholics because of their religion's sinister connections with foreign powers with designs on the liberty of Protestant Englishmen ran very deep.

We cannot be certain how much Marvell knew about the conduct of Cromwell's campaign and therefore the extent to which there was moral complicity in the Lord General's genocidal ferocity. But his 'Ode' was not hagiography and is characterised by a measured tone that oscillates between praise of Cromwell – in terms that seem to portray him now as an elemental force of nature, now as one living precariously by *force majeure* alone – and recognition of the constitutional enormity of what had occurred, sharpened by a picture of the dignity of the monarch he had usurped.

Twentieth-century criticism has subjected this poem to much analysis and commentary. Directly opposing conclusions have been drawn and Marvell's politics continue to elicit powerful and contradictory critiques. A similar pattern of interpretation is found in relation to the other poems in the Marvell canon. Indeed, Marvell criticism has been punctuated by periodic expressions of dismay from the leading scholars in the field, decrying the lack of balance and judicious understanding in many attempts at interpretation. Rare is that finely adjusted, knowledgeable tact that has characterised the best criticism and been so scandalously absent from the worst.[7] One such scholar, John Carey, even went so far as to say: 'The amount of Marvell criticism is growing rapidly, and there is more bad than good.'[8] Long before the emergence of critical theories about the arbitrary signification of texts, Marvell critics were having a field day with interpretation. In one sense, of course, this is a tribute to the complexity of Marvell's art, its refusal of definite closure around one clear meaning, its rich, ambiguous, polysemic texture. It is the prerogative of great art to leave the critic fumbling in its wake, even as we recognise the vital importance of informed criticism in helping to understand texts. And the texts, where Marvell is concerned, are fraught with the possibility of error. Again and again, critics have sought to reduce the poems to philosophical schema or to identify them too closely with the political circumstances of the time (this 'represents' the state of the Church of England; that 'is' the Battle of Marston Moor). The truest readings of the poetry are those which are sensitive to the strangeness of Marvell's genius: its delicate equipoise, held between the sensual and the abstract, its refusal to treat experience too tidily, the uncanny tremor of implication that makes the poems' lucid surfaces shimmer with a sense of something undefined and undefinable just beneath. There may have been political reasons for this. Eliot's 'lukewarm partisan' was not smugly detached from the contemporary political mayhem. In less than a decade he would be sitting on the benches of the House of Commons and he would remain an MP until his death. But it may have been that he saw the function of the artist at a time of revolutionary change as being not a war artist or propagandist but a witness to the true, inner nature of the conflict.

His hesitations, his attention to nuance, his willingness to reflect both sides, his holding of the line for contemplation, may have been not an evasion but a gesture of aesthetic responsibility. Two centuries later another English poet, Matthew Arnold, would argue that a society in the process of rapid change needed at least a few voices prepared to step back from the immediate call to 'lend a hand at uprooting certain definite evils'[9] and to reflect, not as a means of shaking off their responsibilities to act, but to allow the sort of profound critical reflection that would make subsequent acting more effective. It has been suggested that the characteristic motion of a Metaphysical poem is to create images or conceits that juxtapose apparently discordant things ('The most heterogeneous ideas are yoked by violence together,' complained Dr Johnson in his *Life of Cowley*).[10] It is possible – but also possibly too fanciful – to suggest that a society riven by war and unexpected violence might prompt an objective correlative in poetic technique, an attempt at the level of art to manage these disturbing dislocations.

At a more immediate level, a country in the grip of civil war, with its constant demand to take sides, to resolve issues by declaring one's wholehearted support for this or that faction, might prompt the artist to reassert a notion of poetry as something other than propaganda for one or other faction, to recover the sense of it implicit in Wallace Stevens's assertion: 'The poem is the cry of its occasion.' Complexities of this kind, issues of artistic principle and conscience, would have run through Marvell's mind as he approached the subject of treating the most powerful man in the mid-seventeenth-century state.

Marvell's great poem, as its title clearly signals, is modelled on the Odes of Horace, perhaps the most potent single influence on a poet saturated in Latinity. The classical precedent gave the poem a ready-made shape, a stock of usable images, a framework of decorum, that a skilled poet like Marvell could use as a starting point to launch his own individual variations. The poem has a dramatic structure that allows the contradictions of Cromwell's career to be held up for examination and contrasted with those of his opponents. Unlike Marvell's later, and lesser, poems on Cromwell, it does not consist of statement. The Horatian precedent also helped Marvell to attain some distance and avoid the risk of sycophancy or servile praise of the regime.

The very opening lines of the poem refer, in characteristically Marvellian fashion, to the tension between the contemplative and the active life, the need for even the learned young scholar to 'forsake his *Muses* dear' and take up arms. Cromwell too, the country gentleman from the Fens, had to abandon his 'private Gardens, where/He liv'd reserved and austere,/As if his highest plot/To plant the Bergamot' to fulfil his destiny. Marvell represents him as a natural force, uncheckable like a thunderbolt:

> *So restless* Cromwel *could not cease*
> *In the inglorious Arts of Peace,*
> *But through adventrous War*
> *Urged his active Star.*
> *And, like the three-fork'd Lightning, first*

Breaking the Clouds where it was nurst,
Did thorough his own Side
His fiery way divide.

After this, all Cromwell's actions are seen as inevitable, righteous, ordained by a historical necessity to 'cast the Kingdome old/Into another Mold' in spite of the pleas of constitutional monarchists – which Marvell might have been at heart – that the 'antient Rights' were a prohibition against regicide. In the most morally unattractive passage of the poem, Cromwell is shown as the embodiment of a principle that might is right, a seventeenth-century Stalin. Just as nature abhors a vacuum so everything must cede to Cromwell's exerted power, because it is power, and 'must make room/Where greater Spirits come'. Yet these lines are immediately followed by a passage on the comportment of King Charles I on the scaffold on 30 January 1649 that has become as famous as the much quoted stanzas of 'To his Coy Mistress':

He *nothing common did or mean*
Upon that memorable Scene:
  But with his keener Eye
  The Axes edge did try:
Nor call'd the Gods *with vulgar spight*
To vindicate his helpless Right,
  But bow'd his comely Head,
  Down as upon a Bed.

Some details here – the fact that a mattress was laid by the scaffold, and a detail from the famous later account of the execution by the Venetian ambassador Momigliano that referred to the rejection by the King of a proposal to pass a restraining cord around his neck should he not voluntarily submit himself to the blow of the axe – suggest that Marvell might have been an eyewitness to the execution on that bleak Tuesday afternoon in Whitehall.[11]

This passage has attracted much comment as an indication of Marvell's political ambivalence, his possible misgivings about the regicide and Cromwell's implacability, embodied in the latter's famous assertion: 'I tell you we will cut off his head with the crown on it.' But it is less often remarked that these lines on 'the *Royal Actor*' (itself a metaphor opening up the possibility of a stagey, even insincere royal performance) are immediately followed by a resounding endorsement of the 'forc'd Pow'r' that was now triumphant. An allusion to a legend recorded by Pliny in his *Natural History* about a human head being found during the excavation for the foundations of the temple of Jupiter Capitolium in Rome, an augury that Rome should be the capital of the world, presses the decapitation into service as a promising augury for the Cromwellian republic. And the Irish, who are 'asham'd/To see themselves in one Year tam'd', are invited to share in this bloody triumphalism.

It is a characteristic of this poem, however, not to rest in one judgement of its subject for long. The last third of the poem introduces a different note, offering a view of Cromwell not as a vengeful fury or thunderbolt of Jove, but as a potentially fallible human actor, mindful of his accountability to Parliament. The mere mention of his being 'still in the *Republick's* hand' raises the possibility that a day could come when he might not be. His tribute of Ireland as 'A *Kingdome*, for his first years rents' shows that he is expected to, as it were, pay his way as supreme commander. A new metaphor now enters the poem, of falconry. Cromwell is the state's raptor, trained to return to its leather gauntlet, bearing the kill. His forces will also hunt down the Scots – a detail that allows us to assert that the poem was completed before Cromwell's Scottish campaign which started on 22 July 1650 – in their 'tufted brake'. The poem ends on a note, not of triumph, but of warning:

> *The same* Arts *that did* gain
> *A* Pow'r *must it* maintain.

In the end, Marvell is not prepared to give Cromwell a blank cheque. Just as the King came to an unfortunate end, so Cromwell, currently favoured by fortune and men's eyes, could fall out of favour. This concluding couplet is generally regarded by scholars as a political commonplace of the Renaissance. Two years earlier Anthony Ascham, in *A Discourse: Wherein is Examined What is Particularly Lawfull during the Confusions and Revolutions of Government* (July, 1648), had observed: 'the Usurper ... will find himself oblig'd to secure his conquest by the same meanes he obtained it'.[12] Ultimately, the thought is traceable back to Sallust, but its position here as the closing apothegm suggests that it was the closest Marvell would come to a definitive judgement on Cromwell and one that was not without principled reserve about the danger of granting too much to the political leader or surrounding him with the aura of historical inevitability.

Some scholars have seen the influence of the poet Tom May's translation of Lucan's *Pharsalia*, even down to some close verbal parallels, in the 'Ode'. If this is true, then Marvell was profoundly ungrateful, for several months after having composed the Cromwell poem he wrote a savage satire on May who died on 13 November 1650. May, who abandoned the idea of a career in the law because of a speech impediment, was a playwright, poet, historian and translator who had made his reputation at the court of Charles I but who switched allegiance to the Parliamentary cause, his detractors suggested, when he failed to succeed Ben Jonson as Poet Laureate, the job being given instead to Sir William D'Avenant. According to Anthony Wood he was both a freethinker and a free liver: 'He became a debauchee *ad omnia*, entertained ill principles as to religion, spoke often very slightly of the holy Trinity, and kept beastly and atheistical company, of whom Thomas Chaloner the regicide was one.' Wood also describes the manner of May's death: 'going well to bed, he was therein found next morning dead, occasioned, as some say, by tying his nightcap too close under his fat chin and cheeks, which choked him when he turned on the other side'.[13] At the Restoration May's body was removed from Westminster Abbey and his monument taken down as an act of repudiation of the author of *A History of the Long Parliament* (1647), considered as the work of a Parliamentary apologist.

The problem presented by the poem 'Tom May's Death', which was first published in the posthumous 1681 folio, is that Marvell's authorship is not certain and it is puzzling, for it seems to come from the pen of an avowed Royalist, not from an author moving rather rapidly into the embrace of Cromwell and his party. Its mockery of May as a political turncoat has struck some, in the circumstances, as a little rich. Grosart solved the enigma by saying: 'the renegade and purely self-seeking republicanism of May and his evil living were offensive to the high-souled poet'.[14] Closer in style to the poem on Richard Flecknoe with its satirical couplets, the poem mocks May's drunkenness and corpulence and has him visiting, in the Elysian fields, the shade of Ben Jonson who calls him:

'Most servil' wit, and Mercenary Pen'. Jonson accuses May of turning 'the Chronicler to *Spartacus*', a reference either to Fairfax or the Earl of Essex; if the former, the puzzle of the poem deepens because Marvell was shortly to enter Fairfax's employment. The notion that it may have been simply May's character that was under attack rather than his political mobility is suggested by a passage that sets out Marvell's elevated view of the role of the public poet, endorsing the independence of judgement with which the Cromwell ode had recently ended:

When the Sword glitters ore the Judges head,
And fear has Coward Churchmen silenced,
Then is the Poets time, 'tis then he drawes,
And single fights forsaken Vertues cause.
He, when the wheel of Empire, whirleth back,
And though the World's disjointed Axel crack,
Sings still of ancient Rights and better Times,
Seeks wretched good, arraigns successful Crimes.

The strange echo in this passage of the 'antient rights' Charles I was said in the earlier poem to have pleaded in vain at his trial by Cromwell's men only deepens the puzzle. And notwithstanding the stirring call to poetic duty contained in these lines, Marvell was shortly to leave London and its political excitements and poetic opportunities for the rural solitude of Yorkshire (indeed, if he had not done so already). If we assume his spell in London to have been financed by the sale of the Meldreth property, those funds would not last for ever and some form of employment, for a young man soon to turn thirty, would in any case have been a prudent thing to search for. Closet Royalist or lapsed Royalist, his company for the next decade would be unambiguously Puritan.

5

The Batteries of Alluring Sense

My gentler rest is on a Thought,
Conscious of doing what I ought.

On 25 June 1650, five years after the House of Commons appointed him to be Commander-in-Chief of the Parliamentary forces, the Lord General, Thomas, Lord Fairfax, sent a letter resigning his command. He retired to his Yorkshire estates to pursue his scholarly and antiquarian interests and cultivate his garden. He was also concerned about the education of his daughter, Mary, then aged twelve. His choice of tutor was the young poet, Andrew Marvell, who was about nine years his junior. Such an appointment – given Fairfax's love of poetry and learning, and his authorship of a collection of poems called *The Employment of My Solitude* – was inspired. It was also testimony to Marvell's high esteem with the Puritan party, any Royalist dalliance clearly having been put aside. For Marvell, Nun Appleton would offer a relaxed '*atmosphère familiale et puritaine*', as Legouis puts it.[1]

Lord Fairfax clearly had a great deal in common with his new tutor. Although a distinguished and courageous soldier in the Civil War he may have shared some of Marvell's reluctance at the outset to take up the cause. In his autobiographical *Short Memorials*, probably written around 1665, Fairfax – who had been knighted by Charles I in 1640 for his performance in the Scottish wars – declared: 'I must needs say my judgement was for the Parliament, as the King's and Kingdom's, great and safest Council.'[2] This is the tone of someone whose first instinct was the loyalism of a constitutional monarchist and who was dragged reluctantly into 'that unhappy War'. It echoes a much quoted comment of Marvell's written a few years later that has become a crucial piece of evidence in the debate about Marvell's true political allegiance. Writing in the first part of *The Rehearsal Transpros'd* (1672), Marvell, deploying the faintly obsequious tone of a Restoration public figure, declared:

> *Whether it were a War of Religion, or of Liberty, is not worth the labour to enquire. Which-soever was at the top, the other was at the bottom; but upon considering all, I think the Cause was too good to have been fought for. Men ought to have trusted God; they ought and might have trusted the King with that whole matter. The* Arms of the Church are Prayers and Tears, *the Arms of the Subjects are Patience and Petitions. The King himself being of so accurate and piercing a judgement, would soon have felt where it stuck. For men may spare their pains where Nature is at work, and the world will not go the faster for our driving. Even as his present Majesties happy Restauration did it self, so all things else happen in their best and proper time, without any need of our officiousness.*[3]

The orotund smugness of this passage was characteristic of Restoration hindsight (and written under the censorship of Charles II) but it is consistent with Marvell's sense of divine providence in human affairs (''Tis Madness to resist or blame/The force of angry heavens flame'). It has been suggested that the phrase 'the Cause was too good to have been fought for' means not that the Civil War should never have happened or that the King should have been trusted to resolve the political conflict in his own way, but that the cause was so transparently the right and just one that no one should ever have contemplated taking up arms against it.[4] Both interpretations are consistent with a view that trusts to some degree in fate rather than the intervention of human agency. Marvell was not a political revolutionary or Utopian, in an age when plenty of both abounded, and it is likely that he and Fairfax, in their rural sequestration on the banks of the Rivers Wharfe and Ouse at Nun Appleton House, the former Lord General's country seat at the confluence of the two rivers, enjoyed many reflections and discussions on these great issues of state.

Thomas Fairfax had been born on 17 January 1612 at Denton in Yorkshire. From the outset of the Civil War he was a prominent supporter of Parliament in Yorkshire but even when he accepted the appointment as Commander-in-Chief he was, according to his later reflections, diffident about doing so. 'I was so far from desiring it,' he wrote, 'that had not so great an authority [the House of Commons] commanded obedience, being then unseparated from the royal interest, besides the persuasions of nearest friends, not to decline so free and general a call, I should have hid myself among the staff to have avoided so great a charge.'[5] He went on to perform courageously – sometimes recklessly – as a military commander, in spite of frequent ill health. During the siege of Colchester in the summer of 1648, Milton – a far less equivocal and subtle praiser of politicians than Marvell, as his sonnet on Cromwell demonstrates – wrote a sonnet in praise of the Lord General which opened: 'Fairfax, whose name in arms through Europe rings/Filling each mouth with envy, or with praise,/And all her jealous monarchs with amaze', and which celebrated the 'firm unshaken virtue' of Fairfax.[6]

But it was the trial and execution of the King that started the process of withdrawal of Fairfax from the Cromwellian cause. When he was appointed one of the King's judges in 1649, and his name was read out as such, his wife is said to have protested that her husband would never sit as a judge. In the account by Edward Hyde, the Earl of Clarendon, in his *History of the Rebellion,* she called out in the court that her husband 'had more wit than to be there' and a few moments later when the impeachment of the King was read out, making use as it did of the expression 'all the good people of England', she cried out again, 'No, nor the hundreth part of them' before being bundled out of court.[7] Though some historians are sceptical, her husband later claimed that he had not wanted the King to die: 'My afflicted and troubled mind for it and my earnest endeavours to prevent it will sufficiently testify my dislike and abhorrence of the fact,' he insisted in the *Short Memorials.* But Clarendon, a hostile witness of course, observed that Fairfax 'out of the stupidity of his soul' was throughout 'overwitted by Cromwell, and made a property to bring that to pass which could very hardly have been otherwise effected'. The Lord General's misgivings about the Parliamentary Army and its domination by the so-called Agitators (whom he dubbed 'the Forerunners of Confusion and Anarchy') came to a head the year after he had put down a mutiny of Levellers at Burford in the spring of 1649. In the summer of 1650 the council of state wanted to attack Scotland as a pre-emptive strike but Fairfax refused to condone an attack except in defence. 'Human probabilities', he said in his letter of resignation, 'are not sufficient grounds to make war upon a neighbour nation, especially our brethren of Scotland, to whom we are engaged in a solemn league and covenant.' Parliament pleaded with him but he was adamant. Only in his late thirties, Fairfax thus retired to Nun Appleton where he lived for the rest of the Commonwealth and during the Protectorate (though he was MP for the West Riding in the 1654 Parliament).

His love of literature and learning was legendary. John Aubrey, in his brief life of Fairfax, describes the Lord General's action in setting a guard around the Bodleian Library in Oxford when the city was invaded by the Parliamentary forces in 1646: 'He was a lover of Learning, and had he not taken this speciall care, that noble Library had been utterly destroyed, for there were ignorant Senators enough who would have been contented to have had it so.'[8] In retirement he wrote poems, made a collection of coins and engravings, translated from Latin and French, composed a history of the Church to the Reformation, a treatise on the breeding of horses, and a metrical version of the psalms and other parts of the Bible. During the Protectorate there were constant rumours that 'Black Tom' (so called because of his very dark complexion) was engaged in Royalist intrigues against the government, but these appear to have been unfounded.[9]

The selection of Marvell as a tutor – presumably some time after Fairfax's resignation in June 1650, but no more precise date can be given – seems to have been natural enough. They were fellow Yorkshiremen, poets (though not of matched talent) and temperamentally inclined towards the contemplative rather than the active life, whatever their proven distinction in the latter had been or would prove to be. But there may have been a more specific contact between the Fairfaxes and the Marvell kin that caused Marvell to be recommended to this very important post as tutor to the daughter of one of the most famous men in England at that time. When the Reverend Andrew Marvell was curate at Flamborough in the first years of the century, the local Lord of the Manor, Sir William Constable, married Dorothy, daughter of Sir Thomas Fairfax (the Lord General's grandfather). When the Reverend Andrew Marvell moved to Hull in 1624 he was brought into contact with the Alured family, as noted above, who lived next door in the house built on the ruins of the old Carthusian Priory. The Alureds had known the Fairfaxes for many years. The signature of John Alured of Hull, alongside Fairfax's, is found on a petition of 28 July 1640 from the Yorkshire gentry to the King, complaining about the burden on the poor of forced billeting of soldiers on them. John Alured's name (though not Fairfax's) is on the list of fifty-nine who signed the warrant for the King's execution. John Alured, as Colonel Alured, makes several appearances in the *Short Memorials*. Fairfax, in choosing a tutor for his young teenage daughter, would be reassured that he came from a good Yorkshire family known to the Fairfaxes.[10]

Mary Fairfax – not a great beauty if the miniature painted by Samuel Cooper in 1650 is an accurate portrayal – was known as 'Little Moll'. Although Marvell writes of her as a symbol of ideal virtue in 'Upon Appleton House', she would later marry the rakish second Duke of Buckingham in September 1657. Buckingham, son of Charles I's minister, was no Puritan, and proposed to use the marriage as a means of regaining his confiscated estates. Fairfax gave Parliament his personal security for his son-in-law's good behaviour but, after the Restoration, Buckingham became rather more useful to Fairfax as a protector. Mary's early life had been exciting for she had accompanied her father with her nurse on one or two dangerous escapades, including the escape through enemy lines from besieged Bradford in 1643. At Nun Appleton, she was tutored by Marvell in foreign languages.

Dating Marvell's poems – particularly those (the majority) which were not printed until after his death in 1681 – is a perilous activity. A few occasional verses, as has already been seen, can be dated with confidence, but most of the poems on which Marvell's current reputation rests are impossible to pinpoint with accuracy. The long poems, 'Upon Appleton House, to my Lord Fairfax', and 'Upon the Hill and Grove at Bill-borow', obviously belong to this period of rural seclusion, but the garden poems, the pastoral exercises and the religious poems are more uncertain. Given the facts of Marvell's life, there is a strong possibility that he composed these delicate lyrics during these two years of rural seclusion – conditions of leafy tranquillity that are reflected in many of the poems themselves – but this can only be guesswork. There would be a few more years of tutoring before he became increasingly drawn into public and political affairs, when the conditions for such compositions would not be so auspicious. But poets do not always compose in a methodical way. Their poems are often far from being contemporaneous reports on experience. They are picked up and put down. They are redrafted. Earlier fragments are recycled in later compositions. Emotion, in Wordsworth's phrase, is recollected in tranquillity. Writing the poems on Appleton House and Bilborough could even have been a means of bringing back and reliving the experience later. Nor does the fact that Marvell wrote lively political satires mean that he had abandoned more delicate lyric verse. Poets can handle more than one genre at a time. He may have continued circulating in manuscript poems of a kind that would not interest the political public, as the existence of manuscript versions (though not in his own hand) suggests. Nevertheless, with all these caveats, the Nun Appleton period seems the most persuasive date of composition for these pastoral and religious lyrics.

Since Marvell left no other record of this period, except in verse, the precise nature of his relationship with Mary Fairfax can only be guessed at. In 'Upon Appleton House' a passage of fifteen stanzas is explicitly addressed to 'The *young Maria*' which celebrates her youth, her innocence, and her purity:

LXXXVII
'Tis She *that to these Gardens gave*
That wondrous Beauty which they have;
She *streightness on the Woods bestows;*
To Her *the Meadow sweetness owes;*
Nothing could make the River be
So Chrystal-pure but only She*;*
She *yet more Pure, Sweet, Streight, and Fair,*
Then Gardens, Woods, Meads, Rivers are.

Lines such as these – probably handed over immediately to the perusal of Marvell's poet-patron – were conventional praise, but the poet manages, too, a more pointed judgement that suggests that Mary's intellectual accomplishments might be more marked than her personal beauty:

> *For* She, *to higher Beauties rais'd,*
> *Disdains to be for lesser prais'd.*
> She *counts her Beauty to converse*
> *In all the Languages as* hers;

Mary was twelve or thirteen when her young tutor arrived at Nun Appleton. He was twenty-nine, old enough for a proper distance to exist between the two but young enough, perhaps, for a little playful teasing to enter into the relationship between the young daughter of Anne Vere, the strong and fiercely independent-minded mother who had defied the Cromwellian court, and a witty, clever poet, recently arrived from London where he had mixed with the leading poets of the day. Recurring in the lyrics tentatively assigned to this period of his life is the theme of childhood innocence and beauty, celebrated for the most part conventionally but occasionally – as in the poem 'Young Love' – with a faintly unsettling explicitness that can recall for the modern reader the charged ambiguities of *Lolita.* There is a preoccupation with prepubescent innocence in 'A Dialogue Between the Resolved Soul, and Created Pleasure' – a very Puritan debate or verbal tournament between sensuality and purity in which 'a single Soul does fence/The batteries of alluring Sense', progressing through the sequence of human temptations to the ultimate triumph of the 'victorious Soul'. Similar concerns are found in 'The Nymph complaining for the death of her Faun', with its innocent childlike speaker, brushed by the real world with its 'wanton Troopers', a term that entered the language only with the arrival of the covenanting army in 1640. But there is also a parallel preoccupation with love. A conventional poem, 'Eyes and Tears' – Marvell's poems invariably begin from some generic precedent or prior treatment, however deeply individuated, and are almost never a naked utterance or blurt of feeling – contains a phrase, 'The sparkling glance that shoots desire'. An innocent shepherdess exhibits a shy sexual knowingness. The shepherdess Clorinda in 'Clorinda and Damon', who fails to persuade her newly pious swain, Damon, to sport with her in the hay, teases her companion. Did Mary Fairfax in this way tease her young tutor, in their garden walks, sensing his indifference? All these hints and suggestions culminate in 'Young Love'.

The poem is of course derivative in theme. Scholar-critics such as

J.B. Leishman in his essential *The Art of Marvell's Poetry* (1966) have traced the topic from *The Greek Anthology* to Marvell's contemporaries, Randolph and Stow. Perhaps it should be taken as no more than a poetic exercise, written – as many of these lyrics were – to be set to music, a wholly innocent playing with a conventional poetic theme. Or perhaps there was a little more personal pressure behind it:

I

Come little Infant, Love me now,
While thine unsuspected years
Clear thine aged Fathers brow
From cold Jealousie and Fears.

II

Pretty surely 'twere to see
By young Love old Time beguil'd:
While our Sportings are as free
As the Nurses with the Child.

The speaker goes on to argue that 'Common Beauties' must wait until the age of fifteen before experiencing love. His addressee's innocent beauty, however, should be enjoyed now, not as sexual love ('too green/Yet for Lust') but as a more Platonic encounter. Implicated in this theme is the *carpe diem* subject that Marvell would treat so triumphantly in 'To his Coy Mistress': 'Now then love me: time may take/Thee before thy time away'. The co-existence of these poetic moments with the religious lyrics celebrating the defeat of sensuality by the resolved soul, and the likelihood that these were poems written to be read at Nun Appleton by Mary's father, should perhaps persuade us to cancel any thought that they might be anything other than conventional Renaissance tropes.

Several other lyrics of this pastoral group address more directly the theme of disappointed or frustrated love. Again, the frequency of the theme may have more to do with the fact that thwarted rather than fulfilled love was the conventional stuff of poetry than with Marvell's need to deposit his own woes in verse. In 'The Unfortunate Lover' he draws on the Renaissance emblem tradition, specifically here the series drawn by Otto van Veen in *Amorum Emblemata*, published in Antwerp in

1608. The sixteenth- and seventeenth-century emblem books illustrated and expanded various metaphors and allegories from classical or Biblical sources, decorating the picture sometimes with an improving text, and were enormously popular. In this poem Marvell paints a sequence of vivid verbal pictures in a way that shows the great creative potential in the encounter of a fine poetic intelligence with conventional matter, for the poet's treatment is wholly his own. The eponymous lover had a violent birth when his pregnant mother was thrown against a rock after a shipwreck. From this nautical Caesarean the lover never looks back and is subjected to the rough handling of 'Tyrant Love' thereafter. Marvell contrasts the savage actuality of the unfortunate lover's experiences with their literary transformation into a pleasant aesthetic construct ('Musick within every Ear'). 'The Coronet' also expresses a doubt about the worth of art. In this poem the poet, weaving a garland of flowers as a coronet symbolically intended to replace Christ's crown of thorns, finds that the serpent coils of 'Fame and Interest' smother and destroy his pious work of art, rendering its 'curious [skilful] frame' a futile tribute. There is a Puritan iconoclasm here, a doubt about the efficacy or the moral worth of the kind of highly wrought poetry ('set with Skill and chosen out with Care') that Marvell is devoting himself to, a 'curious' art that cannot redeem the world.

A refugee from literary London where he was well connected, the automatic choice for inclusion in any set of commendatory verses or in a celebration of any of the leading poets of the day, Marvell might have been reflecting on his prospects at this time. Surrounded by dedicated public men engaged, or fresh from engagement, with important political issues, he might have thought himself a litte frivolous. He was without a settled career and his only public skill was in the forging of pretty verses. The Puritan in him rather than the aesthete might have felt uncomfortable at this, but before he left Yorkshire there would be further celebrations of landscape and living, the painting of a *paysage moralisé* that would go some way to assuaging these doubts if they existed.

6

Green Thoughts

Society is all but rude
To this delicious Solitude

Nun Appleton House was so called because a Cistercian nunnery once occupied the spot. The house that Marvell celebrated – though it is not the one that stands on the site today, which is owned by a well-known brewing family from Tadcaster – was built from stone taken from the ruined priory. Traditionally it was assumed that Lord Fairfax, whose family had owned the twelfth-century priory since its dissolution in 1542, came to live in a new house started in 1637 or 1638. This is referred to by the antiquarian Ralph Thoresby in his diary for 16 October 1712, where he reports visiting Nun Appleton with an aged local man, Robert Taite. The latter recalled having seen 'the old house pulled down, and a stately new one erected by Thomas Lord Fairfax, the General, and now the most of that pulled down, and a much more convenient (though not quite so large an one) erected by Mr Milner'.[1]

Of these three houses, the first, cobbled together from the stones of the nunnery, is likely to be the one praised by Marvell in 'Upon Appleton House, to my Lord Fairfax'. The second sounds too ostentatious for the modest building in the poem (though it is a poem filled with hyperbole that could make the great small as well as the small great). This second house was engraved by Daniel King somewhere between 1655 and 1660 and shows a cupola that has persuaded some readers of the poem to identify the lines: 'the swelling Hall/Stirs, and the *Square* grows *Spherical*' with this rather new-fangled architectural feature, which would have been unusual in a pre-1650 house. The third, present-day, house was the product of the work done in 1712 and described by Ralph Thoresby.

Lines in a poem by Thomas Fairfax with a clear verbal echo of Marvell's have created further confusion. Fairfax's 'Upon the New-built House at Apleton' (undated) contains the passage: 'Thinke not o Man that dwells herein/This House's a stay but as an Inne' which calls to mind Marvell's 'The House was built upon the Place/Only as for a *Mark of Grace*;/And for an Inn to entertain/Its Lord a while, but not remain.' Although Marvell is making the notion of the house as a temporary earthly resting place or inn into a modest metaphor it might also refer to the fact that Fairfax had already announced plans to rebuild it. Fairfax's lines, if written later, could be an allusion to Marvell's rather than a contemporary endorsement of his conceit, as they have sometimes been regarded. Fairfax could even have been influenced in his designs for the second house by the principles enunciated by Marvell in his poem. In spite of much debate by Marvell scholars and architectural historians there still remains a not wholly discountable degree of doubt about just which house Marvell was referring to, which further researches in local architectural history may one day finally resolve.[2]

Whichever arrangement of stones was behind the poem, its own imaginative construction rests on the surest of foundations. Its vivid scenes recall and make further connections with Marvell's other poems of gardens and conventional pastoral. It is the last in a line of distinguished country house poems of the seventeenth century, which begins with Ben Jonson's 'To Penshurst' and 'Sir Robert Wroth', runs through Thomas Carew's 'To Saxham' and 'To my Friend G.N. from Wrest', Robert Herrick's 'A Country-life' and 'A Panegerick to Sir Lewis Pemberton' and ends with 'Upon Appleton House', which is both a part of and a departure from that tradition.[3] Behind these English models were the Latin poets Horace and Martial, who praised places of residence but without the wider resonances of the English tradition. It was a way of seeing the country house and praising it, not as a rich man's prize, but as the hub of a traditional, ordered, ethical way of life. It stressed the social function of the house in its community and the relationship of this domestic economy to nature. The poet who celebrated this organic community was thus a part of it.

Marvell's emphasis on the indigenous flavour of Nun Appleton's architecture and physical proportions reflects the fact that the professional architect was more or less unknown in the early decades of the seventeenth century. The completion in 1622 of the Banqueting House at Whitehall by Inigo Jones, an architect with a self-conscious awareness of classical styles and Italian methods, marked a turning point, combining with other social changes – which in turn had an impact on architecture – to alter the organic conception described above. The gradual replacement of the great hall, where the landowner dealt directly with his tenants and practised what the sixteenth century called 'housekeeping', by newer architectural features emphasising the separation of the private domestic life from the public role was accompanied by a tendency for the country house to become a place of relaxation, alternating as a home with a fashionable town house. The poems of Jonson and Marvell stress the older role of the house: modest, functional, in harmony with its animate and inanimate surroundings. The concept is idealised, of course, masking quasi-feudal social relationships and deep inequalities of wealth and land ownership, but as a genre it held sway, producing many fine poems.

Marvell's poem begins inside this tradition but develops into something else. It is a poem about the country house, about solitude (that new concept for the seventeenth century, when the great house started to swing away from its communal life towards greater privacy) and about nature. Marvell was influenced in writing it by '*La Solitude*', a poem by the French poet Saint-Amant, whose work he may have encountered during his period in France in the previous decade. The poem was translated by Fairfax himself; another Saint-Amant poem, '*La Jouyssance*', was translated by Thomas Stanley, tutor to William Fairfax, son of Lord Fairfax's great-uncle Edward Fairfax, who in turn had translated Tasso.[4]

The opening stanzas of 'Upon Appleton House, to my Lord Fairfax' immediately set the tone of the poem: wittily hyperbolic, yet at the same time celebrating the modesty and proportion of the early house, which belonged to 'that more sober Age and Mind' when vulgar ostentation, sanctioned by the grandiose 'Forrain *Architect*', was still in the future:

Within this sober Frame expect
Work of no Forrain Architect;
That unto caves the Quarries drew,
And Forrests did to Pastures hew;
Who of his great Design in pain
Did for a Model vault his Brain,
Whose Columnes should so high be rais'd
To arch the Brows that on them gaz'd.

Not only is the house modest in its dimensions, but it is also conscious of function, avoiding wasteful decoration, a very Puritan architectural aesthetic: 'Where ev'ry Thing does answer Use'. The poem alludes to Fairfax's other, more spacious, properties in Yorkshire: Bishop's Hill (the York town house where Mary was born), Denton (where Fairfax was born) and Bilborough. It makes the point that Nature at Nun Appleton has provided spontaneously something that, with all their art, they lack: 'fragrant Gardens, shaddy Woods,/Deep Meadows, and transparent Floods'.

Having set the scene, Marvell then proceeds to recount the family history of the Fairfaxes. In the sixteenth century the heiress and 'blooming Virgin' Isabel Thwaites was shut up in the Nun Appleton priory by her guardian, the Prioress, Lady Anna Langton, to prevent her being courted by William Fairfax. He secured Isabel's release and married her in 1518, the same Prioress being forced at the dissolution of the nunnery to hand the property over to the sons of William and Isabel. The poem dramatises the seductive overtures to Isabel of the '*Suttle Nunns*', who stress the attractions of the celibate life and try to reel in their precious catch. Marvell's Puritan reading of the crafty Catholic nuns, anxious to capture the innocent virgin for Rome, fits perfectly with his notion of Catholicism's project of trying to recruit the best by stealth, as the Jesuits had tried to do with him, briefly, as an undergraduate. Never again would he allow himself to fall victim to the dangerous wiles of that religion and its 'Hypocrite Witches'. The first of many pictures of sexual innocence – an abiding leitmotif in the poem and one connected with the figure of Mary Fairfax whom some critics have seen as its unifying principle[5] – is painted in this section where the nuns invite Isabel to turn her back on men and sleep each night with a selected virgin: 'Where you may lie as chast in Bed,/As Pearls together billeted.' In the description of William Fairfax's hesitation about taking Isabel by force there may be an allusion to the present Lord Fairfax's misgivings about the conduct of the recent war and regicide: 'Sometimes resolv'd his Sword he draws,/But reverenceth then the Laws'. In the end William decides on force, brushing aside the '*Wooden Saints*' and '*Relicks false*' brandished by the nuns. Thus Marvell has established the foundation myth of Nun Appleton: Protestant valour has defeated superstition, restoring the house to its proper function as a Puritan seat: ''Twas no *Religious House* till now.'

Marvell then begins to praise Fairfax's retirement in ambiguous terms that could be taken as a criticism in spite of the virtuous tone of the portrait of one 'who, when retired here to Peace,/His warlike Studies could not cease;/But laid these Gardens out in sport/In the just Figure of a Fort'. Developing the notion of the flowers as ranked military forces ('See how the Flow'rs, as at *Parade*,/Under their *Colours* stand displaid') he compares the garden retreat of Nun Appleton to a lost Edenic scene that, after the rupture of war, can never be retrieved:

Unhappy! shall we never more
That sweet Militia *restore,*
When Gardens only had their Towrs,
And all the Garrisons were Flowrs,
When Roses only Arms might bear,
And Men did rosie Garlands wear?
Tulips, in several Colours barr'd
Were then the Switzers *of our* Guard.

The remaining stanzas of the poem describe the grounds and surrounding landscape of Nun Appleton. Even in Marvell's description of the mowers at work, images of war infiltrate, as well as religious images of redemption – the path of a mower through the grass is compared to the parting of the Red Sea for the Israelites. The recent conflict cannot be put out of mind even in what is ostensibly a gentle landscape portrait. There seem pointers, reminders, here – to Fairfax or the prematurely retired twenty-nine-year-old poet – of the world they have retreated from. Like the birds who nest in the meadow, hoping to shield themselves from sight, they are vulnerable to the mower's scythe. Modest retirement may be no more than an evasion: 'Unhappy Birds! what does it boot/To build below the Grasses Root;/When Lowness is unsafe as Hight'. Even a detail such as the release of the '*Cataracts*' at Denton thirty miles up the River Wharfe – sluices opened to clear ponds, resulting in flooding of the meadows at Nun Appleton[6] – carries an ambiguous charge, as if it is obscurely reminding Fairfax of his abandonment of Denton and, by implication, of wider responsibilities. It also gives Marvell the opportunity for some wonderful conceits ('And Fishes do the Stables scale'), playing with the inversions of the flood. After this, Marvell's retreat into the wood contains more closely observed images of nature which Victorian taste was to light gratefully on:

Then as I carless on the bed
Of gelid Straw-berryes *do tread,*
And through the Hazles thick espy
The hatching Thrastles *shining Eye*
The Heron *from the Ashes top,*
The eldest of its young lets drop,
As if it Stork-like did pretend
That Tribute *to* its Lord *to send.*

Sharp and vivid as the poet's natural observations are, the political allusions never quite disappear. The 'hewel' or woodpecker is seen as slowly undermining the solid oak tree, which has been fatally weakened by a '*Traitor-worm*' just as the state may have been weakened by the betrayals of the Royalists. 'Who could have thought the *tallest Oak*/Should fall by such a *feeble Strok*'!' After the Civil War the most solid institutions, including kingship, must be considered now impermanent.

Marvell's reference to himself as an '*easie Philosopher*' of the wood sets up an echo with his poem 'The Garden' where Neoplatonist thoughts are triggered by nature. Marvell is almost Wordsworthian in his reading of a lesson from the vernal wood: 'Thrice happy he who, not mistook,/Hath read in *Nature's mystick Book*.' The poet who would, before the decade's end, be immured in lodgings off the Strand and moving in the crowded world of Restoration politics, was plainly – however much he mediated it through sophisticated and allusive imagery – a lover of the natural world. Yet he could not leave that sophistication alone, and his choice of image to convey his languid passage through the leaf-canopied wood was one that expressed a Puritan twinge of guilt at over-indulged ease or forgetfulness of decent plainness: 'Under this *antick Cope* I move/Like some great *Prelate of the Grove.*' Even his sensual pleasure in this bucolic recreation must be rendered with a dash of self-lacerating ardour:

Bind me ye Woodbines *in your 'twines,*
Curle me about ye gadding Vines,
And Oh so close your Circles lace,
That I may never leave this Place:
But, lest your Fetters prove too weak,
Ere I your Silken Bondage break,
Do you, O Brambles, *chain me too,*
And courteous Briars *nail me through.*

The poem ends with the arrival of '*young Maria*', who 'like a *sprig of Misleto,/On the Fairfacian Oak* does grow'. She is the only child of the Fairfaxes and Marvell refers to their hopes in her. Disappointed at the absence of a male heir they have made 'their *Destiny* their *Choice*' and placed all their hopes for the future in Mary Fairfax. She would die, childless, as the Duchess of Buckingham in 1704, but for now she is seen as the centre of an imagined, prelapsarian world of beauty and innocence: '*Heaven's Center, Nature's Lap/And Paradice's only Map.*' The sky is now growing dark and they must move in. In a final extravagant image – for which Marvell's knuckles were rapped by T.S. Eliot, but which is one of the most delightful and witty in the poem – the darkening sky is compared to the dark leather coracle that the salmon-fishers hoist: 'And, like *Antipodes* in Shoes,/Have shod their *Heads* in their *Canoos*'.

Marvell's other topographical poem to Fairfax, 'Upon the Hill and Grove at Bill-borow', concerns another house owned by Fairfax at Bilborough, a few miles from Nun Appleton. The hill referred to is, in that flat country, a rather risible eminence of 145 feet which Marvell claims in the poem can be used by seamen on the Humber as a landmark. It is 'a perfect Hemisphere' with 'a soft access and wide' which may be why, as a local farmer told the present author in 1997: 'Folk ski off it in winter.' Again, Marvell alludes to the military past of Fairfax:

Much other Groves, say they, then these
And other Hills him once did please.
Through Groves of Pikes he thunder'd then,
And Mountains rais'd of dying Men.

The poem concludes that Fairfax does not want those hills without the corresponding groves: 'Nor Height but with Retirement loves'. The suggestion seems to be that he needs both the active and the contemplative life and Marvell, in his poems to his patron, seems to be holding him to that balance, reminding him of the world left behind and his duty to it, as well as praising the pleasures of retirement.

'The Garden' grants more allowance to the need for withdrawal. 'How vainly men themselves amaze/To win the palm, the Oke, or Bayes', it begins, continuing in a mode of profound contemplation that does not seek to counterbalance every description of natural beauty with some allusion to politics or society or a call to the active life. It is thus different in temper from the Fairfax poems and may belong to a later date, when the need for calm reflection and quiet may have been more pressing. As a busy politician, Marvell often seemed in his correspondence to be rushed and harried. His letters of that period sometimes contain expressions of determination to go into the country to find the space to think and write. Although living in central London, during his years as an MP he spent some time in a cottage at Highgate, demolished in 1869 and now part of Waterlow Park. A memorial tablet in the wall of Lauderdale House, halfway up Highgate Hill, marks the putative spot of 'Andrew Marvell's Cottage' today. Only one letter is actually dated from Highgate (24 June 1673), but there are several other references to going there in his correspondence. On 24 July 1675, for example, he wrote to his favourite nephew, William Popple, about being 'resolved now to sequester my self one whole Day at *Highgate*'[7] and in another letter he apologised for a late reply to a letter, saying, 'I am much out of Towne'[8] – probably a reference to a further spell in Highgate. His reputation for secrecy may have had as much to do with this need to find time to read and to compose as with darker intrigues.

The exclamation in 'The Garden' – 'Fair quiet, have I found thee here,/And Innocence thy Sister dear!/Mistaken long, I sought you then/In busie Companies of Men' – differs from the playful mock-languor of the Fairfax poems. There is an unqualified relish for seclusion – 'Society is all but rude,/To this delicious Solitude' – and a frank sensual enjoyment of the fruits of the garden – 'The Luscious Clusters of the Vine/Upon my Mouth do crush their Wine'. The governing antithesis of this poem, however, is not the simple Puritan pleasure versus ascetic purity of the pastoral–religious lyrics. From the sensual celebration of the fruits of the earth, Marvell passes not to renunciation or censoriousness. The movement is a transcendent one, to a mystical, disembodied rapture of pure contemplation that has left behind the poor world of mere sense:

Mean while the Mind, from pleasure less,
Withdraws into its happiness:
The Mind, that Ocean where each kind
Does streight its own resemblance find;
Yet it creates, transcending these,
Far other Worlds, and other Seas;
Annihilating all that's made
To a green Thought in a green Shade.

The seductive smoothness and rhythm of these lines draws the reader into a contemplation of Marvell's garden-ecstasy, where all conscious intellectual activity and the world of actual sense melt into a Platonic idea of garden greenness, a sort of distilled essence of natural beauty, a 'green Thought in a green Shade'. In his posthumous volume of *Miscellaneous Poems* Marvell uses the word 'green' an extraordinary number of times, the colour operating as a potent symbol of the contemplative mood. The exalted state Marvell reaches in the poem, where his 'Soul into the boughs does glide' like a bird, is compared with the Edenic state of unsexual bliss where pleasure was solitary: 'Two Paradises 'twere in one/To live in Paradise alone'. Marvell never married and wrote many poems celebrating love without sex and the innocence that precedes sexual knowledge.

Marvell did not stay longer than two years at Nun Appleton, assuming he arrived there some time after November 1650 when he wrote the poem on the death of Tom May, perhaps as late as the beginning of 1651. Early in 1653 he was seeking an official government post, although the post he actually attained during the summer was another tutorial one. Two poems during 1651 can be accurately dated, the first being 'To his worthy Friend Doctor Witty upon his Translation of the Popular Errors'. Witty was a Hull physician who translated a Latin treatise published in 1638 by another Hull doctor, James Primrose. Marvell's poem, together with a Latin one on the same theme, appeared among some commendatory verses to the translation, which seem to have been published very early in 1651, so he was thus still in contact with Hull during his Fairfacian retreat. The poem is of interest chiefly for its insight into Marvell's view of translation. He believed strongly that the translator should be servant of the text and not try to be clever at its expense. Too many translators 'are Authors grown' and, by adding matter unnecessarily, 'make the Book their own', a charge that could still be levelled at some poetic translators today. Translators who muddy the waters of good prose by their prolix additions are worse than those who miss out things from the original: 'He is Translations thief that addeth more,' writes the poet.

The other poem was a Latin verse addressed to Oliver St John, who was chosen in February 1651 to undertake a mission to the United Provinces to negotiate an alliance with the Dutch. He reached the Hague on 17 March, but the mission was unsuccessful and he returned in June. The existence of the poem indicates that in Yorkshire Marvell was not isolated from the political world.

The hints of impatience with rural seclusion in the Fairfax poems make it unsurprising that Marvell was now looking for new employment. It is unlikely that the thirteen-year-old Mary had nothing more to learn in the field of foreign languages, but her tutor was getting restless. It was time to call in some favours. And Marvell's first approach was to another poet, John Milton.

7

A Gentleman Whose Name is Marvell

Cromwell had now dismissed the parliament by the authority of which he had destroyed monarchy, and commenced monarch himself, under the title of protector, but with kingly and more than kingly power.

Dr Johnson, *Life of Milton*

In the period after Lord Fairfax retired to his Yorkshire estate to write poetry and collect medals, Oliver Cromwell had pressed ahead with the military action against the Scots from which Fairfax shrank. The following year, in 1651, Cromwell defeated Charles II at Worcester after his invasion of England, launched from Scotland. Cromwell was consolidating his power throughout this period. In 1653 he dissolved the Rump Parliament, choosing in its place the 'Barebones' Parliament of impeccable Puritans whom he told: 'Truly you are called by God to rule with him and for him.' By December 1653, however, Cromwell had clawed back the powers of the Barebones Parliament and styled himself Lord Protector. He refused the title of King but the matter of his acceptance of the crown continued to be debated and, in the view of some observers, Cromwell began to acquire the airs and graces of a monarch. For uncompromising republicans like Milton, however, Cromwell was the Great Helmsman, enjoying both temporal power and the additional convenience of having the endorsement of God. In his eulogy of Cromwell in the 1654 *Defensio Secunda* – the latest polemical exchange in Milton's propaganda war in defence of the anti-Royalist cause – Milton called his Lord Protector *pater patriae* (father of the fatherland). The unsympathetic Tory, Dr Johnson, later remarked: 'Caesar, when he assumed the perpetual dictatorship, had not more servile or more elegant flattery.'[1]

Only weeks after the beheading of King Charles in 1649, Milton had been appointed Secretary for the Foreign Tongues and in that capacity the now blind poet and functionary dictated a letter to the President of the Council of State, John Bradshaw, on 21 February 1653:

> *. . . there will be with you to morrow upon some occasion of busines a Gentleman whose name is Mr Marvile; a man whom both by report, & the converse I have had with him, of singular desert for the State to make use of; who alsoe offers himselfe, if there be any imployment for him. His father was the Minister of Hull & he hath spent foure yeares abroad in Holland, France, Italy, & Spaine, to very good purpose, as I beleeve, & the gaineing of those 4 languages; besides he is a scholler & well read in the Latin and Greeke authors, & noe doubt of an approved conversation, for he com's now lately out of the house of the Lord Fairfax who was Generall, where he was intrusted to give some instructions in the Languages to the Lady his Daughter. If upon the death of Mr Wakerley the Council shall thinke that I shall need any assistant in the performance of my place . . . it would be hard for them to find a Man soe fit every way for that purpose as this Gentleman.*[2]

Evidently, Milton did not consider the Fairfax connection to be a drawback, in spite of the former general's falling out with the Cromwellians. The letter shows him fully aware of Marvell's linguistic skills and scholarship, Milton's own being so formidable. The senior poet's willingness to praise others was so notoriously constrained that an encomium from him would be doubly valuable. Both author and recipient of this letter were fierce republicans. John Bradshaw had been President of the Parliamentary Commission to try the King in 1649 and his signature had headed the list on Charles's death warrant. The Ashmolean Museum in Oxford keeps the high-crowned beaver hat lined with plated steel to ward off blows that he wore during that turbulent time. In a particularly grisly moment at the Restoration his was one of the corpses dug up and hanged in their coffins at Tyburn on 30 January 1661, the twelfth anniversary of the regicide. Although Bradshaw would later oppose Cromwell's assumption of arbitrary power, he was at the time of Milton's letter an important figure in the government. Milton's entreaty, however, was fruitless. Marvell had to wait another four and a half years before gaining such a post. Perhaps Bradshaw was unwilling to favour a recent employee of the man who, unlike himself, had refused to sign the King's death warrant and whose wife had cried out in open court that he had more wit than to do so. The job went instead to Philip Meadows, later knighted and made ambassador to Denmark.

It is worth noting Milton's spelling of Marvell's name as 'Marvile'. Its spelling on the baptismal register leaves no doubt that we have it right but English orthography was looser in those days and Marvell's name occurs in a variety of forms: Mervill, Mervile, Marvel, Mervail – all these by people who knew him well. Marvail was the spelling used by his fellow Hull MP Colonel Gilby. Current donnish practice is to pronounce Marvell's name with the stress on the second syllable (like the Irish patriot Parnell), but those of us who prefer to pronounce it as if Marvell were what he can so often seem, a prodigy in nature, may have equal warrant.

The letter of February 1653 is the first record of Marvell's acquaintance with Milton. The tradition that they met in Rome, deploring the papacy in the cloisters of the Vatican itself, is absurd, since by the time Marvell reached Rome Milton was back in London, teaching his schoolboy nephews in Aldersgate Street. The connection between the two poets – natural because of their common erudition and classicism, though the political temperature of the two differed markedly – would later serve Milton well when the enthusiastic defender of regicide found himself under threat of retaliation at the Restoration. It proved useful to have a friend in Parliament. When Milton had fallen from grace Marvell would visit him discreetly at his house in Jewin Street, Petty France in the early 1660s but probably less cautiously before the Restoration. Milton's nephew, Edward Phillips, in his *Life of Mr John Milton* (1694) claimed that 'he was frequently visited by persons of Quality . . . and . . . by particular Friends that had a high esteem for him, *viz* Mr Andrew Marvel'.[3] This was probably some time after Milton moved to Petty France on 17 December 1651. John Aubrey's brief life of Milton cites Marvell as being among the senior poet's 'familiar learned Acquaintance'.[4] It has even been suggested that Marvell was the author of an anonymous life of Milton but the usual attribution now is Milton's friend Cyriack Skinner, the relative of the Mrs Skinner who figures in the story of the

Reverend Andrew Marvell's drowning.[5] Marvell is also alleged to have helped Milton to write either his *Eikonoclastes* (1649) or his first *Defensio pro populo Anglicano* in 1651, which would imply an active collaboration between the two before and during the Nun Appleton residence, whereas the tone of Milton's 1653 letter is of one who has recently made Marvell's acquaintance. The evidence for Marvell's involvement in this tract is a letter from Anne Sadleir, Mrs Skinner's sister and an acquaintance of Marvell's father. In a letter to Roger Williams, the New England colonist and pioneer of religious liberty, she wrote: 'as I have heard he [Milton] was faine to have the helpe of one Andrew Marvell or els he could not have finished that most accursed Libell'.[6]

It is clear that Marvell was forging useful contacts close to the government. Either Fairfax or Cyriack Skinner may have brought about the introduction to Milton. Although it was unproductive on this occasion, Milton may have felt moved to help Marvell find something else. In Paris he had met John, Viscount Scudamore, whose daughter would later marry William Dutton, the young man taken under Cromwell's wing with a view to his becoming the husband of his youngest daughter, Frances Cromwell. It may have been Scudamore, at Milton's prompting, who now proposed that Marvell could be tutor to William Dutton. Or it may have come about because of Marvell's connection with the family with whom the orphan Dutton was staying at Eton, the Oxenbridges. Elizabeth Oxenbridge, sister of the Reverend John Oxenbridge, a Fellow of Eton, had in 1645 married Oliver St John, Chief Justice of Common Pleas, to whom Marvell had written his Latin verses at the time of St John's embassy to Holland in the spring of 1651. Marvell was clearly moving closer to the government and would have been drawn increasingly to Cromwell's attention. His new post would complete the process.

It has always been assumed that Marvell went straight to Eton to take up his post as tutor to Dutton, but a memoir of the Dutton family, published privately in 1899, claimed that early in 1653 William Dutton, together with his new tutor, was living as part of Cromwell's household 'at their residence in the Cockpit at Whitehall or at Hampton Court' before moving to Eton in the summer. No biographer has ever reported this hypothesis; it cannot be called a fact because the author of the Dutton family memoir, Blacker Morgan, offers no evidence and there is no mention in any other source of Marvell's presence in Cromwell's

London household.[7] Clearly the tradition existed in the Dutton family and could have a basis in fact. If it were true, it would be an important confirmation of the closeness of Marvell to Cromwell and might explain the absence, in those poems praising the Protector that he was to write later in the decade, of the sort of qualified eulogy that had entered into the 'Horatian Ode'. Marvell came to admire Cromwell personally in the years from 1653 to the latter's death in 1658 and was a *de facto* laureate to the state, a role that Milton might have been expected to fulfil but which his passionate engagement in pamphlet warfare at the time probably prevented him from discharging.

William Dutton was the son of a Royalist who died soon after the surrender of Oxford in 1646. He was left in the care of an exceedingly wealthy uncle, John Dutton of Sherborne Court, Gloucestershire, described by Anthony Wood as 'a learned and a prudent man, and as one of the richest, so one of the meekest men in *England*'. Marvell's former employer, Lord Fairfax, knew Dutton because the general's signature appears on a pass dated 24 June 1646, giving Dutton free passage out of Oxford during the Civil War, though the mystery of why a prominent Cavalier should come to an agreement with the Lord Protector has never been solved. Dutton seems to have admired Cromwell in some fashion and even described the arrangement that they made, linking the two families, as 'a blessing from God'.[8] Thus Cromwell, for no apparent reason other than finding the boy a suitable prospective husband for his daughter, made an agreement that he would become the boy's guardian on John Dutton's death, which eventually happened in January 1657. In return, Dutton would promise to make his nephew heir to the ancestral estate, an arrangement that John Dutton's daughters would have to suffer. Whatever the benefits of this arrangement to the two older men, it was not a success for the young people. Frances Cromwell, then aged fourteen, was a beautiful young woman, deeply in love, not with Dutton but with Robert Rich, grandson of the Earl of Warwick. It was rumoured that the future Charles II also wished to marry her, not least to ease his passage back to the throne by an alliance with the Cromwell dynasty. Frances and Robert eventually married in November 1657 but their happiness was short-lived, Robert dying three months after the marriage. Frances Cromwell lived on into her eighties and William Dutton also died without issue, Sherborne passing to his brother Ralph, later a baronet. The whole elaborate plan had come to nothing.

But at the start of 1653 Cromwell immediately took the boy's education in hand. It was important that he was brought up in a good Puritan atmosphere and the household of the Oxenbridges was perfectly cast. The Reverend John Oxenbridge had been deprived of a tutorship at Magdalen College, Oxford by Archbishop Laud in 1634. They had then gone to the Bermudas to escape this 'prelate's rage' and, on 25 June 1653, Oxenbridge was made one of the seventeen (non-resident) commissioners responsible for the colony. The family's new guest would hear vivid reminiscences from his hosts of their spell as colonists, which may have stimulated him to start to compose his very Puritan poem, 'Bermudas'.

A little earlier than this, Marvell wrote his first political satire. No longer was he the pastoral poet playing with notions of detachment, nor was this a poem embodying the judiciously balanced examinations of the 'Horatian Ode'. It was more in the nature of verse propaganda by a poet who had put his rustic interlude behind him and was busily cementing himself into the new regime. Never again would he write political verse of the subtlety and complex artistry of the 'Horatian Ode'. The poem was probably written after the English victory over the Dutch fleet off Portland on 18–20 February 1653, though it was not actually published until 1665, when it was issued during the later Dutch wars with the addition of some more topical extra lines purporting to have been written by Marvell. This first Dutch war had been in progress since 1652 in consequence of the Navigation Acts of October 1650 and October 1651, which aimed at wresting control of sea trade from the Dutch. Marvell was able to draw on details of his own Dutch travels in the previous decade when writing this poem.

The native of Holderness was apparently unaware of the ironies of 'The Character of Holland' mocking the flat and low-lying physical geography of the Netherlands and the country's attempts to reclaim land from the sea: 'They with mad labour fish'd the *Land* to *Shoar*'. The expressions are vivid; in driving foundation-piles into the sea, the Dutch are said to have 'to the stake a strugling Country bound' and there is much wit in the poem, reminiscent of the Nun Appleton verses. Frequent flooding results, for example, in a situation where 'The Fish oft-times the Burger dispossest,/And sat not as a Meat but as a Guest'. The poem flows smoothly and wittily in those rhyming couplets to which Marvell was addicted. He was a skilled poetic craftsman and a master of the elegantly turned couplet – *pace* the contention of Legouis that he was an 'amateur' – but he was not a radical innovator in the craft of verse. It is one of the ways in which he was John Donne's inferior. He tended to keep with the forms and rhythms he knew and never risked losing control for the sake of a new effect. There are lines in 'The Character of Holland' so smoothly achieved in their balancing wit that they could have been written by Pope, his gibe at the country's obsession with reclaiming land as the only civic good, for example: 'To make a *Bank* was a great *Plot of State*;/Invent a *Shov'l* and be a *Magistrate*.' The mockery and the ceaseless puns go to work on the country's hospitality to religious sects and then its conduct in the recent naval wars. The victory at Portland Bill in February, when seventeen or eighteen Dutch ships were taken along with their crews and with thirty merchantmen, not to mention those ships that were destroyed, sent the country into a frenzy of patriotic joy which culminated in a solemn thanksgiving by order of Parliament on 12 April. Marvell's triumphalist tone reflects this national euphoria. Cromwell would have been well pleased with the poem, had a copy been passed to him.

The two men were in correspondence that summer when Marvell wrote to Cromwell from the Oxenbridges' house at Windsor on 28 July 1653 'to render you some account of Mr Dutton', addressing his letter 'For his Excellence, the Lord General Cromwell'. The tone of the letter is rather pious and even sycophantic ('indeed the onely Ciulity which it is proper for me to practise with so eminent a Person is to obey you') but that may have been no more than the appropriate convention of the time. Marvell told Cromwell that he had examined William several times in the presence of John Oxenbridge. Making use of a metaphor of false and genuine coinage, the tutor admits to what sound like some initial misgivings about Dutton: 'For I thought that there might possibly be some lightness in the Coyn, or errour in the telling, which hereafter I should be bound to make good.' But he promises to bring the best out of the boy in the way Cromwell has already laid down it should be done. He describes Dutton as being 'of a gentle and waxen disposition' and continues piously: 'He hath in him two things which make Youth most easy to be managed, Modesty which is the bridle to Vice, and Emulation which is the Spurr to Virtue.' This spotless youth, it appears, has been put down in an even more blameless household ('so godly a family') ruled over by John Oxenbridge, a man, Marvell unctuously observes, 'whose Doctrine and Example are like a Book and a Map, not onely instructing the Eare but demonstrating to the Ey which way we ought to trauell'. Mrs Oxenbridge is also reported to have exhibited 'a great tendernesse' towards the boy, fitting up his room as a study to work in and feeding him so well that his waxy pallor is disappearing: 'he hath already much mended his Complexion'.[9]

Since John Oxenbridge was a Fellow at Eton, it has been suggested that William may have attended the school for formal academic instruction, leaving Marvell with the responsibility for the boy's general moral welfare. Given the strong Puritan atmosphere of the Oxenbridge household, such a task for Marvell would have been otiose and it is hard to conceive of his not having some more active tutorial role. There would, however, have been plenty of time for carrying on his own studies and for writing poetry. 'Bermudas' shows Marvell's almost hypnotic mastery of rhythm, the rocking verses mirroring the regular motion of the waves and the plashing oars of the Puritan pilgrims: 'And all the way, to guide their Chime,/With falling Oars they kept the time.' The poem expresses the thankful words of the pilgrims at God's providence in sending them to these happy isles 'Safe from the Storms and Prelat's rage'. It embodies that characteristic Marvellian play with Puritan rigour and luscious sensuality. In spite of the intense piety of the divinely favoured occupants of the little boat, the waterborne elect can still relish the pleasures of the taste-buds if not those of the flesh. The divine Provider hurls his bounty at them:

He makes the Figs our mouths to meet;
And throws the Melons at our feet.

Notwithstanding the piety of a poem written to be read, no doubt, by his Puritan hosts as soon as the ink was dry, the poem recalls in its conceits the Fairfacian manner: the clusters of oranges on the trees, glowing in their surround of dark green foliage, are 'Like golden lamps in a green Night'.

While at Eton, Marvell made friends with the poet and musician

Nathaniel Ingelo and with the scholar John Hales. Ingelo had been a Fellow of Eton since 1650 and was passionately fond of music in church services. When he lived in Bristol some local Puritans took exception to this, prompting the reply from Ingelo: 'Take away Music, take away my life.'[10] When Bulstrode Whitlocke was appointed Ambassador Extraordinary to the Court of Sweden in September 1653, with the task of trying to persuade the neutral Swedes to favour the English in their naval war with the Dutch, Ingelo accompanied him as chaplain. Whitlocke sailed to Sweden in November and eventually a treaty was signed at Uppsala on 28 April 1654, establishing a political alliance and free commerce between England and Sweden. Marvell wrote a Latin poem, 'A Letter to Doctor Ingelo', regretting his friend's absence and praising Queen Christina of Sweden. It also contains a reference to '*Victor Oliverus nudum Caput exerit Armus*' (Cromwell in triumph, unhelmeted, takes up arms) and implies that Marvell was only recently acquainted with Ingelo. The poem also contains an interesting reference to a portrait of Queen Christina that Marvell has clearly seen, likely to be the one sent by her to Cromwell as a diplomatic courtesy. This suggests that Marvell enjoyed access to Cromwell's private apartments, where the picture was displayed and where it is said to have aroused the jealousy of Cromwell's wife. A newsletter of 20 May 1653 reports: 'Though our General's lady when she casts her eye on that queenes picture lately presented to his Ex[cellenc]y sighs and sayes, If I were gon that were she that must be the woman.'[11]

Marvell's other new acquaintance at Eton was the theologian, John Hales, originally made a Fellow of the College in 1619 and a learned and bookish man described by Anthony Wood as 'a walking library'. After an early flirtation with Calvinism he had been found a canonry at Windsor by Archbishop Laud, which resulted in his being ejected by the Puritans in 1642 and forced to live in hiding. He eventually lost his fellowship in 1649, after refusing to swear the appropriate oath to the Commonwealth, and died in poverty in 1656. John Aubrey talks of his 'bountifull mind' and notes: 'He loved Canarie; but moderately, to refresh his spirits.'[12] Marvell later recalled Hales, still angry at the way the Civil War had undone him, as 'a most learned Divine . . . most remarkable for his Sufferings in the late times, and his Christian Patience under them . . . I account it no small honour to have grown up into some part of his Acquaintance, and convers'd a while with the living *remains* of one of the clearest heads and best prepared brests in Christendom.'[13] The rough treatment handed out to this gentle scholar rankled with Marvell and helps to explain his unwillingness to look back on the Civil War with any affection.

But in 1654 Marvell was still Cromwell's unofficial laureate. Around April of that year, the date of the signing of a treaty with the Queen of Sweden, he probably wrote the two Latin epigrams, '*In Effigiem Oliveri Cromwell*' – a couplet praising an image that frightens his enemies and provides security to his people – and '*In eandem Reginae Sueciae transmissam*', a slightly longer poem designed to accompany a portrait sent to the Queen (and once attributed to Milton), which praises her as the virgin Queen of the north ('*Bellipotens Virgo*') and Cromwell as the agent of the people's will. He may already have started work on a longer poem celebrating Cromwell's first anniversary as Lord Protector, a title he had assumed on 16 December 1653.

On 2 June, Marvell wrote from Eton to Milton at his home in Petty France in London, referring to having presented a copy of Milton's newly published *Defensio Secunda* to Bradshaw. Marvell's own reaction to this Latin work, a continuation of Milton's defence of the regicides that also contained some autobiographical passages and reflections on his blindness, was not a little hyperbolic: 'I shall now studie it even to the getting of it by Heart: esteeming it to my poor Judgement (which yet I wish it were so right in all Things else) as the most compendious Scale, for so much, to the Height of the Roman eloquence.'[14] After rather more in this vein, including an analogy with the spiralling imperialist narrative of Trajan's column in Rome, which Marvell would have examined in 1645 and 'in whose winding ascent we see imboss'd the severall Monuments of your learned victoryes', Marvell concludes with 'an affectionate Curiosity' to know the latest news about Colonel Overton, who had been Governor of Hull since 1647 and had just met Milton. The letter suggests a regular and continuing intimacy between the two poets, though no other correspondence has survived from this time. Two years more would elapse, however, before they were finally working together.[15]

Marvell's celebration of Cromwell's first year as Lord Protector, 'The First Anniversary of the Government under O.C.', was written presumably to be circulated in time for the anniversary on 16 December 1654 but it was not published until the following year. The printer was Thomas

Newcomb, the government printer, which suggests that Cromwell's men were pleased to see it circulated as propaganda. Its author was not disclosed.

Though not as great a poem as the 'Horatian Ode', the poem is a complex, less dispassionate exploration of Cromwell's rule. Critics have interpreted it, variously, as simple praise, as a call to Cromwell to institute a new kingly dynasty, or as an attempt to portray Cromwell as a Davidic king. It is certainly not crudely propagandist, although it celebrates Cromwell and defends him against the charge that he had assumed arbitrary power and deplores his critics, particularly the radical sectarians who opposed him. It has the same gift for graceful and memorable epithet which marked the 'Ode': ''Tis he the force of scatter'd Time contracts,/And in one Year the work of Ages acts.' After celebrating Cromwell's political virility the poem praises his ability to forge a harmonious polity: 'Such was that wondrous Order and Consent,/When *Cromwell* tun'd the ruling Instrument.' Marvell's readiness to trust in power and the fateful moment is evident in the portrayal:

Hence oft I think, if in some happy Hour
High Grace should meet in one with highest Pow'r,
And then a seasonable People still
Should bend to his, as he to Heavens will,
What we might hope, what wonderful Effect
From such a wish'd Conjuncture might reflect.

Alas, the people are not always seasonable and Utopian hopes are thwarted by human folly. Cromwell's ability to survive 'ponyarding Conspiracies' and a coach accident in Hyde Park (in September of that year) only makes him seem stronger and more predestined. Marvell returns to the theme of Cromwell's selfless abandonment of private life to serve the public good that he had explored in the 'Ode': 'Resigning up thy Privacy so dear,/To turn the headstrong Peoples Charioteer'. Where he was, in the earlier poem, a thunderbolt, he is here 'a small Cloud' that swells to a drenching, beneficent, rainstorm 'Which to the thirsty Land did plenty bring,/But though forewarn'd, o'r-took and wet the King.' This seems a rather weak metaphor to describe the violence of the regicide, but it reveals Marvell's conviction at this time – in contrast to his position twenty years later – that the King's fate was inevitable. Cromwell, in what he did, was a divine agent ('an higher Force him push'd') and strong decisive government is preferred by Marvell to undisciplined plebiscite: ''Tis not a Freedome, that where All command;/Nor Tyranny, where One does them withstand'. For this reason Marvell is bitterly condemnatory of the Fifth Monarchy men and cognate sectarians – 'Accursed Locusts' – who gleefully pounce on every political wobble of the strong leader. After a passage of envious praise put into the mouths of foreign rulers the poem ends with a salute to the man who 'as the *Angel* of our Commonweal,/Troubling the Waters, yearly mak'st them Heal.'

The celebration of Cromwell, buttressed by classical and Biblical allusions that gave it a more epic resonance throughout, would have done Marvell's burgeoning career in the state no harm at all.

8

A Fine and Private Place

Rather at once our Time devour,
Than languish in his slow-chapt pow'r.

The period of the English Civil War and its aftermath was a time of great religious as well as political ferment in England. Millenarian sects – the 'Accursed Locusts' of 'The First Anniversarie' – swarmed around the body politic and even mainstream politicians saw themselves as the instruments of God. In the 1650s the Puritans interpreted their task as establishing the rule of the saints. Ordinary Protestants as well as the millenarians pressed forward with their demands. On 25 May 1653 a petition was presented from the Kentish Churches to Cromwell offering advice, 'judging this a season in which the Lord doth especially call for the free contribution of his people to the work which through so much blood, etc. he hath wrestled into their hands'.[1] There was an expectation, in the more enthused, that at this glorious time many of the last things forecast in the Book of Revelation might come to pass, one of which was the conversion of the Jews. In August 1653 another petition to Parliament suggested that the Jews should be invited into the Commonwealth 'for there [*sic*] time is neere at hand'.[2]

Some scholars have been persuaded by this evidence to see the reference in Marvell's most famous poem, 'To his Coy Mistress', to 'the Conversion of the *Jews*', as evidence of its contemporaneity with that national mood, lending the poem an additional touch of playful irony. Others have taken another reference in the poem to the speaker loving his mistress, did time allow, 'ten years before the Flood', to mean it was written in 1646, because contemporaries like Raleigh in his *History of the World* (1614) forecast the Flood in *anno mundi* 1656.[3] Of the two dates, 1653 is a little more persuasive, but the risk of premature certainty in dating Marvell's poems must always be avoided. It is, however, not unreasonable to consider the poem at this point.

Marvell was aged thirty-two and unmarried. In the opinion of John Aubrey he was a reserved man of few words – not, perhaps, an ardent lover and wooer. 'To his Coy Mistress' inevitably raises the question about the identity of its addressee. There is a long tradition in literary biography of attempting to identify the poet's mistress – Dante's Beatrice, Arnold's Marguerite – which sometimes meets with success, but often is no more than an innocuous and pleasant detective game. Nothing is known, unfortunately, about Marvell's mistress except what can be inferred from the poem itself, which is cast in the form of a highly literary exercise drawing on many traditional devices and themes, though Marvell, characteristically, gives it a wholly individual and original flavour. There could well have been no mistress at all. Unlike the amatory poems of John Donne where the extremity of erotic feeling, the reckless *hubris* of sexual love, is rendered sometimes with a startling intensity that is almost palpable, 'To his Coy Mistress' is never less than controlled, witty, in command of itself, its soaring moments of eloquence just that, not cries of unchecked passion. The extraordinary effect of the writing lies in something else. Two arguments, however, may be exercised on the other side. The first is that poets invariably *do* root their poems in experience, actual lived experience.[4] The second is that the poem contains an oddly specific detail – 'I by the Tide/Of *Humber* would complain' – locating the specific poet in a specific place. Could his mistress have been a young woman from Hull, kept in touch with during the years in London, more easily while in Yorkshire, and again since? He was in contact with the town throughout his life, visiting relatives, taking business advice from in-laws, and, later, acting as its Member of Parliament. To have kept a mistress there would not have been beyond the bounds of possibility. But those who date the poem in 1646, when he was either in Italy or Spain, have cast a young Italian or Spanish woman in the role. Coming to the end of his foreign trip, Marvell would have reason to emphasise the urgency of enjoying a love that might soon have to be cut short. And, finally, there is the question, discussed more fully later, of whether Marvell possessed any ardency at all towards the opposite sex.

Certainly, the literary precedents for the poem are many and obvious. The central theme comes from the famous ode of Horace (Book I.11), with its cry of '*carpe diem, quam minimum credula postero*' (seize this moment, place the least possible trust in the future). The spoor of Marvell's more immediate contemporaries is also found on the poem, in particular, Abraham Cowley's poem 'The Mistress', first published in 1647 in a collection with that name. Cowley (1618–67) was a precocious poet who wrote his first verse-romance at the age of ten. When the Civil War broke out he joined the Royalist side with a satire, 'The Puritan and the Papist', and a political epic, 'The Civil War'. He was later imprisoned as a Royalist spy but at the Restoration was more or less rehabilitated. Charles II said at his death: 'That Mr Cowley had not left a better man behind him in England.' The correspondences between Cowley's poem and Marvell's are thematic and even linguistic. The phrase 'vast *Eternity*' in Cowley passes straight into Marvell's poem but in the seventeenth century, which took for granted allusiveness and echo and reference back to poetic precedent, the charge of plagiarism would not even have arisen.

'To his Coy Mistress', now considered one of the great canonical poems in the English poetic tradition, has attracted a corresponding body of criticism but, like most poems of its kind, its greatness lies in a certain quality of resistance. No one can ever quite manage to have the last word on it and, in spite of its allusiveness, it has an immediate intelligibility, a direct appeal to the reader. Unlike Marvell's satires and long poems it can be read happily without recourse to footnotes. The poet Philip Larkin was probably thinking of this poem when he wrote:

> *What still compels attention to Marvell's work is the ease with which he manages the fundamental paradox of verse – the conflict of natural word usage with metre and rhyme – and marries it either to hallucinatory images within his own unique conventions or to sudden sincerities that are as convincing in our age as in his.*[5]

Those 'hallucinatory images' and 'sudden sincerities' abound in a poem that is structured around an argument or logical syllogism. Numerous grave and censorious scholars have come forward to point out that the strict rules of the syllogism are not properly adhered to by the poet. John Crowe Ransom, a key member of the 1940s movement known as 'the New Criticism', wrote in a book with that title that the poem's argument contains lamentable 'indeterminacies that would be condemned in the prose of scientists, and also of college freshmen'.[6] Were the average college freshman, however, able to write a poem of the calibre of 'To his Coy Mistress' it might prove possible to excuse him.

The poem has, even the New Critics would agree, a witty logic, and falls into three short movements or verse paragraphs:

> *'Had we but World enough, and Time . . .'*
> [there would be no urgency]
>
> *'But at my back I alwaies hear . . .'*
> [the pressure of passing time denies us that leisure]
>
> *'Now therefore . . .'*
> [it is imperative that we seize the moment while we can]

The language of the poem is smoothly flowing and witty. 'My vegetable Love should grow/Vaster then empires, and more slow' is a surprising but nonetheless effective image of the leisurely, incremental growth of a relationship, although some scholars have rebuked the common reader for assuming that this is a culinary rather than a Metaphysical term, offering this (speaking perhaps truer than they purposed) as 'a typical example of how Marvell is misread'.[7] Similarly, the concluding image of the two lovers rolling up all their pleasure and passion into a ball which tears – like a Parliamentary cannonball crashing through the gates of a Cavalier park – 'Thorough the iron gates of Life' is striking and arresting. But the most memorable lines of the poem, falling out with that instant memorability, that sense of inevitability in the phrasing – how could it possibly have been put better? – that characterise the greatest poetry, are the central lines, which point to the need for love to vanquish the force of time and human mortality by doing the one thing in its power: seizing the day.

But at my back I alwaies hear
Times winged Charriot hurrying near:
And yonder all before us lye
Desarts of vast Eternity.
Thy Beauty shall no more be found;
Nor, in thy marble Vault, shall sound
My ecchoing Song: then Worms shall try
That long preserv'd Virginity:
And your quaint Honour turn to dust;
And into ashes all my Lust.
The Grave's a fine and private place,
But none I think do there embrace.

Might not a young poet, still conscious of the need to find himself in the world and settle a career before his thirties were swallowed up, have an extra sense of urgency about getting the most out of life before it was too late?

After Marvell's Cromwellian poems of 1654 we enter another of those dark periods in his biography. Nothing is known of him from the time of the praise of Cromwell written at the end of 1654 until his next appearance in France in January 1656, other than that he was still tutoring William Dutton and it may have been that, at the start of 1655, he had managed to persuade Cromwell to allow him to take the teenager on a Grand Tour, pointing out how advantageous it had been for himself a decade earlier.[8] If language-teaching was Marvell's special gift, a foreign trip would have been an obvious step to take.

On 26 January 1656, Alexander Callander, a Scot living in Saumur, wrote to his friend Joseph Williamson, then a young graduate of Queen's College, Oxford but later a statesman and diplomat, and, after his knighthood, Secretary of State in the reign of Charles II. In Williamson's papers in the Public Record Office the letter from Callander is preserved. The latter says to Williamson (the original letter is written in French): 'If you visit Mr Dutton and Monsieur Merville his tutor (*Gouverneur*) I beg you to give them my humble salutations.'[9] Callander took English pupils in a house owned by his sister at Saumur but was absent on business in England in January 1656 when Williamson came to visit. The latter was accompanied by two pupils of his own. Callander wrote from Paris, either having met Marvell and Dutton there en route to Saumur, or being aware of their expected arrival around this time.

Saumur, a town on the Loire, was no accidental choice for these young Puritan gentlemen and their tutors. It was the home of the celebrated Protestant Academy and, as Legouis points out: 'The intellectual atmosphere of the town was strongly Protestant, even though the Protestants were in a minority.'[10] The French Protestants, however, were generally appalled by the English regicide, and the man in charge of a pupil destined to be the son-in-law of Oliver Cromwell might have experienced some coolness of reception. Given Marvell's domestic circumstances when he left for France, living in a strongly Puritan household and having the charge of a ward of the Protector himself, the sojourn in Saumur would nonetheless have been the natural culmination of his most Puritan phase. Whether he sampled the famous wine of Saumur or, as Legouis suggests, made the acquaintance of Father Abel-Louis St Marthe, the learned Father Superior of a nearby Catholic Oratory, or met the local scholar and *bon viveur* Tallemant and through him the most un-Puritan works of Rabelais, must remain conjectural.[11]

The pair remained at Saumur at least until August and probably until September when the academic year ended. On 15 August, James Scudamore, the English Royalist, wrote to Sir Richard Browne, Charles II's resident at Paris and the father-in-law of the diarist John Evelyn, filling him in on the activities of the English at Saumur. Scudamore was rather disparaging of his compatriots' ability for 'acting anything serviceable' to the Royalist cause. He reported that: 'Many of the English are here but few of Noate.' This small noteworthy company included, however, Dutton whom the French called 'le Genre [*sic*] du Protecteur', his connection with Cromwell thus very public indeed. Scudamore also adds that Dutton's 'Governour' is 'one Mervill a notable English Italo-Machavillian'.[12] This is the first recorded indication of Marvell's reputation of being a rather crafty figure whose cards may not always have been placed on the table. He would later be sent on diplomatic missions of a public and of a more clandestine kind. In this instance, it may be no more than a disgruntled Royalist's observation on a young Puritan who had done rather well for himself by toadying to the Cromwellian camp, but it also implies that Marvell was seen as something more than just a travelling tutor: Dutton's companion was 'notable' in his own right.

What might have secured him this reputation – whether after leaving Nun Appleton he had engaged in some more subtle political intrigue that had upset the Royalists – must remain a mystery.

Certainly, Marvell did not disguise his allegiances and connections while at Saumur. During the summer he carried out a task for Milton by circulating in learned circles copies of the latter's *Defensio Pro Se*, published the previous August. In a letter written on 1 August 1657, Milton asked his friend Henry Oldenburg (later the first secretary of the Royal Society) to distribute further copies for him. Oldenburg, yet another Englishman in Saumur with a pupil, would tactfully advise Milton against drawing any further attention in France to this provocative tract, but in his initial request Milton enthusiastically describes Marvell's success in putting the pamphlet about, although he does not identify his 'friend':

> *A learned man, a friend of mine, spent last summer at Saumur. He wrote to me that the book was in demand in those parts; I sent only one copy; he wrote back that some of the learned to whom he had lent it had been pleased with it hugely. Had I not thought I should be doing a thing agreeable to them, I should have spared you trouble and myself expense.*[13]

Back in Eton probably by the end of 1656, Marvell continued in his duties in the Oxenbridge household as Dutton's tutor. Still closely connected with key figures like Milton and Cromwell, he may have felt that he deserved some more important role in the new order that matched the abilities of a 'notable' thirty-five-year-old, rather than remaining an eternal young gentleman's companion and Latin teacher. But twelve months had still to elapse before he would make that transition to a servant of the State. Early in 1657 he would read the reports of a great English naval victory and see in it the opportunity for a poem. The result – 'On the Victory Obtained by Blake over the Spaniards, in the Bay of Sanctacruze, in the Island of Teneriff' – was a poem that has generally been considered to detract from Marvell's reputation in that it has been seen as a rather questionable attempt to curry favour with Cromwell. Its omission from the edition of Marvell's poems obtained by the Bodleian Library in Oxford in 1945, known familiarly by scholars as

'Eng.poet.d.49' – an edition whose contemporaneous manuscript additions and corrections have given it an air of greater textual authority than the first 1681 Folio edition – has led some scholars to excise the poem from the Marvell canon.[14] According to Legouis, who prints the poem in the standard edition of Marvell's poems: 'It would be no loss to Marvell's reputation, literary and moral, for it smacks of *courtisanerie*.'[15] But Marvellians have sometimes been too ready to drop awkward poems from the canon when they fail to measure up. The balance of probability is that Marvell is the author. It was first published, anonymously, in an anthology in 1674, with the allusions to Cromwell cut out to fit the mood of the time.

The great naval commander, Sir Robert Blake, was one of Cromwell's most able and effective admirals. He had been engaged since May 1655 in blockading the Spanish coast in order to intercept treasure ships returning from America. On 20 April 1657 Blake destroyed a fleet of sixteen Spanish treasure ships at Tenerife in spite of the fact that the bay of Santa Cruz was deep and narrow-mouthed and flanked by shore batteries armed with heavy guns. Not one of the English ships was lost in the action. News of the victory reached England towards the end of May and there was a public thanksgiving in London on 3 June. Blake's health was poor following an earlier battle wound and he died on 7 August, two hours before reaching Plymouth. The poem must therefore have been written at some time between June and early August.

Its tone is triumphalist, scorning the weak fear of the Spanish when faced with the English navy. The line 'The best of Lands should have the best of Kings' has been taken as an endorsement by Marvell of the idea that Cromwell should accept the crown, something he had declined to recommend in his previous poem on Cromwell's first anniversary as Protector. Cromwell had, by the time the poem came to be written, rejected the offer of the crown, so the sentiment was otiose. The climatically blessed Canary Isles, however, are said to lack 'nothing Heaven can afford,/Unless it be, the having you [i.e. Cromwell] their Lord.' The repeated invocations of Cromwell ('For your renown, his conquering Fleet does ride', 'And all assumes your courage in your cause', 'For your resistless genious there did Raign') give the poem a rather sycophantic air that is far removed from the carefully balanced subtleties of the 'Horatian

Ode'. Whether kingly gratitude or aesthetic reservation were uppermost in Cromwell's mind as he read the poem, with its closing couplet 'Whilst fame in every place, her Trumpet blowes,/And tells the World, how much to you it owes', very shortly after its completion the poet was rewarded with the post he sought of Latin Secretary in the Protectorate. At last he had entered the public, political world in which he would remain until his death. His days of tutoring were over.

9

A Good Man For the State to Make Use Of

> *At length, by the interest of* Milton, *to whom he was somewhat agreeable for his ill-natur'd wit, he was made Under-secretary to* Cromwell's *Secretary. Pleas'd with which honour, he publish'd a congratulatory poem in praise of the Tyrant.*
>
> Samuel Parker, *History of His Own Time* [1]

The office that Marvell entered, probably on 2 September 1657, was that of John Thurloe, Secretary to the Council of State. Although Thurloe was strictly his superior in that office, his job was to assist Milton as secretary of Foreign or Latin tongues and therefore he is more usually described as assistant Latin Secretary. Latin was the language of international diplomacy and communication, so Marvell's duties would involve translation between English and Latin, drafting letters and documents, and attending on foreign dignitaries in London as translator.[2] Milton's blindness would obviously hamper him in most respects, so Marvell would have plenty of writing and drafting to do. He would probably also have taken some dictation from Milton and generally deputised for him. Marvell was also a frequent visitor at this time to Milton's house in Petty France. Some of the documents worked on by Marvell survive in the British Library and the Bodleian Library, one of which is a forty-page translation of a political tract by the Swedish envoy to England, Johann Frederick von Friessendorff, done in Marvell's neat, legible hand probably a few months after starting work, at the beginning of 1658. The aim of the tract was to persuade Cromwell to send his navy, with that of Sweden, against Holland and Spain.[3] The historian Christopher Hill says of Marvell: 'Like

Pepys, he was one of the new type of civilian middle-class official who came into their own after the Civil War, during the soberer years of the Protectorate.'[4] Marvell's salary was a comfortable £200 a year. He would find himself at the heart of government, and, since Thurloe was an immensely powerful figure in the administration and head of the overseas intelligence service, he would be gaining an insight into an area in which he would later become personally involved.

His first recorded piece of work was a translation of an official despatch to Thurloe from Hamburg in September 1657.[5] Other documents in his hand that have survived include letters from Cromwell to overseas ambassadors and dignitaries. Among the colonial papers in the Public Record Office is a document recording a petition from a Scottish merchant, Mathias Lynen, on behalf of members of the Guinea Company of Scotland, to Cromwell ('their only remaining refuge under God the righteous') asking for help in recovering a ship 'perfidiously seized' by the Portuguese on its way back from Africa in 1637. The crew had been murdered and the ship had still not been released. On the document is written: 'John Thurloe has desired And. Marvell to write a letter upon this petition to the King of Portugal.'[6] Marvell continued in this work probably until the autumn of 1659.

John Thurloe had been appointed Secretary of State in March 1652 and had helped Cromwell in his ascent into the Protectorate. His charge of intelligence included supervision of the internal and foreign post, and he was reputed to have a strong intelligence network with spies able to intercept letters. According to Bulstrode Whitelocke, he was one of a small knot of friends with whom Cromwell would occasionally relax and 'lay aside his greatness'.[7] At the Restoration, Thurloe was accused of high treason but was released to enjoy his retirement at Great Milton in Oxfordshire, where he was said to be consulted for his vast and privy knowledge of foreign affairs. With the return of Charles II he concealed a vast hoard of papers relating to the Protectorate which were to be rediscovered in the reign of William III in a false ceiling in Lincoln's Inn. It is possible that Marvell visited Thurloe in these retirement years at his chambers in Lincoln's Inn.

Marvell himself dated his involvement in public affairs to this time, denying that he had any prior political engagement, despite his having consorted for several years with leading Puritan figures in ways that had aroused the suspicions of Royalists. In a passage from the second part of *The Rehearsal Transpros'd*, published in 1673 when Marvell was distancing himself from these associations, he wrote:

> *for as to myself, I never had any, not the remotest relation to publick matters, nor correspondence with the persons then predominant, until the year 1657, when indeed I enter'd into an imployment, for which I was not altogether improper, and which I consider'd to be the most innocent and inoffensive towards his Majesties affairs of any in that usurped and irregular Government, to which all men were then exposed. And this I accordingly discharg'd without disobliging any one person, there having been opportunity and indeavours since his Majesties happy return to have discover'd had it been otherwise.*[8]

This is a very dubious passage, which contains a straight lie: we have already seen several examples of his 'correspondence with the persons then predominant'. His representation of himself as someone who reluctantly took up a civil service post because it was the best use of his abilities, and exercised it in strict neutrality without any endorsement of the administration, always with a disinterested care for 'his Majesties affairs', is laughable if it is not something worse. 'He was Latin secretary to Oliver, and very intimate and conversant with that person,' wrote Anthony Wood of the reluctant civil servant.[9] Even his reference to 'that usurped and irregular Government' – one in which he eagerly served and sought preferment and whose poetic propagandist he became – is a slippery piece of hindsight that does him little credit.

Meanwhile two marriages took place that autumn. The first was of his former pupil at Nun Appleton, Mary Fairfax, who on 15 September married the second Duke of Buckingham, George Villiers, a rake later satirised by John Dryden as Zimri in *Absalom and Achitophel* (1681). Cromwell disapproved of the match, unsurprisingly, if Bishop Burnet's brief character sketch of the groom is a true one: 'He had no principles of religion, vertue, or friendship. Pleasure, frolick, or extravagant diversion was all that he laid to heart. He was true to nothing.'[10] It was an unfortunate fate for the innocent emblem of ideal virtue celebrated in the poems written at Nun Appleton House. Two months later, on 19 November, Cromwell's third daughter, also called Mary, married Thomas Belasyse, second Viscount Fauconberg, a kinsman of Lord Fairfax, at Hampton Court and Marvell composed two songs for what was probably a musical entertainment devised for the occasion ('Two Songs at the Marriage of the Lord Fauconberg and Lady Mary Cromwell'). They are both in the pastoral mode that Marvell loved, the first a dialogue between the shepherd, Endymion, and the moon, Cynthia, the second between three rustics, Hobbinol, Phillis, and Tomalin. The first contains an oblique reference to the marriage of Frances Cromwell to Robert Rich, frustrating Cromwell's plans to have her marry William Dutton. The second alludes to Fauconberg's Yorkshire origins by calling him '*the Northern Shepheard's Son*'. Listening to the applause die away after the performance of these songs, Marvell might reflect on the marriages of all these young people he had known and contrast them with his own increasingly confirmed bachelor status.

The fact that, amid all his official duties and political tribute poems, Marvell was still writing pastoral verses is a reminder that poems like 'The Garden', or, as some have suggested,[11] 'Upon the Hill and Grove at Bill-borow', could have been written after the Yorkshire period to which they are customarily assigned.

The pastoral mode was commonly used by poets in the seventeenth century and, without an appreciation of its conventions and properties, one cannot fully appreciate Marvell's way of reanimating conventional material. The case against pastoral is plain enough and the prevailing eighteenth-century view was expressed with his habitual trenchancy by Dr Johnson when he argued that the pastoral machinery of Milton's elegy *Lycidas* was inconsistent with 'the effusion of real passion' and that: 'Where there is leisure for fiction there is little grief.'[12] Such naive views of poetic spontaneity, which were also a characteristic of English poetry in the postwar period – one thinks of Larkin's denunciations of 'the myth-kitty' – may have receded in the more complicated critical climate of the late twentieth century, although some readers may still have difficulty with a poetry that is not plain utterance but that speaks through a poetic convention. The special pleasure of Marvell's poetry lies often precisely in this play with tradition. Understanding it is the key to enjoying him. The critic J.B. Leishman put it well when he wrote: 'For, although Marvell's poetry is highly original and, at its best, unmistakably his own and no one else's, he is almost always acting upon hints and suggestions provided by earlier poets, and almost never writing entirely, as children would say, out of his own head.'[13]

Marvell was also a learned classicist and would be familiar with the origins of the pastoral tradition in the *Idylls* of Theocritus, the third-century BC Sicilian poet who laid the groundwork of this bucolic genre where shepherds and shepherdesses acted out their little dramas with an interesting mixture of idealisation and realism that Marvell's talent readily embraced. Virgil's eclogues and the second-century AD Greek poem by Longus, *Daphnis and Chloe*, developed the tradition which, after disappearing in the middle ages, returned at the Renaissance in the poetry of Torquato Tasso, Miguel de Cervantes, Sir Philip Sidney, William Browne and many others. The genre eventually expired when the Romantic poets rediscovered a more naturalistic response to rural life, throwing the convention aside to commune directly, as they supposed, with nature. But Marvell, as well as drawing on the historical tradition of the genre, also played with and echoed the work of his contemporaries working with the same matter. Sometimes he appears even to be answering their poetic arguments in his own variations. As the Marvell scholar and critic Frank Kermode put it: 'It seems to have been Marvell's habit to assume in his readers an acquaintance with the other poems of the genres in which he chose to work.'[14] A modern reader, impatient with these conventions – which can admittedly invite on occasion a wry or satiric response – could reflect that much popular entertainment in late twentieth-century culture, particularly television comedy, practises an identical generic parasitism.

Grouped together in the 1681 Folio, and probably intended to be read as a sequence, are four poems where a mower rather than a shepherd is the pastoral protagonist. The poems play with the theme of art versus nature – the mower's work being, symbolically, to disturb the latter in pursuit of the former. Poems by Thomas Randolph, Ben Jonson, William Shakespeare's *Winter's Tale*, and Christopher Marlowe, as well as Horace, Ovid, Seneca, Pliny and Theocritus, signal their presence under the surface of these poems. The first of the sequence, 'The Mower Against Gardens', is a diatribe by the mower against 'Luxurious' (lecherous or voluptuous) man who corrupted the simplicity of naturally occurring flora by creating gardens, artificially cordoned-off zones of corrupt pleasure where plant-breeding, grafting, importation of new species – and even statuary – become the signs of moral delinquency. To this Puritan argument against decoration (a bone of contention between the Puritan party and Archbishop Laud in the Church of England, where church architecture, rite and even church organs became a contested issue) is added a sexual undertone. The gardener has 'dealt' – acted as a pander – 'between the Bark and Tree' by grafting:

> *'Tis all enforc'd; the Fountain and the Grot;*
> *While the sweet Fields do lye forgot:*
> *Where willing Nature does to all dispence*
> *A wild and fragrant Innocence.*

The paradox of a highly artificial poem celebrating natural simplicity against artifice is not meant to be missed. Marvell, in the Nun Appleton poems and others, would celebrate the garden, its very artificiality, the comparison of ranked flowers with military drill yielding up memorable conceits. He loved gardens, their formality, their sensual pleasures ('Stumbling on Melons, as I pass'), the way they stood as emblems of moderate civility. The poem is thus a carefully crafted argument, a form of aesthetic play, a tease, a gesture towards the pleasures of poetic genre. Yet there is, like a vein of colour in marble, as always with this poet, the tinge of a serious argument that links it to the real political world. It is a characteristic Marvellian movement, from art to society and back again, the mediation being done through the conventions of an informed literary tradition. The personal tension, too, is there, between an artistic sensibility that relished richness and 'luxuriousness' and a more dutiful social conscience.

As well as the great contest between King and Parliament, the seventeenth century witnessed a philosophical tussle between the old philosophy and the new. It was a great age of scientific inquiry, of hostility to the dying scholasticism and of hospitality to the new age of rational inquiry. Francis Bacon announced himself as *buccinator novi temporis* – the herald of the new age – dismissing, in *The Advancement of Learning*, the traditional thinkers, 'their wits being shut up in the cells of a few authors (chiefly Aristotle their dictator)', in favour of an empirical, inquiring spirit. A similar movement was going on among the exponents of 'rational theology', trying to reconcile science with religion. The great seventeenth-century prose writer, Sir Thomas Browne, called man the 'great amphibium', thinking scientifically and religiously, trying to live reasonably in the two elements.

Marvell would find himself – at any rate at the level of language – in conflict with some of these trends, as a prose writer who loved rich expressions, linguistic borrowings, subtle allusions. His later antagonist, Samuel Parker, would rebuke him for his refusal of plain speech. In an attack on Platonism in philosophy, published in the year of the Great Fire, Parker declared: 'Though a huge lushious style may relish sweet to childish and liquorish Fancies, yet it rather loaths and nauceats a discreet understanding then forms and nourishes it.'[15] A Saussurean before his time, Parker believed language was a system of arbitrary signs: 'The use of Words is not to explain the Natures of Things, but only to stand as marks and signs in their stead, as Arithmetical figures are only notes of Numbers.' So, in these seemingly innocent pastoral poems, one of the finest poets of the age explored, reflected, illuminated – and, above all made into poetry – all these contested questions, but he did so by holding the various elements in suspension. His effects have often been diminished by critics who try to convert them into reductive exegesis, pinning them down too tightly to specific referents that can be at best only hypothetical.

On 23 April 1658 Jane Oxenbridge, who had taken such good care of Marvell's charge, William Dutton, died at Eton. Marvell composed for her a Latin epitaph that was carved on black marble and erected in Eton College Chapel. At the Restoration it was painted over and later it was removed altogether. Anthony Wood dismissed it as a 'large canting inscription',[16] presumably hinting at the overelaboration of a monument for the wife of a Puritan minister. It was printed in the 1681 Folio.

Several months later, news would come of a far more significant death that would draw from Marvell not lapidary platitudes but a major, and in parts unusually heartfelt, poem. On 3 September 1658, Oliver Cromwell died of pneumonia, the day after a violent storm that was immediately seen as symbolic. His health had been failing since the beginning of the year and after the blow of his favourite daughter Elizabeth's death from cancer in August he lived on for less than a month. His body lay in state for weeks while people filed past to pay their respects. One of them was the Quaker, Edward Burrough, who was appalled by this outbreak of hero worship for one 'who too much sought the greatness and the honour of the world, and loved the praise of men, and took flattering titles and vain respects of deceitful men'.[17]

There was, however, one man who knew that he would have to offer his tribute, and notwithstanding his later claim to have abhorred Cromwell and his circle, it was done with an unforced will.

10

I Saw Him Dead

So have I seen a Vine, whose lasting Age
Of many a Winter hath surviv'd the rage.

The death of Cromwell, under whose influence Marvell had flourished throughout the mid-1650s, was a personal blow but also an omen for the future. Presumably Marvell and his friends at the centre of the administration would have made their calculations. In the wake of the fall of a strong political leader, powerful undercurrents start to run. The Royalists, waiting in the wings, would have taken heart. Doubts about the ability of Cromwell's son Richard to take over would surface. Almost a year to the day after entering government service, Marvell's patron had been whisked away, and the future, suddenly, would look less hopeful. New political masters might want to install their own civil servants and his past associations might tell against him. In spite of those alliances, at heart he was not a revolutionary and would, in an ideal world, have chosen the path of supporting a constitutional monarchy. He could live with a restoration, but would it want to live with him?

Whatever his thoughts about his personal prospects, Marvell must have known that a panegyric would be expected of him. From the poem that emerged it seems likely that he needed no external prompting, for it is one of the few from Marvell's hand that contains any expression of direct, personal feeling. It was almost certainly written in the immediate aftermath of Cromwell's death because a volume of tributes, including

Marvell's, was entered in the Stationers' Register by the publisher Henry Herringman on 20 January 1659. It was called simply 'A Poem upon the Death of O.C.'.

Once again the Cromwell of this poem is represented as the reluctant actor who would have preferred a quiet life but whom 'angry Heaven unto War had sway'd'. It recounts, in dignified, moving couplets, the known public events leading up to his death, including the death of his daughter and his love of her and the presaging storm of the night before his death. His victories at Dunbar in 1650 and Worcester in 1651 – both of which shared the date of his death, 3 September – are recalled. Marvell's fatalism has already been noted. It was a complex thing that resulted in a tendency both to defer to the present power (first Cromwell, then Charles II) and to justify apparent shifts in allegiance (though, of course, Marvell became part of the Parliamentary Opposition to Charles, even if he did not challenge his kingship) by arguing that it was not his business to challenge the legitimacy of rulers. Loyalism rather than consistency was his standard of value. Thus, Cromwell is seen once again as an inevitable force, blessed by the stars, and, through the pathetic fallacy, his death marked by the sympathetic natural elements:

> O Cromwell, Heavens Favorite! *To none*
> *Have such high honours from above been shown:*
> *For whom the Elements we Mourners see,*
> *And* Heav'n *it self would the great* Herald *be;*

This is, of course, a public funeral elegy and a certain excess of praise is demanded by the genre. Copious allusions to classical models such as Virgil's *Georgics* abound and Cromwell is celebrated in terms that suggest that his valour exceeds anything in the Arthurian legends and his piety that of Edward the Confessor. His sanctioning of religious war is approved ('He first put Armes into *Religions* hand') and his magnanimity is asserted. Towards the end of the poem a more personal note enters ('All, all is gone of ours or his delight'), suggesting that the poet is writing from personal and intimate knowledge of Cromwell. Not in the remotest sense a confessional poet, Marvell here nonetheless lets his personal emotions show at last:

I saw him dead, a leaden slumber lyes,
And mortal sleep over those wakefull eyes:
Those gentle rays under the lids were fled,
Which through his looks that piercing sweetness shed;
That port which so majestique was and strong,
Loose and depriv'd of vigour, stretch'd along:
All wither'd, all discolour'd, pale and wan.
How much another thing, no more than man?

With just a hint at the controversial status of Cromwell's pre-eminence, the poet predicts that future ages will see him more clearly as an exemplar of courage, 'When truth shall be allow'd, and faction cease'. He is now in Heaven, leaving behind his mourners 'lost in tears'. The poem closes with an allusion to Cromwell's son, Richard, who assumed the Protectorate as if Cromwell had been a hereditary monarch. The reference to Richard's 'milder beams' implies delicately that he will not be able to match his father's authority and power. His absence from the struggle to date is glossed as another example of Cromwellian reserve, waiting in silence until the call of duty comes. When it does, being a Cromwell, he will rise to the occasion: 'A Cromwell in an houre a prince will grow.' Richard survived, in fact, little over six months before his government collapsed in April 1659 to be followed by the restored Rump Parliament.

A surviving document in the Public Record Office shows the detailed arrangements that were made for the funeral. It records the amount of mourning cloth allotted to each of the principal mourners:

9	*6*	*Mr. John Milton*	
9	*6*	*Mr. Merville*	*Lattin*
9	*6*	*Sir Philip Meadows*	*Secryes*
		Mr. Sterry	
9	*0*	*Mr. Drayden*[1]	

'Mr. Drayden' is the poet John Dryden. The figures in the far left column are the number of yards of black cloth proposed and those in the next column the amount actually allocated (though an alternative interpretation is that the two columns represent the shillings and pence granted to buy the cloth).[2] In the event, only the Lord Mayor of London and prominent City officials were granted the full nine yards of mourning cloth. Another document listing those who walked in the funeral procession shows that in the Privy Chamber at Somerset House, where the official mourners assembled before moving off down the Strand, was a party described as 'Secretarys of ye ffrench & Latin Tongs'. This little company of poets and scholars included Dryden, Marvell, Milton, Nathaniel Sterry (another assistant Latin Secretary drafted in to replace Sir Philip Meadows, the man who had beaten Marvell to the post in 1653 and who was now a diplomat) and Samuel Hartlib, a friend of Milton and occasional government servant. As they all moved off down the Strand towards Westminster Abbey, 'Mr. Merville', whose name was next to Milton's in the official list, would have been able to steer the blind poet's steps during the foot procession towards the Abbey.

When Cromwell died, his body had been embalmed and removed from Whitehall to Somerset House, where it lay for many weeks in state, dressed in royal robes of purple and ermine with a golden sceptre in the hand and a crown on the head. The body was privately buried in the chapel of Henry VII in Westminster Abbey on 26 September, but the public funeral in which Marvell and Milton took part was held on 23 November. It was done with magnificent pomp at a cost of £60,000, which caused controversy within the Republican camp. The route taken by the mourners from Somerset House to the Abbey was lined by soldiers in new red coats with black buttons. A king would not have received a more lavish send-off.

Marvell retained his post as a Latin Secretary during the rule of Richard Cromwell and for some little time after, but it is clear that he was already contemplating a move from the civil service to a career in Parliamentary politics. If he were to stand as an MP then Hull, the town where he had so many associations and connections, was the obvious choice. Invariably shrewd in his career moves, Marvell may already have sensed that Richard Cromwell was not going to survive and that the era of powerful authoritarian rule by one man was over. A stronger Parliament, if not a Restoration, was more than likely. At the end of December Marvell set the wheels in motion for selection as a candidate with a request to his sister's husband, the local merchant Edmund Popple, to get him elected a burgess of the Hull Corporation. In the records of that body, the 'Bench Books', 28 December 1658 has the following entry: 'This day Mr Edmund

Popple Sheriffe of this Towne came into this Board and acquainted them that his brother in law Mr Andrew Marvell made it his request that the Board would please to make him a free Burgesse of this Corporation, which the Bench takeing into consideration and accompting the good service he hath allready done for this Towne, they are pleased to grant him his freedome.'[3] The reference to the service Marvell had done for the town is intriguing and suggests that he may have used either his connections with Fairfax or his subsequent government connections to perform favours of some kind for Hull, possibly using his in-laws as the conduit.

Two weeks later, Richard Cromwell summoned a Parliament and Marvell stood as a candidate. He was elected on 10 January 1659 as one of a pair of representatives for Hull, his fellow MP being John Ramsden, the most significant merchant in the town. It was hardly a universal suffrage, the choice being made by the 500 or so freemen of the City, with Edmund Popple a prominent ally and canvasser on that body. Five days later Marvell wrote to Popple – in a letter that has survived as a puzzling fragment only – about some piece of politicking among the burgesses: 'Pray, what say our 86 men of the businesse & of me?'[4] But in spite of his ability to pull strings locally, Marvell lost his seat to the Republican Sir Henry Vane four months later when the Rump Parliament was temporarily restored in May in the wake of Richard Cromwell's political demise. During this period, however, he retained his civil service post, and continued to draw a salary for it. So far from being inconvenienced by the restored Rump – whose existence was to some degree a repudiation of the Cromwellians – Marvell was actually granted official lodgings in Whitehall on 14 July.[5] His superior, Thurloe, by contrast, was dismissed in May. As ever, Marvell was a survivor. Thurloe's replacement was the regicide Thomas Scott, a Republican with far less regard for Cromwell than his Latin Secretary, who continued in his employment until at least the autumn when the Council of State was dissolved by the army. On 25 October the Council issued an order for payment to Milton and Marvell of £86 12s each in arrears of pay, covering the period since Thurloe's fall in May.[6]

During the early months of 1659, however, when Marvell was riding two horses, he wrote two letters that have survived and give his views (or, strictly, those of Thurloe) about the political situation under Richard.

Both are written to Sir George Downing, the British resident at the Hague who had headed the move for offering the crown to Cromwell. On 11 February, Marvell wrote rather scathingly about the Republican argument in Parliament that power resided in the people and should not be handed over to another Protector. Their logic was: 'That it reuerted into this house by the death of his Highnesse, that Mr Speaker is Protector in possession and it will not be his wisdome to part with it easily, that this house is all England.'[7] Marvell was unimpressed by this democratic essentialism and observed tartly: 'But we know well enough what they mean.' In spite of the anti-Richard faction's use of 'all the tricks of Parliament' Marvell was optimistic that his side had a two-thirds majority that would 'weare them out at the long runne'. Again on 25 March Marvell gave Downing another routine update of Parliamentary business. The bill fully recognising Richard's Protectorship was passed on 14 February.

While in London, and out of Parliament again, during the second half of 1659 and the early months of 1660, Marvell is said to have taken part in meetings of the 'Rota' and spoken there. This political club was founded by his friend James Harrington, the political theorist and author, in 1656, of the *Commonwealth of Oceana*, dedicated to Cromwell. The work was mentioned later by David Hume in his *Idea of a Perfect Commonwealth* as 'the only valuable model of a Commonwealth' extant. Harrington's notion was that power depends on the balance of property ownership and his treatise, in offering an economic interpretation of history, has led to his being called the first Marxist. Like Marvell he was impressed by the traditional Elizabethan notion of the body politic, and the continuity of the natural and social order in contrast to the more ruthlessly pragmatic political vision of Hobbes. Although a Republican, he took no active part in the Civil War and was said to have been deeply shocked by the execution of the King. His moderation would have made him attractive to Marvell. The Rota Club met regularly from November 1659 to February 1660 and was attended by Cyriack Skinner, Henry Neville (the political writer and translator of Macchiavelli), and John Aubrey, who wrote a brief life of Harrington in which it was revealed that Harrington wrote poetry 'but his Muse was rough' and Neville had to talk him out of persisting with it. He also described the meetings of the Club, which Marvell attended that winter:

> *. . . the beginning of Michaelmas-terme, he had ever night a meeting at the (then) Turke's head in the New Pallace-yard, where was made purposely a large ovall-table, with a passage in the middle for Miles to deliver his Coffee. About it sate his Disciples, and the Virtuosi. The Discourses in this Kind were the most ingeniose, and smart, that ever I heard, or expect to heare, and bandied with great eagernesse: the Arguments in the Parliament howse were but flatt to it.*[8]

The Club was formally organised with a ballot box in which votes or tentamens (experiments) were cast. Although Aubrey said that at this time 'as to human foresight, there was no possibility of the King's returne' the Club seems to have been hated by the Parliamentarians, particularly for its advocacy of gradual rotation of membership of Parliament by regular balloting, which would result in complete replacement of the House every nine years. Sometimes, when the party at the Turk's Head broke up, Harrington would declare: 'Well, the King will come in.' Unfortunately, Harrington went mad, imagining that 'his Perspiration turned to Flies, and sometimes to Bees'.

Richard Cromwell fell in part because he failed to secure the support of the army, the final blow being the defection of his generals, Lambert, Fleetwood and Desborough. In October 1659 a Committee of Safety, effectively a military dictatorship, was imposed. In December this Committee again gave way to the Rump Parliament, which admitted seventy-three of the members of the former Long Parliament who had been expelled or 'secluded' in 1648. This enlarged Rump called what was known as the Convention Parliament, which met for the first time on 25 April 1660. Although the balance of power between Parliament and the King would never again revert to what it was in the 1640s, the restoration of the King – promising to submit to Parliamentary terms once restored – had become inevitable. The country was no doubt tired of war, dissension and the failure to secure a viable alternative form of government. On 29 May 1660, Charles II returned to London in triumph.

Marvell was in that Parliament elected on 2 April. Once again John Ramsden was his fellow MP, with a massive majority over his nearest rival, Marvell, who in turn saw off the challenge of Edward Barnard of Gray's Inn, William Lister (a former Hull MP during the first and second

Protectorate), Matthew Alured (to whom he was of course related but whose uncompromising republicanism told against him) and Francis Thorpe (a judge under the Commonwealth).[9] Marvell would remain an MP for Hull until his death in 1678.

Marvell continued to write poetry, with his immersion in the political world producing, inevitably, a number of satires. He also turned for the first time to prose and pamphlet warfare. But it would be wrong to assume that his political career signalled the death of the lyric poet. Uncertainty about dating the poems should counsel caution about such generalisations. The conventional assumption that the lyric, pastoral and garden verse belongs to the early 1650s is persuasive, but it is an assumption nonetheless. There is no reason in principle why he could not have written some of this poetry during the 1660s. Some writers on Marvell, scenting a conspiracy of conservative academics keen to distance their hero from the contaminations of politics by privileging the lyric over the political verse, have accused the latter of a process of 'hypercanonisation', an ugly piece of jargon denoting the selective winnowing of the canon to exclude unwelcome political verses.[10] There is something in this, but, important as both the Cromwell poems and the later satires are, and remembering that Marvell was always an intensely political poet, nothing can boldly be assigned to the period of his Parliamentary career that can equal those poems where his wit and formal elegance are most forcefully on display. To minimise the skill and insight and judgement of his best political poems is grossly to misrepresent his art, but fewer of these later poems captivate the reader in the same way as 'To his Coy Mistress' or the 'Horatian Ode'.

11

His Majesties Happy Return

If Marvell's picture does not look so lively and witty as you might expect, it is from the chagrin and awe he had of the Restoration then just effected.
Thomas Hollis[1]

On 29 May 1660 Charles II entered London to scenes of popular rejoicing. Old-fashioned historians have always relished this particular episode in the national narrative. Writing in 1936 (the year of the Jarrow March), the author of the relevant volume of the *Oxford History of England*, G.N. Clark, painted a picture of Merrie England stirring its sleepy limbs to raise maypoles, propose drunkenly extravagant loyal toasts, and mock the defeated Puritans. Clark wrote warmly of the King's procession making its way from the harbour at Dover through south-east England to Whitehall, deploying an antique diction to realise the feudal scene: 'Noblemen and gentlemen attended on horseback, mayors and aldermen in their gowns, country-folk were morris-dancing on the greens; maidens strewed flowers and sweet herbs before the cavalcade.'[2] Although the truth may have been a little more undifferentiated, there is little doubt that the Restoration was welcomed. The country had had enough and was at the very least eager to come out and see the spectacle. Perhaps the young King, whose thirtieth birthday this was, could offer, if not a return to the old days, a period of stability. In London bonfires lit up the night sky, some of them immolating effigies of Cromwell. The diarist John Evelyn wrote that night: 'I stood in the Strand and beheld it and blessed God.'[3]

Marvell, in spite of his later retouching of the record, had been closely associated with the anti-Royalist cause for almost the whole of the 1650s. His superior, Thurloe, was under arrest on a charge of high treason. His close friend and associate in Thurloe's office, Milton, for whom he spoke up bravely in his first months in Parliament, spent a brief period in jail in the autumn of 1659 and saw his books burnt by the public hangman. Marvell, had he not had better luck, might have followed him, if not to jail, then into the political wilderness. Although he began the decade in the company of a moderate Parliamentarian, Lord Fairfax, he had increasingly moved towards the core of the Cromwellian administration and had made many enemies who would be watching him for the future. His life was often in danger on the rough streets of Restoration London as he made his way back from Westminster to his lodgings in Maiden Lane, Covent Garden. Marvell has been criticised for the rapidity with which he embraced loyalty to the King, but he justified it with a more elevated argument than mere opportunism. And if he accepted as a *fait accompli* the restoration of constitutional monarchy he remained a member of the opposition to the court party. His anonymous verse satires were not designed to flatter the leading figures in the regime, and his controversial pamphlets were unsparing in their attacks on the established clergy. Skilled in the arts of self-preservation, he was not a toady.

One of Marvell's first tasks in the Convention Parliament, which had met for the first time on 25 April, was to compose a Latin reply to the Prince Elector Palatine of the Rhine, the King's first cousin, who had written with his congratulations on the Restoration. It has been suggested that the decision of the House on 23 July to ask 'Mr *Marvell*, a member of this House . . . together with the members that serve for the Universities'[4] to prepare a reply on behalf of the King was a deliberate act of mockery directed at Cromwell's scribe by a triumphantly Royalist Commons. In fact it may have been no more than a practical recognition of a skilled Latinist's well-advertised suitability for the task.

Marvell sat on various select committees in the Convention Parliament and was, from the outset, a diligent MP. Even in his brief stint in Richard Cromwell's Parliament the previous year he had been placed on five committees: to examine a petition from Elizabeth Lilborne (5 February 1659); to consider how the five northern counties could be supplied with 'a learned, pious, sufficient and able ministry' (5 February); to examine whether the county palatine of Durham should be represented in Parliament (31 March); to examine a petition of the disbanded forces in Lancashire (13 April); and to consider how to remove and where to place records then at Worcester House, which was to be returned to its owner (13 April). In the Convention Parliament he was put on to no fewer than ten committees between June and November considering, variously, reparations to landowners, spending money to redeem captives at Algiers and Tunis, draining of the Fens, settling the militia, and examining 'a bill for preventing the voluntary separation and living apart of married persons'.[5] Marvell was both industrious and attentive to the detail of what must have been on occasion tedious business for someone of his lively wit. His letters to his constituents show a passion for the intricacies of Parliamentary business. This diligence may have helped his reputation in the House, though he would always have enemies ready to exploit any perceived failings.

On 15 November, and again on the 27th, he reported to the House the work done by his select committee on a bill to erect and endow vicarages out of rectories that had been impropriated. This was a measure of redistribution of Church revenues that failed to win approval from the Lords, where it was blocked by the bishops. The measure was proposed again, without success, several times during the next two decades. Marvell would never take the side of the Church Establishment and was vigorous in his praise of the King for his Declaration of Indulgence, issued on 14 April 1660 at Breda where he held his court when still in exile. This promised 'that no man shall be disquieted or called in question for differences of opinion in matters of religion'. On his return the King promoted this Declaration, in Marvell's view, 'as far as the Passions and Influences of the contrary Party would give leave for'. He also praised the King for his Act of Indemnity, passed on 29 August, which drew a line under what had happened in 'the late Combustions'. Always vigorously anti-clerical, the clergyman's son had little doubt about who was to blame for attempts to block the King's measures of religious toleration:

> *For, though I am sorry to speak it, yet it is a sad truth, that the Animosities and Obstinacy of some of the Clergy have in all Ages been*

> *the greatest Obstacle to the Clemency, Prudence and good intentions of Princes, and the Establishment of their Affairs.*[6]

Although diligent as an MP in reporting back to his electors, the Hull Corporation, Marvell rarely indicated the way he had voted or gave an account of the speeches he had made. His tone was an interesting and paradoxical mixture of the servile and the exacting; he would indicate his willingness to write to them at any cost (on one occasion forgoing his supper to do so), but he would also instruct them sternly not to speak of certain matters or give them uncompromising instructions about how they should handle a particular issue. The earliest letter we have to the Corporation from its new MP was written on 17 November 1660, although it refers to an earlier letter, which has not survived, written to the Mayor on the first day of the sitting. It was addressed to Mayor Christopher Richardson and 'the Aldermen his Brethren'. The piece of business that Marvell thought concerned them most was the question of the settling of the militia. Eight regiments needed to be disbanded now that the wars were over and Marvell was on a select committeee dealing with the issue. He was not in favour of a standing army, telling the Corporation: ''Tis better to trust his Mtyes moderation.'[7] He predicted: 'I doubt not but ere we rise to see the whole army disbanded &, according to the Act, hope to see your Town once more ungarrisond.'[8] This prompted a memory that he shared with the Corporation: 'For I can not but remember, though then a child, those blessed days when the youth of your own town were trained for your militia, and did methought become their arms much better then any soldiers that I haue seen there since.' He went on to point out his lack of importance as a 'private member', notwithstanding which 'though I can promise litle yet I intend all things for your service'. He was thus going to be an independent back-bencher, who would give a good account of himself to his constituency. The letters helped to make him feel that he was not wasting his time in Parliament: ''Tis much refreshment to me after our long sittings daily to give you account of what we do,' he wrote at the end of November.[9] In December the Corporation showed its appreciation of the two MPs by sending them a present of Yorkshire ale. Marvell quipped: 'the quantity is so great that it might make sober men forgetfull'.[10]

His letters tell of the important issues of state but also matters of more parochial interest to Hull, such as the attempt by local worthy Henry Hildyard to regain the Manor House, a large mansion inside the Hull walls that had been rented from him by Charles I, turned into a fort and granted to the town by the Parliament in 1648. A letter on this matter, signed by Marvell and Ramsden but in the latter's hand, refers to the Civil War, prompted by Hildyard's predicament: 'the iniquitie of those tymes was to be lamented but it had been as in great earthquakes, or ovrfloweings where bounds had been generally removed, & possessions washt away one from anothr'.[11] The image of natural disturbance here is reminiscent of the famous observation on the Civil War by Edward Hyde, the Earl of Clarendon, in his *History of the Rebellion*:

> *a small, scarce discernible cloud arose in the north, which was shortly after attended with such a storm, that never gave over raging till it had shaken, and even rooted up, the greatest and tallest cedars of the three nations; blasted all its beauty and fruitfulness; brought its strength to decay and its glory to reproach, and almost to desolation . . .*[12]

The recent employee of Cromwell was happy to lend his signature to Ramsden's account of 'the late Combustions'. Increasingly loyalist in temper towards the King, Marvell was not sycophantic, refusing just before Christmas to approve a bill asking for the 'voluntary benevolence' of the country in meeting the expenses of the King's coronation. 'For though nothing be too much for so gracious a Prince as his Majesty has been all along to us,' he suggested, 'yet 'tis good to leave something to give hereafter & not to indanger the peoples good will by taking their benevolence.'[13] In case this was a little too free, he quickly added: 'God hath laid a soare affliction upon his Mtyes family & therein upon the whole nation.'

If Marvell can sometimes seem a little too anxious to please in these letters to his constituents, he was at the same time ready to take risks for an old friendship. At this precise historical moment, any declaration of friendship for Milton, the unabashed defender of regicide, was most certainly a risk. Tradition has it that Marvell was a constant, though at certain times rather a discreet, visitor to Milton at his London home. In the latter part of 1660, however, Milton was in jail. The Act of Indemnity did not include him and he had been imprisoned in October. On 15

December Milton was released by order of Parliament and immediately protested that the House of Commons Serjeant-at-Arms had imposed excessive jail fees on him. Marvell bravely took up his case, complaining that the £150 demanded was extortionate. In the *Parliamentary History of England* published in 1808 by Thomas Hansard, the following account is given:

> *The celebrated Mr John Milton having now laid long in custody of the serjeant at arms was released by order of the House . . . Soon after, Mr Andrew Marvel* [sic] *complained that the serjeant had exacted 150l. fees of Mr Milton; which was seconded by col. King and col. Shapcot. On the contrary, sir Heneage Finch observed, That Milton was Latin secretary to Cromwell, and deserved hanging. However, this matter was referred to the committee of privileges to examine and decide the difference.*[14]

Having been told by the solicitor-general, Finch, that the man he was defending 'deserved hanging', Marvell would have had cause to reflect seriously on the safety of his own position. According to Milton's nephew, Edward Phillips, in his *Life of Mr John Milton* (1694): '*Mr Andrew Marvel*, a member for Hull, acted vigorously in his behalf, and made a considerable party for him.'[15]

Marvell's pay as an MP – apart from the barrels of ale sent down from Hull – was 6s 8d for every day's attendance and it came from the Hull Corporation. This was presumably the 'honourable pension' referred to by Aubrey. It has been estimated, however, that his total remuneration from 1659–78 amounted to no more than around £525.[16] Largely as a result of the disparaging comments of Samuel Parker, who seemed to think that the taking of a wage was a mean act of money-grubbing, a legend grew up that Marvell was the last MP to receive wages from his constituents in this way.[17] In fact the practice, though not widespread, continued until the end of the century, when two Bristol MPs, Sir Richard Hart and Sir John Knight, are recorded as receiving a regular allowance in the Parliament of 1690–95. Marvell's successor as MP after his death, William Ramsden, also received a wage. Corporations like Hull saw it as a good investment and the money was raised by a local tax known as 'knight's pence'.

The early letters of Marvell as MP demonstrate a vigilant attention to the growing presence of the Excise and the likely costs of various measures being considered. He saw his role very clearly as being to advance the interests of Hull businessmen before anything else. His satirical poem 'The Last Instructions to a Painter' draws a picture of a 'portly Burgess' who 'through the weather hot,/Does for his Corporation sweat and trot'. An earlier Hull MP, Peregrine Pelham, had written to the Corporation in 1645 making the point plainly enough: 'I am confident you neede not feare any committee to doe you any prejudice. I doe not spend 500 li p'ann' here for nothing.'[18] MPs would be expected to write letters, report back on legislation touching local business interests, interview people, negotiate on the Corporation's behalf, and even arrange bribes. At the Restoration the return of the country gentry to Parliament in greater numbers – with their lordly indifference to stipend – resulted in a decline in a practice chiefly seen in the urban constituencies and the ports. Parker's objection to Marvell's taking of wages had, therefore, an element of snobbery.

Marvell's reputation continued to be one of honest poverty. A description of him as an MP, which first surfaced in an article in the *Gentleman's Magazine* in 1738, although its source is not given, is a memorable one and a telling example of the eighteenth-century construction of a Marvell legend of patriotic sanctity:

> *Andrew Marvel, one of the most disinterested patriots in the reign of Charles II, by managing a very narrow patrimony, kept himself above corruption: and there is a story of him which though it may seem but ordinary, deserves to be everlastingly remembered: he dined usually at a great ordinary in the Strand, where having eat heartily of boiled beef, and some roast pigeons and asparagus, he drank his pint of port; and on the coming in of the reckoning, taking a piece out of his pocket, and holding it between his thumb and finger: 'Gentlemen, said he, who would let himself for hire while he can have such a dinner for half a crown?'*[19]

Marvell would have received far less as an MP than the £200 he had been receiving as a civil servant before entering Parliament. Some have speculated that his in-laws in Hull – rich merchants and traders who could make good use of a reliable man in London and Westminster – may have offered Marvell an additional stipend even though, as members of the

Corporation, they were doing this already. Often in his letters he reports himself as being very busy, sometimes on business 'out of towne', yet his Parliamentary activity cannot have been as demanding as it would be for a Hull MP today, with long daily sessions and extensive constituency duties. He spoke rarely in Parliament and, as a member of the Opposition, was not at the centre of the administration, or a holder of posts. It is not clear what this business was (unless it was a reference to his writing) but it could well have been ancillary, and perhaps necessarily discreet, activity carried out on behalf of his friends in Hull. The legend of his poverty may have been no more than a legend.

12

A Breach of the Peace

And if you can but get scent of anything that smells of a Priest, away you run with full Cry and open Mouth.[1]

Marvell celebrated his fortieth birthday on 31 March 1661. The following day he was re-elected to what became known as the Cavalier Parliament, where he would achieve a moderately active public profile. Over his seventeen-year career in this Parliament he would be appointed to 120 committees, act as teller in 8 divisions, and make 14 speeches, a diligent enough record for the day.[2]

Even before his re-election, Marvell was settling in to a good relationship with the Hull burgesses. His letters continued to be shrewd, attentive and compliant. 'I have no greater delight than to be serviceable to you,'[3] he wrote in one letter, concluding: 'It is hard for me to write short to you. It seems to me when I haue once begun that I am making a step to Hull & can not easily part from so good company.' His references to the King are unimpeachable. After 'an ugly false report' of an attempt on the life of the King he told the Corporation: 'I doubt not but the same extraordinary hand that hath hitherto guided him will still be his Protection against all attempts of discontented persons or partyes.'[4] The most prominent of those 'discontented partyes' was that of the Fifth Monarchy Men. This millenarian sect was at its most powerful in the 1640s and 1650s, when its belief in the revelation of the Book of Daniel that the return of Christ would occur at the overthrow of the last four earthly monarchies (Babylon, Egypt, Rome, and the Pope) captured the imagination of many zealots. They saw the Civil War as enacting the violent end of the fourth monarchy and heralding the arrival of the Fifth Monarch, Jesus. Although their moment had passed, a final attempt at insurrection, led by Thomas Venner, a Fifth Monarchist preacher, took place on 7 January. Ten days later, Marvell reported briefly: 'The Prisoners of the fift Monarchy men in this late insurrection haue been found guilty today upon their triall . . . The next week 'tis expected they should all be executed.'[5]

After the King's initial attempts at reconciliation, something like a Royalist backlash against the Presbyterians as well as the sectarians was growing and it would be reflected in the imminent elections, but Marvell continued to work away at the parochial concerns of Hull. In February he requested that he be kept discreetly informed about the interests of the Corporation in terms that suggest he had felt underconsulted by them: 'Pray let me in all things that are not of too nice a nature be informd somthing particularly & with the first that I may serve you the better.'[6] His close relationship with his twenty-seven-year-old nephew, William Popple, is revealed by a request made the next month that the Corporation address Marvell's correspondence to him, marking the envelope '*to be left with William Popple Merchant London* & not one word more of street signe or lodging'.[7] If he was receiving his mail at his nephew's hands on a regular basis Marvell may thus have been engaged in business with Popple and was in such close contact that doing this meant 'I can haue them out the first minute the maile comes. Otherwise the seuerall Porters carry them about in their walks & so much time is losst.'

Marvell's diligence paid off at the general election in April 1661. His fellow MP John Ramsden, who had triumphed so clearly at the election a year previously, sank to the bottom of the poll – his poor attendance record telling against him – and his seat was taken by Anthony Gilby, the Royalist colonel and captain of the Hull garrison. It was an interesting combination, the former Cromwellian and the Royalist representing the town together for the next seventeen years. Both MPs, however, shared a strong anti-Catholicism. Gilby later advocated strong measures against Catholics and supported the bill to exclude them from Parliament 'that now our laws will be made by those of our own religion'.[8] To any Catholic constituents who protested he said bluntly: 'they may thank themselves for it'. Gilby waived his wages for the first session of the Cavalier Parliament, although the Corporation presented his wife with a piece of plate, but he subsequently agreed, like Marvell, to be paid in cash and ale for his Parliamentary duties.

Marvell seems to have been very confident of his position as an MP, for his reaction to the news of his re-election bordered on the complacent. 'I perceive by a letter from Mr Mayor,' he told the Corporation a few days after the election, almost as an afterthought before signing off, 'that you have again (as if it were grown a thing of course) made choice of me now the third time, to serve for you in Parlament.'[9] Parochial as these letters generally were, Marvell occasionally gestured towards the wider world. On this same occasion he thus reported: ''Tis two days news upon the Exchange that some French in the Bay of Canada haue discoverd the long lookd for Northwest passage to the East Indyes.' Was it Popple who reported the news from the Exchange or was he there himself engaged on business?

The Cavalier Parliament met for the first time on 8 May 1661. A week later tensions between Marvell and Colonel Gilby began to surface. Marvell's regular despatches to Hull had always been a joint effort with John Ramsden but, given the latter's poor attendance record, they were probably the work of Marvell. On 16 May, however, Marvell wrote to Mayor Richardson delicately pointing out that his new partner preferred to make his own line of communication with Hull: 'I would not haue you suspect any misintelligence between my partner & me because we write not to you joyntly as Mr Ramsden & I used. For there is all civility betwixt us. But it was his sense that we should each be left to his own discretion for writing except upon some answer unto your Letters & that to be joyntly.'[10] How far the Corporation believed in that 'civility' may be guessed at. They would be fully aware of the sharply contrasting political backgrounds of the two Members. In fact, relations steadily worsened during the first weeks of the new Parliament until, on 1 June, Marvell was forced to write again:

> *Gentlemen my worthy friends,*
>
> *The bonds of civility betwixt Colonell Gilby and my selfe being unhappily snappd in pieces, and in such manner that I can not see how it is possible euer to knit them again, the onely trouble that I*

> *haue, is least by our misintelligence your businesse should receive any disadvantage.*[11]

Marvell explained that the cause of the rupture was 'some crudityes and undigested matter remaining upon the stomach euer since our Election' and described it as 'this unlucky falling out'. He regretted that the Corporation's interests might be adversely affected by this rumpus and pledged: 'if I wanted my right hand yet I would scribble to you with my left rather then neglect your businesse'. Two days before this, he had already reported to them his profound concern for their affairs when finding himself too busy to give his normal full account: 'I am something bound up that I can not write about your publick affairs but I assure you they break my sleepe.'[12] The major political events of the day, such as the order for the burning of the Covenant by the public hangman on 17 May – the Covenant was the oath to defend the Parliamentary cause and reform the Church of England on anti-episcopalian lines – usually merit a brief reference in Marvell's letters.

Around this time Marvell wrote his first recorded letter to the Trinity House Corporation in Hull. Trinity House had developed out of an amalgamation of the mediaeval guild of the Holy Trinity and the Shipman's Guild and consisted of twelve Elder Brethren, six Assistants, and an unlimited number of Younger Brethren. The Elder Brethren chose two Wardens and one of these was Edmund Popple, Marvell's brother-in-law, to whom he also wrote from time to time in a personal capacity. Marvell himself was never chosen as an Elder Brother. Trinity House was the chief authority for the port of Hull and maintained charities for 'decayed' seamen. Its income came from endowments and from the levying of primage on vessels using the port, a right abolished in the nineteenth century.[13] Marvell would be as assiduous in his pursuit of the interests of Trinity House – particularly in relation to a long drawn-out wrangle over the erection of a lighthouse at Spurn Head in the 1670s – as he was of the interests of the city Corporation. Sixty-nine letters to the Brethren have survived. In 1674 Marvell also became a member of a similar body on the Thames, Trinity House at Deptford, which had jurisdiction over pilotage for the Port of London. As the chief authority for lighthouses in England and Wales, it caused some degree of conflict of interest to Marvell over the Spurn Head project. On 18 May, Marvell – this time securing the joint signature of his reluctant partner Gilby – wrote his first letter to Trinity House, indicating his willingness to be of assistance and flattering the House as 'so considerable a body in your selues and so honourable a limbe of the Towne'.[14]

Although Marvell flattered the Corporation excessively ('I account all things I can do for your service to be meere trifles & not worth taking notice of in respect of what I ow you . . . I haue in the things concerning your town no other sense or affection but what is yours as farr as I can understand it'[15]) he could handle the burgesses firmly when it was needed. 'Be pleased to let me distinctly & fully know your minds in these points so materiall that I may not for want of resolution from you to be exposed when it comes to the pinch,'[16] he demanded on one occasion. On another he reprimanded them: 'It would behoue you to be speedy and punctuall in your correspondence.'[17] There is a note of impatience here with his provincial masters. But the prevailing note was unctuous courtesy and high sentiment. Reporting a bill being brought in by King Charles which would allow him to appoint and dismiss magistrates in the Corporations and one that would give him the sole right to command the militia and armed forces, Marvell intones as a loyal subject and a mere weak member of the House: 'I hope his Majesty will as he has done hitherto help us out of these straits of our own minds; otherwise we may stick in the Briars.'[18]

On 16 June Marvell supported the first reading of a bill to make Holy Trinity Church, Hull a separate parish from its mother church of Hessle, reserving the advowson (right of patronage) for the Corporation. At first that right was not granted, so Marvell said he could not support the second reading, ticking off the Corporation for not giving him clearer instructions about how he should vote. The bill was eventually passed on 29 June.

Marvell's secure position with his constituency base was important for his political survival. During the early summer of 1661, in a House where the court party was becoming increasingly confident that the tide was running in its direction, the underlying mistrust that existed towards people with Marvell's political history increased. On 20 June he wrote to Hull: 'I must beseech you also to listen to no little storyes concerning my selfe. For I belieue you know by this time that you haue lately heard some very false concerning me.'[19] It is not clear what these rumours were but they were plainly more than grumbles from Gilby and were widespread enough that Marvell could take it for granted they had independently reached the ears of the Corporation.

Nothing more is heard of these rumours for the remainder of the year (although there is an eight-month gap in Marvell's surviving correspondence between June 1661 and February 1662, the month in which he acted as a teller for a proviso to the poor bill on behalf of garrison towns, which was lost). But early in 1662, a more serious incident occurred in the House of Commons, reported in the *Journals of the House* for 18 March 1662:

> Ordered, *That the Difference between Mr* Marvell *and Mr* Clifford, *Two Members of this House, be referred to Mr Speaker, to examine; and, to that End, to hear Mr* Scott, *another Member of this House, who was present when this Difference did happen; and to mediate and reconcile the same between them if he can; or else to report it to the House, with his Opinion therein.*[20]

Thomas Clifford was the MP for Totnes in Devon, a closet Catholic, and later stalwart of the court party granted estates by Charles II as a reward for supporting his plans to establish Catholicism in England in 1669. He became Lord Clifford of Chudleigh in 1672, his initial 'C' contributing to the famous 'Cabal' administration of Clifford, Ashley, Buckingham, Arlington and Lauderdale between 1670 and 1673. He eventually resigned as Lord Treasurer in 1673 rather than sign the Test Act. Two obvious reasons for a clash with Marvell were his crypto-Catholicism and his aggression; Pepys refers to 'his rudeness of tongue and passions when angry'.[21] But Marvell also, in spite of his quietness and reserve, seems to have had a quick temper. During the nineteen years of Marvell's Parliamentary career from 1659 to 1678 only six such quarrels are noted in the Parliamentary records so the incident was a serious one. After the Speaker's investigation the matter was resolved, with Marvell having been found guilty of the first provocation and being instructed, in spite of his reluctance, to apologise:

> *Mr Speaker reports, That he had examined the matter of difference between Mr* Marvell *and Mr* Clifford*; and found that Mr* Marvell *had given the first provocation that begot the difference: and that his opinion was that Mr* Marvell *should declare his sorrow for being the first occasion of the difference; and then Mr* Clifford *to declare, that he was sorry for the consequences of it: And that Mr* Clifford *was willing to yield to this determination, but that Mr* Marvell *refused.*
>
> *And the House thereupon directing the said Mr* Marvell *and Mr* Clifford *to withdraw; and taking the matter into debate;*
>
> Resolved, *That the said Mr* Marvell *and Mr* Clifford *be called into their places: and that each of them shall have a reprehension from Mr Speaker, for breach of the peace and privilege of the House; and according to Mr Speaker's report, be enjoined to declare their sorrow for it; and to crave the pardon of the House.*
>
> *And the said Mr* Marvell *and Mr* Clifford *being accordingly called in to their places; and having received a grave reprehension from Mr Speaker, and Mr* Marvell *declaring that he was sorry, that he should give the first provocation of the difference; and Mr* Clifford *acknowledging that he was sorry for what ensued; and both of them engaged to keep the peace and privilege of the House for the future; and not to renew this difference, but to have the same correspondence they had before it did happen: with which the House was well satisfied; and did remit the breach of privilege.*[22]

This was not, however, to be Marvell's last physical encounter with another Member in the House, nor was Clifford to be allowed to get away with a formal rebuff from the Speaker. In his satire written five years later, 'The last Instructions to a Painter', Marvell has a portrait of Clifford, by then the Comptroller of the Household: 'With *Hook* then, through the *microscope*, take aim/Where, like the new *Controller*, all men laugh/To see a tall Lowse brandish the white Staff.' In another poem of 1673 attributed to Marvell, 'An Historicall Poem', there is an allusion to his tragic end: 'Clifford and Hide before has lost the day,/One hang'd himself, the other fled away.'

The Speaker, Sir Edward Turner, was not forgiven either for this humiliation. He appears in 'The last Instructions', mercilessly cast:

Paint him in Golden Gown, with Mace's Brain:
Bright Hair, fair Face, obscure and dull of Head;
Like Knife with Iv'ry haft and edge of Lead.
At Pray'rs, his Eyes turn up the Pious white,
But all the while his Private-Bill*'s in sight.*
In Chair, he smoaking sits like Master-Cook,
And a Poll-Bill *does like his Apron look.*
Well was he skill'd to season any question,
And make a sawce fit for Whitehall's *digestion:*
Whence ev'ry day, the Palat more to tickle;
Court-mushrumps *ready are sent in in pickle.*
When Grievance *urg'd he swells like squatted Toad,*
Frisks like a Frog to croak a Taxes *load.*
His patient Piss, he could hold longer then
An Urinal, and sit like any Hen.
At Table, jolly as a Country-Host,
And soaks his Sack with Norfolk *like a Toast.*
At night, than Canticleer *more brisk and hot,*
And Serjeants Wife serves him for Partelott.

ll 866–84

Marvell's love of 'reverend Chaucer'[23] is once again attested in this passage. The poem would appear anonymously and for now he had no choice but to defer to the power of the Speaker and reflect on the extent of the animosity towards him in parts of the House.

13

Beyond Sea

If one were to choose a date for the beginning of the modern world, probably July 15, 1662, would be the best to fix upon. For on that day the Royal Society was founded, and the place of Science in civilization became a definite and recognized thing.

Lytton Strachey[1]

Marvell's education had been in the classics and, just as in politics he seems to have been happiest occupying the middle ground, his intellect seems to have been poised between the old and the new, between the traditional values of a classicist and a student of the Bible and the scientific values of the new age of inquiry. There is evidence in his writing of familiarity with Hobbes 'whose half-mediaeval, half-modern mind was the dominating influence over intellects which came to maturity in the middle years of the century', according to Strachey. Hobbes's materialist philosophy – 'The universe, that is, the whole mass of things that are, is corporeal', as he put it in his famous work, *Leviathan* (1651) – did not naturally consort with the idealist tendency of Marvell's thought. The poet who wrote of a dialogue between the soul and the body would have few points of contact with a philosopher who rejected the notion of the soul as mediaeval 'vain philosophy'. 'The accepted tradition of centuries past, blended out of Platonic, Aristotelian, Neoplatonic, Stoic and Christian elements, spoke with seemingly overwhelming authority for the soul as a spiritual and even divine essence, informing the body, but existing in its own right, separable, and consequently immortal,' wrote Basil Willey, a modern historian of seventeenth-century thought.[2]

At the dawning of the great age of modern science and reason, Marvell – though he lived at the centre of the turbulent political events of his epoch – was not wholly emancipated from the old philosophy nor eager to seize the role of *buccinator novi temporis.* He was, however, according to Aubrey, a friend of the mathematician John Pell, who invented the division sign in mathematics. Pell was a precocious scholar favoured by Cromwell, who sent him on a political mission to Switzerland in 1654. He later took orders and, like John Aubrey, was not greatly competent in managing his affairs and never quite lived up to his initial promise. The new science, as well as the contemporary confusion of astrology and astronomy, entered into Marvell's poems where mathematical and geometrical metaphors abound, such as the 'perfect Hemisphere' of Bilborough Hill or the '*holy Mathematicks*' of 'Upon Appleton House'.

Whatever his appetite for intellectual exploration, Marvell was always a keen physical traveller. By the spring of 1662, he had been at home for at least five years and would have been getting restless. Malicious gossip in the House, made worse by his recent public dressing-down from the Speaker, may well have persuaded him to look for a change of scene and the opportunity now appeared to present itself. The mission that he undertook was a mysterious one. Marvell's references to it at this time are brief and enigmatic. Writing to the Brethren of Trinity House on 22 March, he apologised for managing only a brief letter, citing in excuse 'some avocations lately in mine own particular'[3] that had preoccupied him. A week later he asked for 'a dormant credit for an hundred pound'[4] to oil the wheels of their business – the beginnings of the long-running Spurn Head lighthouse project.

One of the navigational duties of Trinity House was the provision of aids to navigation. In the sixteenth century a beacon was set up, later followed by a buoy that enabled the House to collect buoyage charges. There had been a light on Spurn Head as early as 1427, when it was maintained by a hermit, but it was not until the late sixteenth and early seventeenth centuries that speculators began to be attracted to the idea of seeking patents to erect a lighthouse and charge tolls on passing ships. Such schemes were consistently opposed by Trinity House, although their colleagues in Newcastle supported the idea to help their coal trade. In 1618, 1637 and 1657 the House opposed schemes, until in 1660 Philip Frowde was given leave to promote a bill in Parliament, then in 1662 Trinity House introduced its own bill to erect a lighthouse on Spurn Head. Its principal argument was that the revenues would benefit the poor. The House was joined by various other speculators including Justinian Angell, who later actually managed to erect lights with voluntary support. Both Trinity House Hull and Deptford objected to this on the grounds that the lights were badly sited, trying in 1675 to get them extinguished. Hull Corporation, however, opposed this move. Later, in 1675, Angell obtained a patent giving him the right to charge a farthing a ton on all passing ships. This rose to a halfpenny in 1678, the year of Marvell's death.[5]

Marvell made this apparently very ordinary scheme take on an air of delicate intrigue, warning the Brethren on 8 May that it was not 'safe . . . to speake too cleare by the Post'.[6] He was hopeful of completing his work on their behalf soon but had an announcement to make:

> *But that whch troubles me is that by the interest of some persons too potent for me to refuse & who haue a great direction & influence upon my counsells & fortune I am obliged to go beyond sea before I haue perfected it [i.e. their business].*

The offer that Marvell was unable to refuse was to carry out some sort of clandestine political mission to Holland at the request of Charles Howard, Earl of Carlisle, a Privy Counsellor. Marvell told the Brethren that Carlisle had been apprised of their business so that during his absence Carlisle would be 'absolutely yours'. He went on: 'And my journy is but into Holland from whence I shall weekly correspond euen as if I were at London with all the rest of my friends toward the effecting of your businesse.' On 9 January he did just that, writing from Vianen to assure the Brethren that 'your businesse shall not receive any detriment by my absence'.[7] He implied that 'mine own private affairs' – an odd way to refer to what must have been official government business or government-sanctioned activity – were subservient to the needs of his constituents and that he could return in person if it became necessary.

Not everyone was happy about this mission, which took away from Hull, if only temporarily, a useful operator. Throughout Marvell's Parliamentary career there would always be those ready to take advantage of any action that could be turned against him. On this occasion it was the Governor of Hull, Lord Belasyse, a Royalist and a Catholic, who gave voice to the public criticism of this unwarranted excursion by the town's MP. Marvell sailed for Holland probably in May and did not return until perhaps as late as March 1663 in time to be present in Parliament on 2 April. The nature and purpose of the mission is unknown, but on arrival at the Hague he stayed with Sir George Downing, with whom he had corresponded in his first days in Thurloe's office.[8] The involvement of Downing and Carlisle confirms that it was an important mission on behalf of the government. Expanding British colonial trade and the need to protect it against its sea rivals, the Dutch, would lead to war in less than two years. Marvell may have been involved in some form of intelligence work connected with these national rivalries.[9] In February, Belasyse wrote to the Corporation, complaining about the MP's continued absence, with the implication that they should consider replacing him.[10] They were not eager to do so, writing instead to warn Marvell of the resentment building up against him. He took the point and, if he had not already planned to do so, set off back to England. Replying on 12 March to their letter prompted by Belasyse's intervention, Marvell observed that his own conscience made him always put his duties to 'the publick & your service' above his 'private concernements' and that he was 'making all the speed possible back, and that with Gods assistance in a very short time you may expecte to heare of me at the Parliament House'.[11] On 2 April Marvell was indeed back in Parliament, writing this time (rather breathlessly for he was 'newly arrived in Town and full of businesse')[12] to the new Mayor of Hull, Richard Wilson. He added rather tartly that he had been to the House and 'found my place empty; though it seems as I now heare that some persons would haue been so courteous as to haue filled it for me'.

Marvell's relationship with Carlisle was not over. Within two months he was off again in his service, presumably having distinguished himself in Holland. Carlisle's politics were as ambivalent as Marvell's. He had originally borne arms for the King but during the Civil War switched to the Parliamentary side, distinguishing himself at the Battle of Worcester where he was wounded. In his twenties he had been captain of Cromwell's bodyguard, although he was later arrested and imprisoned in the Tower for treason, suspected of having been involved in Sir George Booth's insurrection of 1658. He was eventually released without trial. He had been elected as MP for Cumberland at the same time that Marvell was returned for Hull and shortly afterwards made a Privy Counsellor. He was created Earl of Carlisle in April 1661 and later became Governor of Jamaica. It seems likely that Carlisle, eight years younger than Marvell, would have had much in common with the poet. Carlisle would also have been a useful man for Marvell to have on his side.

Marvell's letters both to the Corporation and to Trinity House in the weeks after his return were even more ingratiating than ever, referring to 'the great delight I take in writing to you'[13] when in fact he was extremely busy and must have found such long letters something of a chore. Not that sittings of the House were long by late twentieth-century standards. 'We sate which is unusuall with us till 6 at night,'[14] he reported in May, letting fall, as a casual aside: 'The Earle of Carlisle is going upon an Extraordinary Ambassage to Muscovy in order to setting up the English trade again there: from hence he is to goe to Sweden & Denmark.' That Marvell might have a personal interest in this mission is not yet mentioned; perhaps he was quietly preparing the ground for another controversial absence. The letter in which he reported Carlisle's plans is signed 'St Jones' instead of his usual 'Westminster'. This is St John Street, Clerkenwell, where Marvell had lodged in the spring of 1642 (the heroine of Defoe's *Moll Flanders* mentions taking 'a private lodging in St John Street, or as it is vulgarly called, St Jones's, near Clerkenwell'). Marvell appears to have lodged there again between his return from Holland and his second departure with Carlisle. Many of the anecdotes of Marvell's life after the Restoration appear to be set in these City districts. If there was a dark side to Marvell, a less reputable existence than that of the esteemed poet, diligent Member of Parliament, and defender of true religion, it would have found its expression here, in the taverns, ordinaries and stews of mid-century London. His later detractors, such as Samuel Parker and the tribe of anonymous pamphleteers who responded to his *Rehearsal Transpros'd*, paint a consistent portrait of Marvell the low-life adventurer. Though it gains no warrant from the documentary evidence we have about Marvell, it should not be dismissed out of hand. Scattergun as Parker's approach was, the fact that certain themes keep emerging in his and in the other portraits suggests some possible grounds in fact for these lurid touches. Here is Parker in full flight, caricaturing Marvell on his return from Europe in the 1640s:

> *and so return'd as accomplish'd as he went out, tries his fortune once more at the Ordinaries, plays too high for a Gentleman of his private condition, and so is at length cheated of all at Picquet. And so having neither Money nor employment, he is forced to loiter up and down about* Charing-Cross *and in* Lincolns-Inn fields, *where he had leisure and opportunity to make Remarques (among other Subjects) upon the wheel of Fortune . . .*[15]

Parker also refers to Marvell having 'been employed in Embassies abroad, and acquainted with Intrigues of State at home' and generally the details in his account conform with the facts where these are known, however derisive the tone ('Go your way for a smutty lubber,'[16] was one of Parker's more vivid imprecations). Marvell may well, therefore, have been a gambler and a drinker. Aubrey similarly referred to his drinking habits, although implying that they were of a more solitary nature: 'He kept bottles of wine at his lodgeing, and many times he would drink liberally by himselfe to refresh his spirits, and exalt his Muse.'[17] Parker's ill will towards Marvell grew as the years went by. His attack became more abusive:

> *Amongst these lewd Revilers, the lewdest was one whose name was* Marvel. *As he had liv'd in all manner of wickedness from his youth, so being of a singular impudence and petulancy of nature, he exercised the province of a Satyrist . . . A vagabond, ragged, hungry Poetaster, being beaten at every tavern, he daily received the rewards of his sowerness in kicks and blows . . . But the King being restor'd, this wretched man falling into his former poverty, did, for the sake of a livelihood, procure himself to be chosen Member of Parliament for a Borough . . . [for the sake of 5s a day, a custom] long antiquated and out of date, Gentlemen despising so vile a stipend that was given like alms to the poor . . . yet he requir'd it for the sake of a bare subsistence, altho' in this mean poverty he was nevertheless haughty and insolent.*[18]

Another respondent, Richard Leigh, author of *The Transproser Rehears'd*, mockingly granted Marvell's superior knowledge of 'Rabble-Affairs . . . as having been a frequent & assiduous Spectator of these little broyles of the

Rascality',[19] but Parker and his associates remain our only witnesses to Marvell's putative low-life activities in Clerkenwell or Covent Garden.

By June 1663 Marvell was dropping heavier and heavier hints about his extra-Parliamentary activity. 'I am forced by some private occasions but relating to the publick to be something lesse assiduous at the House then heretofore,'[20] he explained to Mayor Wilson. He offered no more elucidation, which suggests that his activities were too secret to be divulged. A fortnight later, he finally anounced his plans:

> *The relation I haue to your affaires and the intimacy of that affection I ow you do both incline and oblige me to communicate to you that there is a probability I may very shortly haue occasion again to go beyond sea. For my Lord Carlisle being chosen by his Majesty his Embassadour Extraordinary to Muscovy Sweden and Denmarke hath used his power which ought to be very great with me to make me goe along with him Secretary in those Embassages.*[21]

Marvell's tone with the Corporation was defensive. He explained carefully that it was 'no new thing for members of our house to be dispens'd with for the service of the King and the Nation in forain parts'. He added that he would not 'stirre without speciall leave of the House that so you may be free from any possibility of being importuned or tempted to make any other choice in my absence'. Marvell was clearly taking no chances on this occasion. It was to be a longer trip this time – 'The time allotted for the embassy is not much above a year' – and he wanted to ensure that no attempts would be made to unseat him in his absence. In the event the embassy lasted until the end of January 1665, but there were no attempts this time to take advantage of his removal.

14

Peasants and Mechanicks

Our Liveries were so rich, and so well-trim'd that the Pages Liveries amongst others cost near thirty pounds sterling a piece, being almost covered quite over with silver lace.[1]

On 20 July 1663 Marvell was on board a man-of-war at Gravesend, eager to depart for Archangel. According to the nineteen-year-old Swiss under-secretary to the embassy, Guy Miège, the other vessel making up the party, a merchantman, had already attempted to sail on 15 July but, after a week of violent storms during which the Master's refusal to put ashore earned him the title of '*Amphibium*' from the drenched passengers, it had been driven back to Newcastle to make repairs.[2] In his eve-of-departure letters to the Hull Corporation and to Trinity House, Marvell described 'taking barge for Grauesend'[3] that day, although the man-of-war did not actually sail until 22 July. He repeated his expectation that the voyage would finish 'within twelve moneths', which proved to be rather optimistic. His letter to Mayor Wilson was florid and ingratiating, but at the same time careful to make the point that this was an officially sanctioned mission and one that the Corporation had approved: 'I undertake this voyage with the order and good liking of his Majesty and by leaue given me from the house and entered in the journall, and hauing received moreover your approbation I go therefore with much more ease and satisfaction of mind and augurate to my selfe the happier successe in all my proceedings.' He also left a sly warning to handle Colonel Gilby robustly, so that he might serve them properly in his absence.

To the Brethren of Trinity House he again stressed the official backing for his mission but also indicated that he saw it as personally beneficial – 'so advantageous to my selfe upon all respects and not unusefull to the public'.[4] This would be the last letter he wrote to either body for more than eighteen months – given the impracticability of doing so while at sea and travelling on land – and he was keen to reassure the Brethren that their business would not suffer in his absence. Indeed, his short disappearance to Holland had proved, in the event, not to have needed his cutting the trip short: 'Neither do I now go abroade againe but with a probability of coming back before your opposers can haue any hope of effecting their former pretensions.' He suggested that the balance of the money he had asked them to deposit with him to facilitate his work for them in the lighthouse business could now be returned. Will Popple could arrange that for them. And then he was off.

Marvell's certainty that this mission would do his career some good was well founded. His clash in the House with Clifford had taken place more than a year previously but he would be aware that he still had enemies at Westminster who remained suspicious of the past he himself had so easily disowned. A mission on behalf of the King to a foreign power, in the company of a favoured young aristocrat, would surely remove once and for all any doubts about his loyalty. Further commissions might follow.

The voyage from Gravesend to the port of Archangel took a month, the frigate making much quicker progress than the merchantman which did not arrive until 5 September. Guy Miège described the whole embassy in often very vivid detail in *A Relation of Three Embassies from His Sacred Majesty Charles II to the Great Duke of Muscovie, The King of Sweden and the King of Denmark Performed by the Right Ho'ble the Earle of Carlisle in the Years 1663 & 1664*, which was published anonymously in 1669, 'with his Lordships approbation'. It was a popular work that went through several editions and translations. Miège, who was born in Lausanne in 1644, went on to publish in 1691 a *New State of England* – a sort of anatomy of Britain – and various French dictionaries and grammars. He was a shrewd and observant writer. The purpose of the embassy he described was to bring about the restoration of certain trade privileges that English merchants had previously enjoyed in Russia but which the Tsar had cancelled after the execution of the King. Miège wrote that the present ruler of 'Moscovy', Alexey Michailovitz, had a great 'abhorrency of the murther of King Charles the First' so the embassy would have its work cut out. Back in England, the King had already held a lavish reception for the Russian ambassadors, but a personal visit of his representatives was necessary. Another aim of the embassy was to restore a special English privilege of paying no impost when using the port of Archangel in recognition of their having originally discovered the port. Two reasons were proffered for winning back these privileges: the fact that the rebellion was over and that 'these very Priviledges were the basis and foundation, upon which the Amity betwixt the two Crowns of England and Moscovy were superstructures'.

The embassy was led by the dashing young Carlisle, aged thirty-four and with 'a peculiar grace and vivacity in his discourse'. Throughout, he deployed the maximum amount of display and pomp in order to ingratiate himself with the Duke of Moscovy:

> *His Train consisted of near fourscore persons, amongst which he had ten Gentlemen, six Pages, two Trumpets, and twelve Footmen. He had also a Chaplain, several Interpreters, a Chirurgeon, six Musicians, besides many Tradesmen that were very necessary in Muscovy.*

The ships were weighted down with items of furniture and catering equipment and they had brought also 'a magnificent canopy of red Damask, surrounded with a gold and silver Fringe, and having on the back in a large circle the Arms of the King of England, richly embroidered with silver'. On arrival at the bar of Archangel on 19 August Carlisle immediately set in train the arrangements for the triumphal entry of this splendid retinue:

> *He sent Mr* Marvel *his Secretary, into the Town. Of whose landing the Governour having notice, ordered him to be conducted by six Gentlemen to the Castle, through a Regiment of six hundred men, and the next day he sent sixteen boats guarded by several hundreds of men, under the command of a Collonel, to receive his Excellence, and bring him ashore.*

After this display, the ambassador himself, Lord Carlisle, finally entered the town of Archangel on 23 August, though some obscure breach of protocol in this heavy pageantry created some dismay in his hosts. Several English and Dutch merchant ships, happening to be in the harbour, had fired cannon salutes, a practice not approved of by the Russians. Nevertheless, the stay at Archangel augured well and the embassy was treated to 'all manner of Good entertainment'.

On 12 September the party left Archangel in six barges 'of which one was set apart for his Kitchin, and a hearth and Chimney contrived in it'. The Earl, an Englishman abroad, had taken great care to bring his creature comforts with him. The barges, hauled by serfs not horses, moved slowly up the Duina and Sucagna rivers via Colmogro, Arsinoa, Yagrish, Ustiga, Tetma and Chousca, reaching Vologda on 17 October. As the Russian winter was setting in Marvell and his compatriots fortified themselves against the cold with furs and sheepskins; there was some anxiety that the rivers might freeze, halting the snail-like progress entirely. To pass the time the English party went ashore to shoot duck and pigeon. On arrival at the small villages the local priest would often come out to the barge with a present of fish or gooseberries in the hope of some reward, which usually turned out to be aqua vitae. The result of this was that he commonly went home again drunk. Feeling colder and colder, they huddled in their furs and now felt that 'our Voiage began to be grievous and insupportable'. On arrival at Vologda they decided to lodge there for three months until the snow had frozen sufficiently to support sledges. There was some diversion there in the form of music and dancing. Guy Fawkes Night was celebrated on 5 November and 'The Buttlers wife was brought to bed, having been big with child before she came out of London.'

On 7 January the party moved off again by sledge via Yaroslaf, Rostof, Peroslaf and Troitza, reaching a little village near Moscow called Yawes on 3 February. Various encounters along the way had taught the English party that the Russians were sticklers for protocol, at least in relation to themselves. As they prepared for their entry into Moscow the behaviour of minor local officials sent out to negotiate the arrangements provoked irritation and offered 'tokens of indignity and contempt'. Carlisle's patience was becoming exhausted and he instructed Marvell to compose a letter in Latin to the Tsar 'in which he should inform him of the principal circumstances of this disorder'. The letter complained of the 'misfortune, if not an indignity' of their treatment, and complained rather querulously of their sojourn at Yawes 'in this pitiful village, amidst all kinds of inconveniences, and swarms of troublesome Insects'. Carlisle demanded, through Marvell's Latin, satisfaction for these 'barbarous and inhumane' treatments and was apparently mollified by the response.

On 6 February, almost seven months after leaving England, the embassy entered Moscow in splendour: 'It was reported every where in the Court that the City of Mosco never saw the Entry of any Ambassador so glorious as this.' Two hundred sledges made up the procession. A few days later, on 11 February, a formal audience with the Tsar took place, Carlisle arriving in a sledge in which Marvell was also riding: 'In the Ambassadors sledge there was the Secretary and the chief Interpreter standing and uncovered, the Secretarie carrying in his hands upon a yard of red Damask his Letters of Credence written in parchment, whose Superscription contained all the tiles of the *Tzar* in letters of Gold.' The Tsar's adornment of jewels made him seem 'like a sparkling Sun' and the English party coming into his presence were 'like those who coming suddainly out of the dark are dazled with the brightness of the Sun'. The Tsar, at thirty-four, was the same age as the English Ambassador. His first question was about the Queen Mother: 'How doth the desolate Widow of that glorious Martyr *Charles* the First?' Various florid Latin speeches, composed and delivered by Marvell, were offered from the English side, and gifts were presented, including a gun used by the royal martyr and a pair of pistols worn by Charles II when 'after so long adversity he rid in his triumphant Entry into His Metropolitan City of London'.

A second audience took place on 13 February at which, in spite of its being the first opportunity to get down to the essential business that had brought them there, the ambassadors were still complaining about the slights they had received from the Russian officials. The Tsar reproved them for these complaints before informing them that he was refusing their substantive request on the grounds that the English Company of Archangel who wished to see their former privileges restored had supported the rebellion. An English informer, Luke Nightingale, had, the Tsar claimed, been sent by Charles I with this information. He went on to suggest that the English planned to rob him and had abused trading rules to line their own pockets at the expense of the Russians. To cap it all the Tsar then announced that he took grave exception to being described in Marvell's Latin address as 'Illustrissime' rather than 'Serenissime'.

After this brutal setback, the English returned on 29 Feburary to try to win a change of heart. Still pressing for an apology for the slight given by the Tsar's officials – apparently not considering it tactful to let this go in the difficult circumstances – Carlisle attempted to demolish the Russian objections. The Tsar was informed smoothly by Carlisle – who had been wounded at the Battle of Worcester fighting for Cromwell – that 'though all the *English* were involved in the calamatie of that Rebellion, but the better part alwayes free from the guilt thereof'. This was a very Marvellian argument. Carlisle next attempted to destroy the credibility of Luke Nightingale, calling him 'a broken merchant, a perjured fellow and a grosse Imposter'. On the impropriety of the Latin address – and speaking no doubt to a learned brief drafted by Marvell, who may have actually delivered all this matter in his own Latin – Carlisle pointed out that 'the word Serenus signifieth nothing but still & calme'. He added that Cicero had called the night serene, and similar usages could be found in Lucretius. Carlisle's final riposte was that, if titles were in dispute, why was his king not accorded by the Russians that of Defender of the Faith? On 19 March the Tsar replied that the King offered him no help against his enemies 'the *Pole* and the Grim Tartar'. At a final private audience on 22 April that lasted until one o'clock in the morning Carlisle saw defeat staring him in the face. The whole elaborate embassy, with all its pomp and circumstance, had been a total failure.

After a final public audience on 24 June, the party finally left Moscow, having witnessed the exchange of coloured eggs at the Orthodox Easter. Carlisle wrote a letter to Secretary of State Henry Bennet, later Earl of Arlington, a member of the Cabal, after the final private audience in which he expressed his irritation: 'What else was to be expected in a country where all other beasts change their colours twice a yeare but the rationall beasts change their soules thrice a day.'[5]

On 3 August the ambassadors arrived at Riga on the next leg of their journey to Sweden. They travelled on horseback, with three coaches and 200 waggons, in more clement weather, but they were still complaining. This time it was the hard Russian saddles, the tents in which they had to sleep, the restricted diet – 'nothing but Beef and Mutton' – and the 'persecution of the flies'. But at least the passing scenery diverted them. They were forced to concede 'the delight of beholding the Rivers gliding through these vast wildernesses'. And the natives were a pleasant curiosity:

> *Our habits appeared so unusual to the Peasants, that they no sooner saw two or three of my Lord's Servants on horse-back, but away they run in all haste to their houses, clapping their doors after them, as if we had been so many ominous Birds, or Spirits come on purpose to fright them.*

But, generally speaking, 'the small civility we found in this barbarous Nation, and the natural disposition each of us had to be returning towards his own Country, prevailed with us to leave Moscovy with much pleasure and satisfaction'. They rested for fifteen days in Riga until on 22 August they set sail in a man-of-war via the Baltic to Stockholm, nearly running short of provisions on the voyage. Arriving at Stockholm, Carlisle 'dispatched Mr Marvel his Secretary, and Mr Taylor his Steward in the Boat . . . The Secretary was sent to give notice of the Ambassadors arrival and to inform himself at what time he was to make his Entry into the Town.' The reception of the embassy by the Swedes on 8 September was less extravagant than that offered by the Russians but had, they felt, more genuine civility. They spent five weeks in Stockholm at the court of the nine-year-old King Charles XI, to whom Marvell delivered a Latin address after Carlisle had delivered it in English. Marvell then offered it in French to the Queen Mother. Guy Miège was impressed by Marvell's artfulness as a rhetorician for, in delivering his farewell address to the Queen Mother, Carlisle said at one point 'That the boldest eloquence would lose its speech' then paused as if he was genuinely lost for words in praising her excellence. When Marvell delivered the same speech in French, Miège noticed that he also paused in the same place and realised that this was in fact a carefully contrived effect. In spite of all these arts, however, the Swedish mission, diplomatically speaking, was as fruitless as the Russian one and the hapless embassy set sail on a ship called the *Centurion* on 13 October for Denmark, arriving at Copenhagen two weeks later. During the voyage they had been entertained by two tame bears from Moscow which wrestled playfully and sucked the fingers of anyone who dared.

On arrival at Copenhagen, Marvell was despatched, as usual, to give notice of Carlisle's arrival 'and to carry his Credentials to the Chancellor'. On 27 October Carlisle made his solemn entry into the town where 'The King of Denmark appeared to us very grave and Majestick.' Soon after this Carlisle's wife gave birth to a son. They left – again failing in their mission to secure Danish support in preparations for war against the United Provinces – on 15 December. The sea being frozen, they travelled by land, after an initial attempt to go by sea from Elsinore had failed. Their numbers were now thinned out as they pressed on home overland, a little anxious because the hostilities of the Dutch War were just beginning, passing through the town of Bockstoud near Hamburg where another incident displayed Marvell's hot temper. It was in the first days of January, just after dinner, when the party was due to set off to complete a further three or four leagues that night. Marvell's waggoner said he would not go unless a friend of his, another waggoner, went along with him. Marvell was having none of this:

> *The secretary not able to bring them to reason by fair means, tried what he could by foul, and by clapping a pistol to his head would have forced him along with him. But immediately his pistol was wrested from him, and as they were putting themselves into a posture to abuse him, we interposed so effectually that he was rescued out of their hands.*

The circumstances in Miège's account are not clear enough to be certain who the aggressor was on this occasion, but once again Marvell seems to have been prone to getting himself into a violent incident. Perhaps tempers were frayed after the strain of this long, fruitless mission. After Marvell was rescued 'out of the hands of a barbarous rout of Peasants and Mechanicks' he set off to protest to the governor of the town about the disorder. While he was gone his companions found themselves 'beset by above a hundred of them endeavouring to rob us of our goods, and others to do violence to our persons'. In the fracas 'a Page lost his Periwig' and 'the rabble took particular delight to toss him up and down with his Furs in the snow'. At this point Carlisle returned and order was quickly restored.

The embassy arrived back in England on 30 January 1665 – the anniversary of the King's execution – having returned via Munster, Cologne, Malines, Brussels, Calais, and Gravesend. Charles II asked

Carlisle to record in full what had happened in order to enable him to challenge the accounts arriving from the Russian ambassadors, who were complaining of the insolence of the English mission. Miège was commissioned to perform the task. That he did so with such competence has provided Marvell's biographers with an account of a period of nearly eighteen months that would otherwise have remained teasingly blank, for Marvell himself left no record of the trip.

15

Sober English Valour

> Holland, *that scarce deserves the name of* Land,
> *As but th'Off-scouring of the* British Sand.

During Marvell's absence in Russia the threat of naval war with the Dutch had become an imminent reality. The Commons had voted £2.5 million for the war and shortly after Marvell returned to England the Second Dutch War began in March 1665. He had also missed the first attempts to impeach the Lord Chancellor, Clarendon. Both events would loom large in the satires Marvell began to write in the mid-1660s, prompted by disillusion with the government of Charles II and its growing intolerance of dissent. The dislocations and turbulence of war and an unsettled national politics would be accompanied in 1665 by a major outbreak of bubonic plague, followed in turn by the Great Fire that ravaged London in 1666. For a poet who had always displayed a satiric vein and who was at the heart of the political world and keenly attentive to its every nuance, Marvell's shift to satire at this time is wholly unsurprising.

Marvell plunged straight back into political business in February 1665. His signature appears on the 4th, together with that of Colonel Gilby, John Ramsden and John Cresset, witnessing a Trinity House document.[1] A month later the Hull Bench Books record that an order was made on 16 March for the payment to him of £10 6s 8d for thirty-one days' attendance at the last session of Parliament.[2] Marvell would have been kept at the government's expense throughout the latter half of 1663 and 1664 (he was officially noted as a court dependant)[3] but the Parliamentary wages would now be needed to enable him to survive back in London. He was in the habit of occasionally handing over his wages to his brother-in-law Edmund Popple, who acted as banker, investment adviser and general man of business for him. The Bench Books record such payments being made on 2 March 1661, 3 December 1663 (when Marvell was riding out the Russian winter at Vologda), 14 December 1665 and 21 April 1670.[4]

The outbreak of plague in London forced the Cavalier Parliament to meet for a short fifth session at Oxford in the autumn of 1665. It was from there that Marvell wrote the first letter to the Hull Corporation and its latest mayor, Robert Bloome, since his return from Russia, though he had been back in London for seven or eight months now. During the spring someone had arranged for the publication of part of the poem he had written during an earlier engagement with the Dutch in 1653, 'The Character of Holland'. The first 100 lines, with a further eight-line conclusion bolted on to make the poem relate to the moment, were entered on the Stationers' Register on 13 June, ten days after the English victory under the Duke of York at Solebay. This original pamphlet, printed for Robert Horn, at the sign of the Angel in Pope's Head Alley, has disappeared, but it was issued again by Horn in 1672, once more for topical reasons, and is in the collection of manuscripts and pamphlets assembled by Robert Harley and printed in the eighteenth century as *The Harleian Miscellany*. According to an early editor of Marvell's work, G.A. Aitken, 'a printer, on the side of the Court, impudently adapted Marvell's poem to the occasion'.[5] The deeds of the early commanders of 1653, Deane, Blake, and Monck, were edited out and replaced with what Aitken rightly calls eight lines of 'doggerel' in praise of the Duke of York and the heroes of 1665:

Vainly did this slap-dragon fury hope
With sober English valour e'er to cope;
Not though they prim'd their barb'rous morning's draught
With powder, and with pipes of brandy fraught;
Yet Rupert, Sandwich, and, of all, the Duke,
The Duke has made their sea-sick courage puke;
Like the three comets sent from heaven down
With fiery flails, to swinge th'ungrateful clown.

It is safe to assume that Marvell was not the author of this conclusion, nor is it likely that he gave his assent to the publication, but the reference to Prince Rupert recalls the anecdote of an early Marvell editor, Thomas Cooke, who in 1726 referred to 'the great regard Prince Rupert always had to his counsels'.[6] Prince Rupert, son of Elizabeth Queen of Bohemia and Frederick V, elector palatine, had been a general of Charles I, gaining the first victory of the Civil War at Worcester, on the opposite side from the Earl of Carlisle. Exiled after the wars he returned at the Restoration to be made a Privy Counsellor and commissioner for the government of Tangier. He had a distinguished naval career and was a vice admiral at the outbreak of the Dutch War of 1672. According to Cooke, who claimed the privilege of having spoken with members of Marvell's family before writing his account of the poet's life:

> *It is reported of that Prince, whenever he voted according to the sentiments of Marvell, which he often did, it was a saying of the adverse party,* He has been with his tutor. *The intimacy betwixt him and Mr Marvell was so great, that when it was unsafe for the latter to have it known where he lived, for fear of losing his life by treachery, which was often the case, his royal friend would frequently renew his visits in the habit of a private person. For he was often in such danger, that he was forced to have his letters directed to him in another name, to prevent any discovery that way.*

It is worth remembering that Cooke made errors about very basic details of Marvell's career, such as suggesting that his embassy was not to Russia but Constantinople – a search of the relevant papers at the Public Record Office has produced no trace of the latter – but if Cooke's anecdote is reliable it suggests two things. The first is that Marvell's easy crossing of political barriers was never trammelled by past associations or inconveniences in the record: he was not abhorred by every member of the court party. The second is that his life as a politician, as has already been suggested, was a dangerous one. Cooke referred to 'the insuperable hatred of his foes to him, and their designs of murdering him'.[7] He claimed to have seen 'a private letter . . . written to a friend from Highgate' (which has not survived) in which Marvell confesses his fear of these enemies, quoting the Latin: '*Praeterea magis occidere metuo quam occidi; non quod vitam tanti aestimem, sed ne imparatus moriar*' (a difficult and possibly incorrectly transcribed piece of Latin which means something like: 'I shrink from killing more than from being killed; not so much because of the value I put on life as from being unprepared to die'). Cooke argued that this made Marvell 'very cautious with whom he contracted a friendship'. Aubrey confirms this when he says that Marvell, though fond of wine, would be cautious about how much he drank in company and 'was wont to say that, he would not play the gooodfellow in any man's company in whose hands he would not trust his life'.[8] This permanent caution, added to a natural reserve and taciturnity, contributed to the air of mystery and apartness that clung to this solitary man. 'He had not a generall acquaintance,' Aubrey noted. Later, at the time of his clashes with Samuel Parker in the early 1670s, he was the recipient of another lost letter, dated 3 November 1673, said to have been left for him at a friend's house and to have been signed with the mysterious initials 'JG'. It concluded: 'If thou darest to print any lie or libel against Dr Parker, by the eternal God, I will cut thy throat.'[9] Marvell's gift for making friends in unexpected places was matched by an equal talent for making cordial enemies in whatever business he was engaged.

In his first letter to Mayor Bloome, Marvell complained that the burgesses had not replied to his letter written before the Oxford session began (their response, written two days previously, was in fact in the post). He provided a short political briefing explaining that the House had voted the King more money to prosecute the Dutch War. He also reported on the Five Mile Bill which, when enacted, would restrain 'nonconformists ejected ministers from liuing neare towns corporate'.[10] He predicted a brief sitting: 'We shall haue a short session I belieue not aboue a moneth.' The Oxford term began on 18 November, by which time the MPs would expect to be gone. In fact the Courts of Justice were held in Oxford in November. Marvell observed that there was in fact 'litle to be done', but added in the same breath: 'I am in some hast.' Once again, he seems to have had several irons in the fire, the immediate Parliamentary business eclipsed by private matters. The presence of the Bodleian Library was one such call on his attention in Oxford. His signature appears in the Library's admission register of 30 September as a visitor, or one of the *extranei nobiles et generosi*, the only other name recorded in this category being, on 4 October, that of Sir Winston Churchill, the politician and father of the 1st Duke of Marlborough.[11] The Library at that time kept no record of books issued but it is safe to assume that the scholarly poet, deprived of access to library resources during his eighteen months abroad, was making good use of the opportunity.

A week after his first letter, Marvell gave the Mayor the latest news: 'Our nauy is speeding to chase the Dutch again of our Seas.'[12] On 2 November he reported that a bill aimed at checking the spread of the plague had fallen 'because the Lords would not agree with us that their houses if infected should be shut up'.[13] The national emergency had evidently contributed to some degree of abatement of the tension between King and Commons, for the former 'was pleased at our departure [from Oxford] to witness his great satisfaction in all our proceedings'. The King prorogued the Parliament until 20 February 1666.

Marvell was thus back in London by the end of 1665 but there is a gap in his public and private correspondence until the beginning of October 1666. It can be assumed that he witnessed, a month earlier, a calamity even more extraordinary than the plague, for on 2 September, in the small hours between about 1 and 2 a.m., a fire broke out at the house of Thomas Farrinor, the King's baker, in Pudding Lane, between Eastcheap and Lower Thames Street. The diarist, Samuel Pepys, was woken at about 3 a.m. by his servants, who had seen the signs of a great fire raging in the city. At first he dismissed it and went back to bed. The Mayor, Sir Thomas Bloodworth, protesting at having been dragged out of bed to see the fire, observed grumpily: 'A woman might piss it out.' But when Pepys woke again at 7 a.m. the extent of the fire was brought home to him. He walked to the Tower to get a full view of the devastation, then went down to the Thames to catch a boat from where he could see the real dimensions of this 'lamentable fire':

> *Everybody endeavouring to remove their goods, and flinging into the river, or bringing them into lighters that lay off; poor people staying in their houses as long as till the very fire touched them, and then running into boats, or clambering from one pair of stairs, by the waterside to another. And, among other things, the poor pigeons, I perceive, were loath to leave their houses, but hovered about the windows and balconies, till they burned their wings and fell down.*[14]

Aided by a preceding long dry spell and an easterly wind, the fire swept through the city. In four days more than 13,000 houses were destroyed, together with the adjacent churches and public buildings. Millions of pounds of damage was done to property in an era before fire insurance. One hundred thousand people were homeless. The stress on a nation already involved in a costly war and still waiting for the predicted Dutch booty was telling. As the fire abated, the search for scapegoats began. Plague, fire, war were seen by the religious zealots as God's punishment on a sinful nation. The politicians – against a background of hysteria and xenophobia during which several foreigners were randomly lynched – seemed to incline towards the traditional explanation for such things: a popish plot. Clarendon would later conclude that there was no evidence 'of any other cause of that woeful fire, except by the displeasure of Almighty God', but the Privy Council held long sessions examining suspect after suspect.

Parliament met on 18 September. One of its first tasks was to appoint a committee 'to inquire into the causes of the late fire'. According to the Journals of the House it was ordered on 2 October 'that Sir Maurice Berkley, Mr Pepis, Sir Thom. Allen, Mr Morice, Sir Richard Everard, Mr Crouch, Mr Marvell, Sir Wm Hickman, Sir Adam Browne, Serjeant Mainard be added to the Committee'.[15] (The prompt action of Samuel Pepys in reporting directly to the King had resulted in a royal order to start pulling down buildings in the path of the fire.) Appointed on 25 September, and meeting in the Speaker's chamber under the chairmanship of Sir Robert Brook, the committee had evidently felt the need very shortly to acquire extra members. On 20 December Marvell and another MP called Jolliff were given the task of examining a Mrs Eves of Enfield to hear what she had to say about the suspicious case of Mrs St George, a palpable papist.

Shortly before the fire broke out Mrs Rebecca Eves claimed to have been told by Mrs St George about a plot for 'firing the city'. A little later, Mrs St George's daughter paid Mrs Eves a visit to ask what her mother had said, clearly anxious about her garrulous parent. After the fire the daughter again told Mrs Eves that 'she had much ado to keep her mother in at the time of the fire, lest she should speak some things she should be questioned for'.[16] Mrs Eves's summing up on the St George family was that: 'They are all great Papists, and there are many more in the neighbourhood.' Even an ardent Catholic conspiracy theorist like Marvell must have concluded that such tittle-tattle was a waste of the committee's time. The full committee report was published on 22 January 1667 but Parliament was prorogued two weeks later before it could properly discuss the matter. No single culprit was ever found and the most likely suspect was a spark from a baker's oven, dry hay in a neighbouring inn and close-packed streets of timber houses on a dry late summer evening with a good wind to fan the flames.

As usual, Marvell's constituency letters at this time are found pleading that 'busynesse dos so multiply of late that I can scarce snatch time to write to you'.[17] As well as the committee on the causes of the fire, he refers to another on which he seems to have been a member, tasked 'to receiue informations of the insolence of Popish Priests & Jesuites & of the increase of Popery'. The strong English tradition of anti-popery was always linked to paranoia about secret conspiracies with co-religionists among the European powers. At a time of war, when France was an enemy, conspiracy theories would find a more fertile soil and anti-popery could be made to seem a patriotic gesture. The committee recommended to the King a range of punitive measures against Catholics, such as the expulsion of non-native 'Popish Priests and Jesuits', the removal of all civil and military office-holders who refused the oath of allegiance and the oath of supremacy and an insistence that all MPs took these oaths. 'Many informations are daily brought in to the two Committees about the Fire of London & the insolence of Papists,'[18] Marvell reported to the latest Mayor of Hull, Richard Franke, at the end of October. Marvell was ready to believe that there was a Catholic plot involved in the fire and promised the Hull burgesses that the reports about to be published would contain 'things of extraordinary weight and which if they were not true might haue bin thought incredible'.[19]

The other major preoccupation of the House was raising further money to prosecute the Dutch War, which was costing much more than anyone could have guessed. Members ran through a range of revenue-raising options that included foreign and domestic excise, a poll bill, land taxes and a chimney tax. The dilemma for Marvell, as for his fellow MPs, was how to meet the King's necessity for money, which at a time of war was clearly also the nation's need, without adding to the tax burden on his provincial merchant electorate. The King was seeking £1.8 million. 'For indeed as the urgency of his Majestyes affairs exacts the mony so the sense of the nations extreme necessity makes us exceedingly tender whereupon to fasten our resolutions,' he explained delicately to Mayor Franke. 'One thing I observe that as the house is much in earnest to furnish his Majestyes present occasions so they are very carefull to prevent the perpetuating of any Imposition.'[20] A poll tax was proposed of one shilling a head payable (two shillings for 'all nonconformists and papists') and a highly ingenious measure for supporting the domestic wool trade against foreign competition: 'That all persons shall be buried in woollen for these next six or seuen years.'[21] Coupled to a recent measure in support of the native flax trade, it was hoped this device would result in £100,000 a year being diverted to domestic wool rather than 'forain linnen'. Marvell's dedication to these financial and commercial matters is impressive. Although he depended on the Corporation for his 'knight's pence' and could thus not afford to appear neglectful of their interests, he seems to have had a genuine feel for the minutiae of public and business affairs, nourished perhaps by regular conversations with his nephew William Popple.

At the end of the year, just before Christmas, the Corporation once again expressed its appreciation of their MP's efforts. He wrote back graciously on 22 December: 'I thank you for your kind present of our Hull liquor.'[22]

16

An Idol of State

Here lies the sacred Bones
Of Paul *late gelded of his Stones.*
Here lie Golden Briberies,
The price of ruin'd Families.

By the start of 1667 English euphoria about the Dutch War – which had reached its peak eighteen months earlier in the great naval triumph off Lowestoft, when sixteen ships of the Dutch fleet were sunk and nine more captured with the loss of 2,000 lives – began to ebb. It was costing a great deal of money and the enemy was recouping its strength, though no one could have predicted the great national humiliation that would come in June and bring the war to an abrupt end. One significant opponent of the war, the Chancellor, Clarendon, would become one of its principal casualties. Marvell would take an active part in attempts at his impeachment.

The new session of Parliament in January began with the old rancour over revenue and a new clash between Commons and Lords, the latter resolving to ignore the Poll Tax Bill and to make its own recommendations to the King on the matter, an act that Marvell found 'unparlamentary and a dangerous precedent'.[1] Although these disagreements occurred in the public sphere, Marvell displayed an odd reticence in his reporting of them to Hull. His account was 'fit for your privacy if not secrecy',[2] he advised the Corporation, referring ten days later to it as 'a silent alarme'[3] that was now patched up. Perhaps he was reluctant to encourage negative rumours about Parliament at this difficult time, though he generally needed little incentive to practise reticence and caution.

There was no restraint, however, about the combined reports of the Great Fire and the 'insolence of Papists'. The former, Marvell promised, would be 'full of manifest testimonys that it was by a wicked designe'.[4] He was convinced that it was no accident and that he knew the general identity of the likely culprits. When a spate of small fires at Hull was reported to him in February, Marvell warned his constituents to take care. 'We haue had so much of them here in the South,'[5] he advised, 'that it makes me almost superstitious. But indeed as sometimes there arise new diseases, so there are seasons of more particular judgements such as that of fires seems of late to have been upon this Nation.' A more practical measure was the bill for the rebuilding of the City after the devastation of the fire, funded in part by the imposition of a tax on coal imports. A bill 'against Atheisme & prophane Swearing'[6] was also under consideration.

Early in 1667 the government resolved to enter into negotiations to secure peace in a war that had little justification other than commercial greed and rivalry. Louis XIV of France was about to invade the Spanish Netherlands and was easily persuadable out of his alliance with the Dutch because hostility to England was not necessary to his grander design. 'We haue some hope of a good alliance or of a Peace God grant it,'[7] Marvell told Hull on 2 February. But two months later, in a letter to Lord Wharton in April, he reported: 'The Dutch are in great preparation for warre . . . So that upon the Change, our Merchants are but in ill heart and hope very litle of peace.'[8] Peace would indeed come, confirmed by the treaty signed at Breda on 31 July, but as a result of something altogether more disagreeable. On 12 June 1667 the Dutch fleet boldly sailed up the River Medway, broke through the protective boom that guarded Chatham harbour, burnt four ships of the line and towed away the *Royal Charles*, at 80 guns the largest vessel of the fleet. This unexpected humiliation by the Dutch effectively ended the war. 'The Peace truly I think is concluded,'[9] Marvell reported to Hull on 25 July. Parliament was prorogued until October but the political repercussions were only just beginning. Clarendon was dismissed, but it did not assuage the public anger at what they perceived as mismanagement of the war. Cromwell's great naval victories had not been forgotten and there was a suspicion that not all the money voted for the war had necessarily found its way to the naval struggle. The damage to the King's reputation was considerable. Any satirist worth his salt would now be thinking of setting pen to paper.

But Marvell's first satire of the reign of Charles II was the poem 'Clarindon's House-Warming'. His authorship of this poem is disputed. It is certainly not among his best and illustrates the problem that modern readers have with Marvell's satires. Copious contemporary references and allusions are the stuff of political satire, in the present day as much as in Marvell's, but appreciation of the wit and nuance of poems addressed to the political situation of the 1660s and 1670s requires historical knowledge. These are poems that demand to be read with explanatory footnotes, but by impeding the flow of attention they can qualify the enthusiasm of many readers.

Edward Hyde, the first Earl of Clarendon, was a lawyer by profession and had been a friend of the poets Ben Jonson and Edmund Waller. He was always opposed to what he called 'the rebellion' and advised Charles I on legal and constitutional matters, as well as serving as Charles II's closest adviser both before and after the Restoration. From 1660 onwards he was probably the most powerful figure in the government, but by 1667 his dominance was nearly over. Court intrigue and the hostility of Parliament – which Marvell naturally shared – led to his dismissal as Chancellor in 1667 and subsequent impeachment. Before he could be imprisoned he fled to France where, after completing his *History of the Rebellion* and his autobiography, he died at Rouen in 1674.

In 1664 Clarendon had begun building an impressive house near St James. Its grandeur and pretension, and the soaring bill for its construction, became notorious; it ended up costing three times the original estimate. It was from here that Clarendon fled to France. On the eve of his departure he was visited by the diarist John Evelyn who described the great, gouty English conservative 'in his garden at his new-built palace, sitting in his gout wheel-chair, and seeing the gates setting up towards the north and the fields. He looked and spoke very disconsolately . . . Next morning he was gone.'[10] Clarendon himself was to confess that the building project had 'infinitely discomposed his whole Affairs and broken his estate'.[11] Because of his involvement in the controversial sale of Dunkirk in 1662 for 500,000 pistoles it was

THE BRITISH LIBRARY

Above: Winestead-in-Holderness Parish Church, Yorkshire, where the poet's father, the Reverend Andrew Marvell senior, baptised his son on 31 March 1621.

Below: 'By the Tide of Humber'. Wenceslaus Hollar's famous engraving of Hull, the town with which Marvell was associated throughout his life.

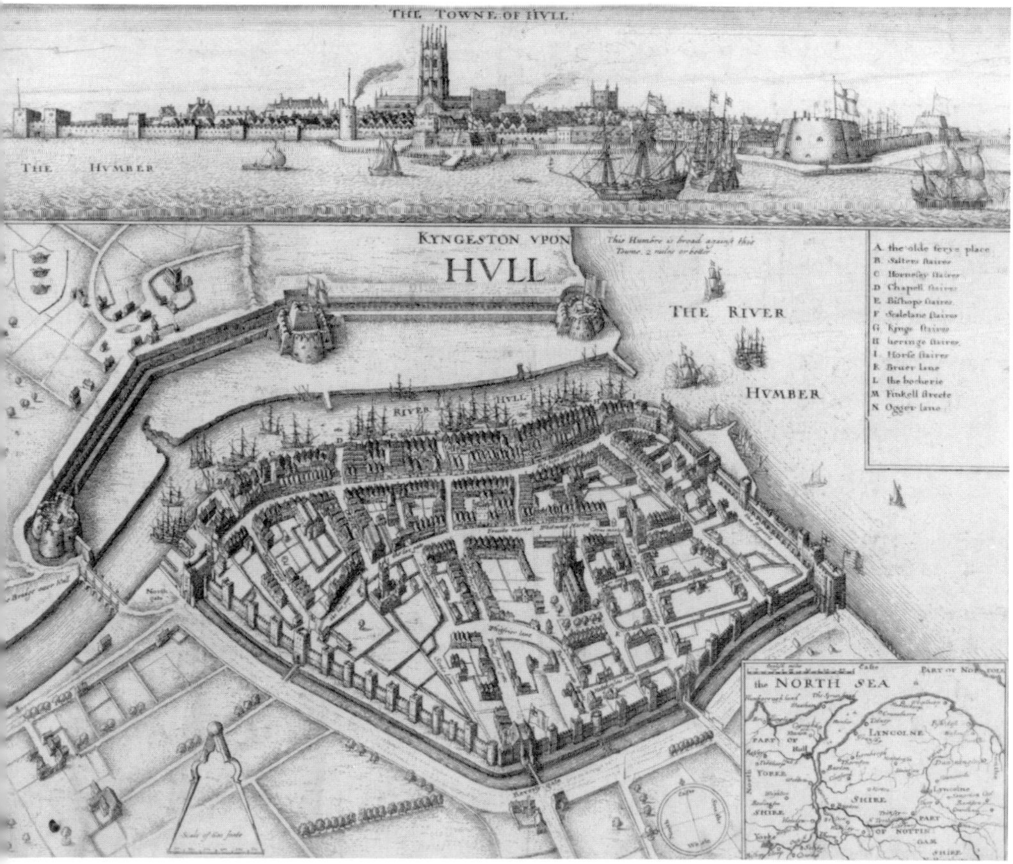

THE BRITISH LIBRARY

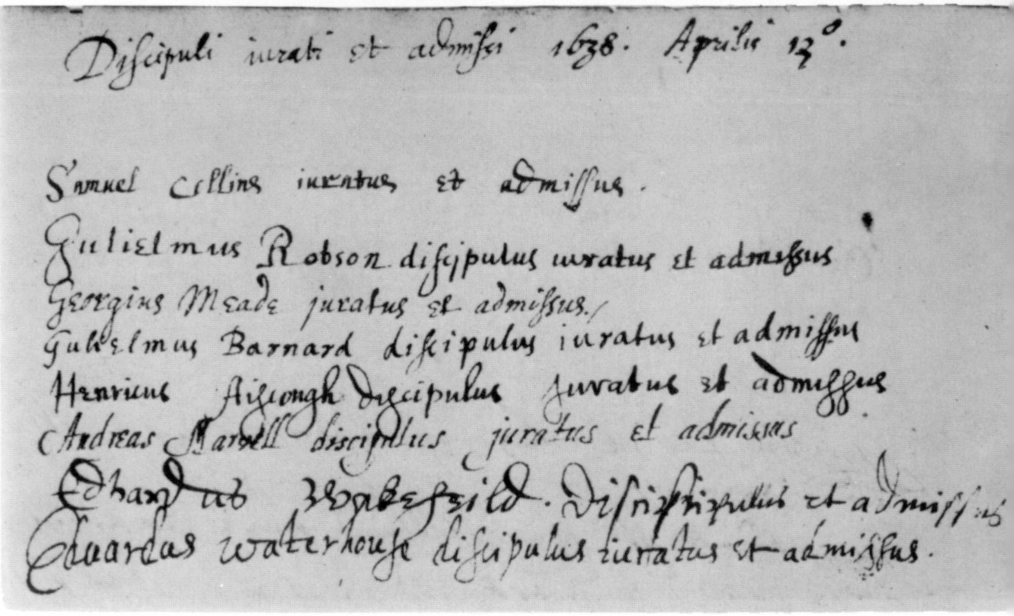

Discipuli iurati et admissi 1638. Aprilis 13°.

Samuel Collins iuratus et admissus.
Gulielmus Robson discipulus iuratus et admissus
Georgius Meade juratus et admissus.
Gulielmus Barnard discipulus iuratus et admissus
Henricus Aiscough discipulus juratus et admissus.
Andreas Marvell discipulus juratus et admissus
Edwardus Wakefeild. discipulus et admissus
Edwardus waterhouse discipulus iuratus et admissus.

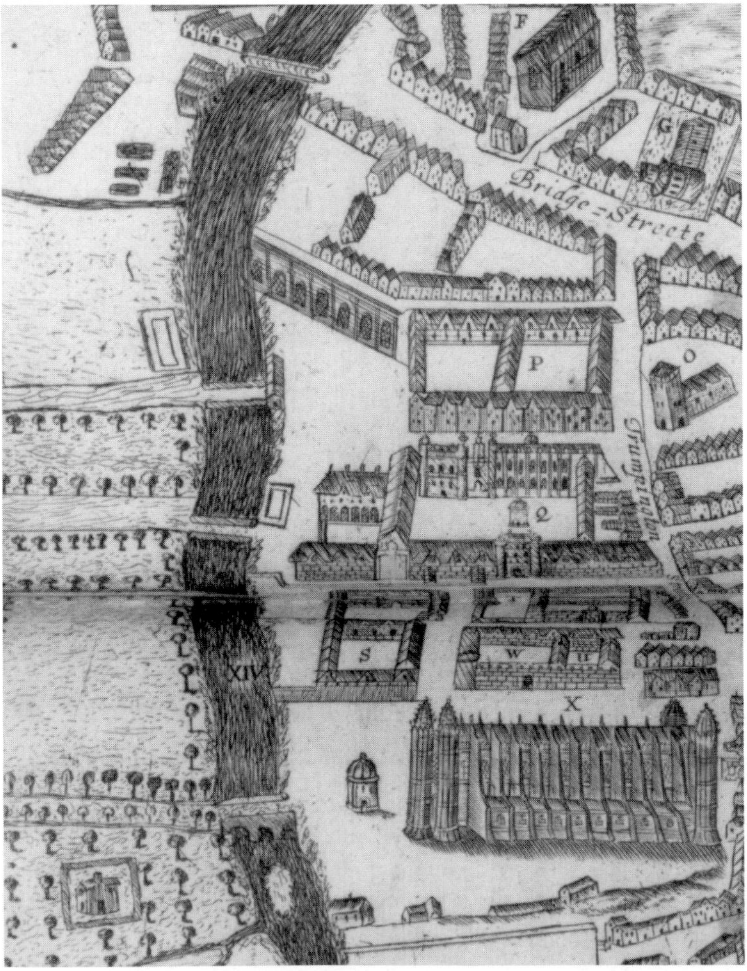

Above: A very rare example of Marvell's own hand: his entry in the Trinity College, Cambridge Admissions Book, 13 April 1638.

Left: An engraving of Trinity College, where Marvell was an undergraduate from 1633 to 1641.

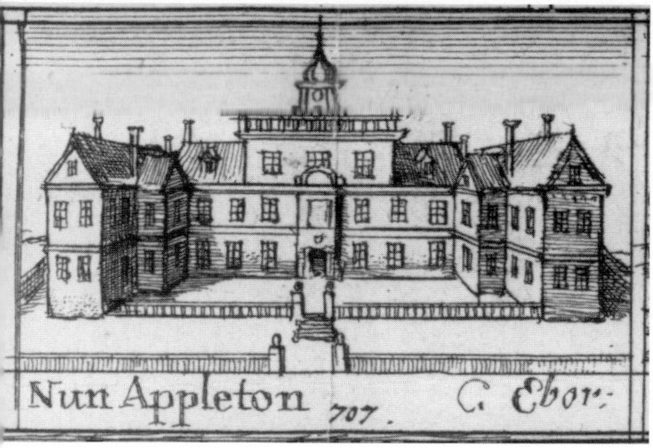

lbove left: Nun Appleton House, c.1655–60, the home of Thomas, 3rd Baron Fairfax, where Marvell wrote some of his inest poetry. *Right:* A watercolour miniature of Marvell's pupil, Mary Fairfax, by Samuel Cooper, 1650. *Below:* An engraving of Thomas Fairfax by W. Marshall after Edward Bower.

E.T. ARCHIVE

AKG LONDON

Above left: Charles I before the Civil War, when Marvell was still more sympathetic to the Royalists than he later became. *Right:* Oliver Cromwell, the Protector, whom Marvell served an eulogised in verse. *Below:* 'But bow'd his comely head/Down as upon a bed.' The execution of Charles I in 1649.

MARY EVANS PICTURE LIBRARY

HULTON GETTY

E.T. ARCHIVE

Above left: The poet John Milton, Marvell's friend and fellow civil servant in the Commonwealth.
Right: Charles II displays the full confidence of the Restoration, when Marvell was an MP.
Below: Landseer's visualisation of the poet and patriot at home in London after the Restoration.

MARY EVANS PICTURE LIBRARY

THE BRITISH LIBRARY

Marvell's personal seal, bearing the image of a stag, which he used on his correspondence.

AKG LONDON

Edward Hyde, Earl of Clarendon, statesman, historian and butt of Marvell's cruellest satire

HULTON GETTY

The house at Highgate, long since destroyed, where Marvell sought occasional respite from h public duties.

THE NATIONAL PORTRAIT GALLERY

The only portrait of Marvell that can confidently be pronounced genuine, painted by an unknown artist in 1660.

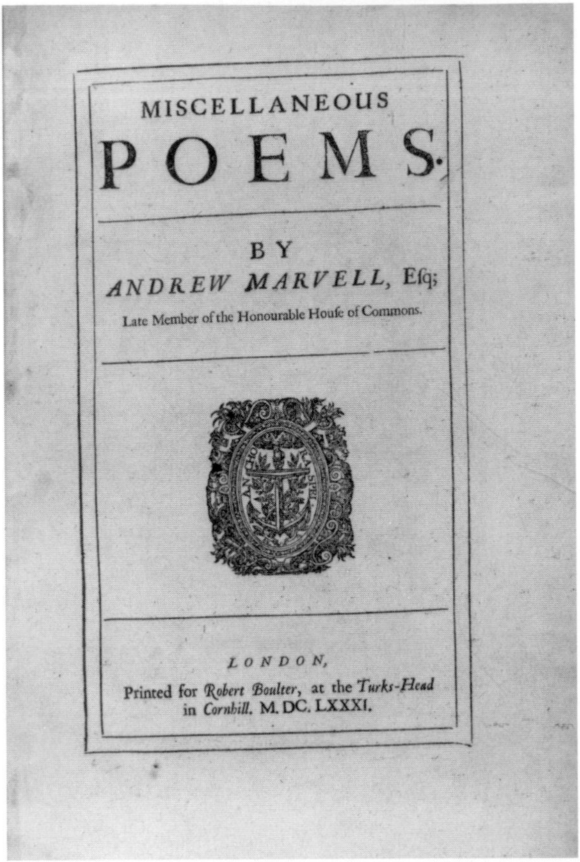

MISCELLANEOUS

POEMS.

BY

ANDREW MARVELL, Esq;

Late Member of the Honourable House of Commons.

LONDON,

Printed for *Robert Boulter*, at the *Turks-Head* in *Cornhill*. M.DC.LXXXI.

Left: The title page of the posthumous collection of Marvell's poems, published in 1681.

Below: The eighteenth-century monument to Marvell in the Church of St Giles-in-the-Fields, London.

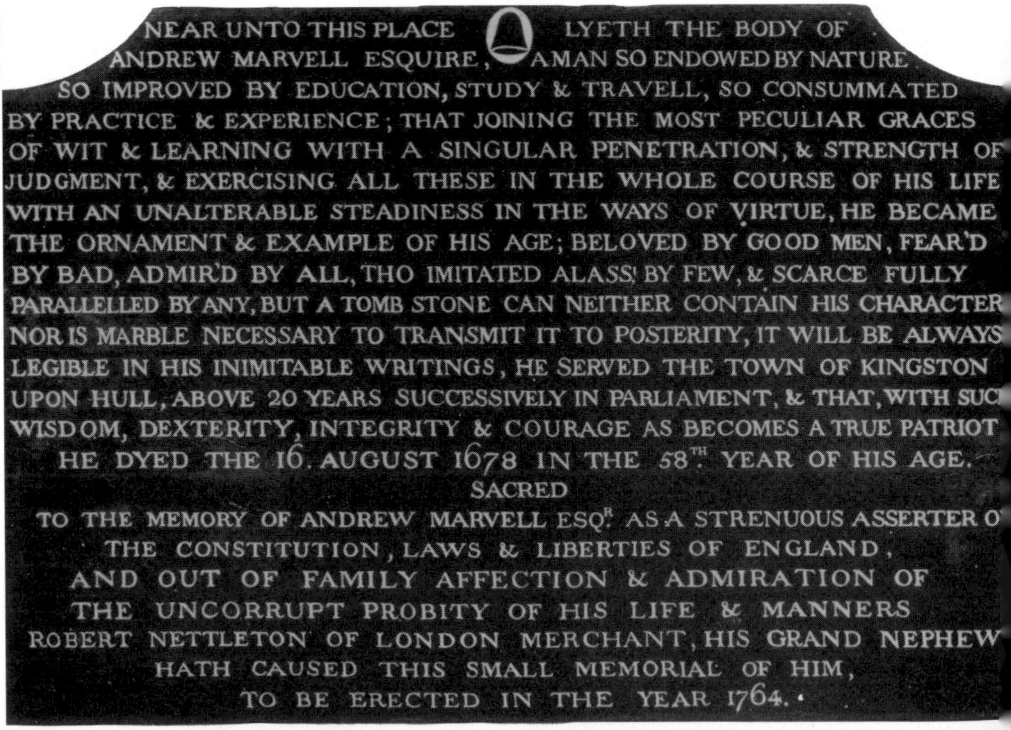
NEAR UNTO THIS PLACE LYETH THE BODY OF
ANDREW MARVELL ESQUIRE, A MAN SO ENDOWED BY NATURE
SO IMPROVED BY EDUCATION, STUDY & TRAVELL, SO CONSUMMATED
BY PRACTICE & EXPERIENCE; THAT JOINING THE MOST PECULIAR GRACES
OF WIT & LEARNING WITH A SINGULAR PENETRATION, & STRENGTH OF
JUDGMENT, & EXERCISING ALL THESE IN THE WHOLE COURSE OF HIS LIFE
WITH AN UNALTERABLE STEADINESS IN THE WAYS OF VIRTUE, HE BECAME
THE ORNAMENT & EXAMPLE OF HIS AGE; BELOVED BY GOOD MEN, FEAR'D
BY BAD, ADMIR'D BY ALL, THO IMITATED ALASS! BY FEW, & SCARCE FULLY
PARALLELLED BY ANY, BUT A TOMB STONE CAN NEITHER CONTAIN HIS CHARACTER
NOR IS MARBLE NECESSARY TO TRANSMIT IT TO POSTERITY, IT WILL BE ALWAYS
LEGIBLE IN HIS INIMITABLE WRITINGS, HE SERVED THE TOWN OF KINGSTON
UPON HULL, ABOVE 20 YEARS SUCCESSIVELY IN PARLIAMENT, & THAT, WITH SUC
WISDOM, DEXTERITY, INTEGRITY & COURAGE AS BECOMES A TRUE PATRIOT
HE DYED THE 16. AUGUST 1678 IN THE 58TH YEAR OF HIS AGE.
SACRED
TO THE MEMORY OF ANDREW MARVELL ESQR AS A STRENUOUS ASSERTER O
THE CONSTITUTION, LAWS & LIBERTIES OF ENGLAND,
AND OUT OF FAMILY AFFECTION & ADMIRATION OF
THE UNCORRUPT PROBITY OF HIS LIFE & MANNERS
ROBERT NETTLETON OF LONDON MERCHANT, HIS GRAND NEPHEW
HATH CAUSED THIS SMALL MEMORIAL OF HIM,
TO BE ERECTED IN THE YEAR 1764.

nicknamed Dunkirk House. On 14 June, Pepys wrote in his diary that: 'some rude people have been . . . at my Lord Chancellor's where they have cut down the trees before his house and broke his windows; and a gibbet either set up before or painted upon his gate, and these words writ: "Three sights to be seen: Dunkirk, Tangier, and a barren Queen."'[12] (Tangier was part of the dowry of Catherine of Braganza whom the King had married in 1661 hoping that she would bring him an heir, but she proved barren.) Clarendon, unpopular and widely blamed for more than he was actually culpable, was thus a soft target for a satirist.

Marvell's poem – if it was his – was written between the summoning of Parliament on 25 June and its first meeting on St James's Day, 25 July. The underlying theme is that Clarendon House has been built on the spoils of a corrupt political career – 'His Friends in the Navy would not be ingrate,/To grudge him some Timber who fram'd them the War' – and the satire is generally unsophisticated, mildly scatological, and little more than routinely derisive. Formally, it is crude in its jogging rhythms and sometimes laboured rhymes. There is no trace of the playful wit, inventive imagery, verbal felicity, or political insight that characterised the great political poems Marvell wrote in the 1650s. Far more considerable as a poem is 'The last Instructions to a Painter' which Marvell – again, if he was truly its author – wrote later in the summer, between 30 August when Clarendon resigned his seals, and 29 November when he fled to France.

On 26 June 1656, elated by a naval victory over the Turks in a war that had dragged on for ten years, the Venetians threw themselves into a frenzy of celebration. The city rulers appointed a committee to choose a painter to record the scene. The successful candidate was Pietro Liberi, whose work was to be displayed in the Sala dello Scrutino in the Doges' Palace where it can still be seen. It is entitled *Battaglia dei Dardanelli* or, more familiarly, *Lo Schiavo* because of the large nude figure of a slave that dominates the picture. The poet Giovanni Francesco Busenello, also greatly excited by the victory in the Dardanelles and eager to celebrate the victory, addressed a poem to Liberi, either to help him secure the commission or to congratulate him on his success. It was a novel idea for a poem to be designed in the form of instructions to a painter on the elements and proportion of a picture. Two years later the poem was translated by Sir Thomas Higgons, a diplomat and man of letters, as 'A Prospective of the Naval Triumph of the Venetians over the Turk: To Signor Pietro Liberi that Renowned and famous Painter by Gio. Francesco Busenello'. The Italian original was a revision and expansion of a poem written immediately after the naval victory by Busenello, initially in the Venetian dialect.

Both the poem and Higgons's translation might have remained minor historical curiosities had the poet Edmund Waller not decided to appropriate the genre in his 'Instructions to a Painter' of 1666. Between that date and the end of the century the genre had a vigorous flowering. It was seen as a useful device for holding together a great deal of otherwise disparate material. Its uses were satirical rather than celebratory and, according to one historian of the genre, these satires are 'direct and fierce, marked by a bitter invective, savage indictments, scurrility and coarseness'.[13] In December 1666 Samuel Pepys had been presented with an anonymous example of this now flourishing genre which he called 'the lampoon, or the *Mock Advice to a Painter*, abusing the Duke of York and my Lord Sandwich, Pen, and everybody, and the King himself, and all the matters of the navy and war'.[14] Pepys describes what appears to be a typical product of the genre. It was in fact a follow-up to Waller's poem, called 'Second Advice to a Painter, For Drawing the History of our Navall Business; In Imitation of Mr Waller'. The same author produced a 'Third Advice to a Painter' early in January 1667, and both these sequels to Waller infuriated the censors of the Stationers' Company when they were printed by a Francis Smith of the Elephant and Castle in the Strand. Two more followed, the 'Fourth Advice to the Painter' and the 'Fifth Advice', and all four were published in 1667 as *Directions To a Painter For Describing our Naval Business: In Imitation of Mr Waller Being The Last Works of Sir John Denham.* The book also appended 'Clarindon's House-Warming' 'By an Unknown Author'. The attribution to Denham has generally been doubted and may be there simply to lend dignity to an unlicensed publication or distract attention from the true author. Marvell's contemporaries, John Aubrey and Anthony Wood, believed that the real author of the *Advices* attributed to Denham was Marvell and some modern editors have agreed with them (at any rate so far as the 'Second' and 'Third' advices are concerned).[15] In his entry on Denham in the *Athenae Oxoniensis,* Wood says: 'To which *Directions,* tho' sir John Denham's name is set, yet they were thought by many to have been written by Andr. Marvell, esq. The printer that printed them, being discover'd, stood in the pillory for the same.'[16] It is probably prudent to concur with the editors of the standard Oxford edition of the poems that 'The last Instructions to a Painter' is the only one of this sequence that is reliably Marvell's – though they attribute to him also a later poem, of 1671, 'Further Advice to a Painter'.

The poem illustrates Marvell's view of public affairs in the second half of the 1660s, when the excitement of a new dawn felt at the Restoration had begun to evaporate and be replaced by a perspective of political sleaze and national self-doubt. It benefits from his closeness to affairs and is unsparing in the lash of its satire. It recalls the baneful events of 1666 and early 1667, such as the Dutch fleet's sailing up the Medway and the fall of Clarendon (though written just too early to record his flight). According to Aubrey, Marvell admired the satires of the rakish poet Rochester: 'I remember I have heard him say that the Earle of Rochester was the only man in England that had the true veine of Satyre.'[17] Rochester reciprocated the admiration in his poem 'Tunbridge-Wells' in 1675, where he saluted Marvell's treatment (in prose) of Samuel Parker ('Tho' *Marvel* has enough expos'd his Folly'). The 'true veine' in a poem such as Rochester's 'A Satyr against Mankind', where the satire deals not merely with the petty events of the day that clutter the genre of the painter poems but the general human condition, was never quite reached by Marvell in his satires of the reign of Charles II. The gift for generalised observation that marks his finest lyrics seemed to desert him in these late satires, which seldom transcend their specific context. Perhaps Marvell, as a practical politician, was too close to the events he described to stand back and take a more reflective view.

'The last Instructions to a Painter', however, is vastly superior to a poem like 'Clarindon's House-Warming' and has many fine satiric touches, such as the portrait of Henry Jermyn, Earl of St Albans, a gambler and *bon viveur* rumoured to have had an affair with the Queen Mother, Henrietta Maria. John Evelyn observed, many years later, of St Albans that: 'He ate and drank with extraordinary appetite. He is a prudent old courtier, and much enriched since his majesty's return.'[18] Marvell painted the old rake with relish:

> *Paint then St* Albans *full of soup and gold,*
> *The new* Courts *pattern, Stallion of the old.*
> *Him neither Wit nor Courage did exalt,*
> *But Fortune chose him for her pleasure salt.*
> *Paint him with* Drayman's *Shoulders, butchers* Mien,
> *Member'd like Mules, with Elephantine chine.*
> *Well he the Title of St* Albans *bore,*
> *For never* Bacon *study'd Nature more.*

The physicality of the description (and the recurrence of Marvell's preoccupation with the human posterior which at least one critic has suggested merits psychoanalytic investigation)[19] is even more evident in the lines on Clarendon's daughter, Anne Hyde, who in a private marriage ceremony at his residence in the Strand, Worcester House, on 3 September 1660 had become Duchess of York. Clarendon, who did not really approve of this match with the King's brother, James, later attributed to it in part his downfall. Rather like a cartoon strip, or a panning camera, the advice-to-a-painter genre allows the poet to present a series of otherwise unconnected caricatures. Anne Hyde is followed by the King's mistress, Barbara Villiers, Countess of Castlemaine whose taste for sex with her servants is satirised:

> *She through her Lacquies Drawers as he ran,*
> *Discern'd Love's Cause, and a new Flame began.*
> *Her wonted joys thenceforth and* Court *she shuns,*
> *And still within her mind the Footman runs:*
> *His brazen Calves, his brawny Thighs, (the Face*
> *She slights) his Feet shapt for a smoother race.*

This is all a far cry from the tender verses enfolding Mary Fairfax and the delicate pastoral dialogues of the 1650s.

After these pen portraits, the painter is invited to imagine the House of Commons in the form of a gaming parlour with the court and country parties no better than a pair of backgammon players in a tavern game in which 'The Dice betwixt them must the Fate divide.' Here the ruling party is motivated by avarice using the Excise as its means. The latter is a many-handed, many-eyed devouring monster prowling the streets by day: 'And flies like Batts with leathern Wings by Night'. In his letters to Hull, Marvell would always reveal himself to be a sworn enemy of the Excise, an essential posture for a member of the country party, opposed to the extravagance and profligacy of the metropolitan court. The poem reels off the names of a catalogue of long-forgotten politicians and makes much of the incompetence of the government in its handling of the Dutch War and its bungled attempts at a peace, which culminated in the shame of the Dutch raid: '*Ruyter* the while, that had our Ocean curb'd,/Sail'd now among our rivers undisturb'd.' At the heart of the poem is a picture of Archibald Douglas, captain of a Scottish regiment, who refused to desert his ship *The Royal Oak* when it was burnt in the Dutch attack and who thus died aboard it. The lines that describe him were later excerpted and framed by lines from another hand to appear as a new poem, 'The Loyall Scot', in 1697. The panegyric is a shift in tone from the satirical temper of the poem up to this point. Douglas is shown as a paragon of male beauty 'on whose lovely chin/The early Down but newly did begin;/And modest Beauty yet his Sex did Veil,/While envious Virgins hope he is a Male'. Once again, Marvell's notion of sexual allure is bound up with innocence and sexlessness.[20]

After the account of the Dutch raid the poem turns to the assigning of blame and by a witty play with rhyme mocks the making of a scapegoat out of Peter Pett, Commander of the Naval Dockyard at Chatham. The real culprit, however, turns out to be Clarendon. The poem – by far Marvell's longest – draws to a close with a dream-sequence in which the King is visited by the shade of his grandfather and then by his father, 'ghastly *Charles*', the latter, 'turning his Collar low,/The purple thread about his neck does show'. Waking from his dream: 'The wondrous Night the pensive *King* revolves,/And rising, straight on *Hyde's* Disgrace resolves.' With a closing reminder that 'scratching *Courtiers* undermine a *Realm*' the poet appears to advocate, as an alternative to the King's current cabal, an aristocratic elite of courtiers rich enough to be above venal bribery and genuinely noble ('large Souls').

Whatever part the poem played in the national debate about the events of 1666–7, its desired end came on 29 November when Clarendon, after dark, left London by coach for Erith in Kent. From there, he took a boat to France, landing in Calais after a journey that took three days because the wind was 'indifferently good'.[21] The search for new scapegoats would now begin.

17

The Faults and the Person

The Raising and Destroying of Favourits and Creatures is the sport of Kings not to be medled with by us.[1]

Marvell's involvement in the impeachment of Clarendon was not confined to the composition of nearly 1,000 lines in rhyming couplets. He entered fully into the Commons debate on the matter, and his interventions were marked by a characteristic independence of judgement. He was never wholly predictable as a politician, although he generally came down on the side of the Opposition forming around the figure of Clarendon's opponent, the Duke of Buckingham, who had married his former pupil Mary Fairfax.

Some time before Parliament met to consider these matters on 10 October 1667, Marvell wrote to Sir John Trott, MP for Andover.[2] Trott's son Edmund had died of smallpox on 11 August, not long after his older brother John, also a young Oxford graduate, had died from the same disease. Since Marvell's correspondence is mostly about political and business affairs, this letter of condolence is of interest in showing a more human side of the poet. Although placing his sympathy in a stern Christian context of acceptance of 'your Sons happiness' (in going to meet his Maker) the letter is one of feeling. 'I know the contagion of grief,' Marvell wrote, 'and infection of Tears, and especially when it runs in a blood. And I my self could sooner imitate then blame those innocent relentings of Nature, so that they spring from tenderness only and humanity, not from an implacable sorrow.'[3] In Marvell's grief, however, there is leisure for fiction, and the letter is a very rhetorical one. It also contains an allusion, masked in a Biblical analogy, to the political situation, and expresses the fear that, in the wake of the Dutch raid, greater calamities were in store for English Protestants from a court that may have done secret deals with the papists. Marvell concludes by enumerating the things that should console a Christian father grieving for his son: 'The word of God: The society of good men: and the books of the Ancients. There is one way more, which is by diversion, business, and activity; which are also necessary to be used in their season.' Marvell is aware that in writing to a father about the loss of his son he is writing of a condition he has not experienced and never will experience. With that nuance, but ostensibly writing about their respective public roles, he writes: 'But I my self, who live to so little purpose, can have little authority or ability to advise you.' Marvell composed two Latin epitaphs – one for each son, the one to Edmund described in this letter as 'this sorry Elogie of your Son' – that are set in tablets in the north wall of the chancel of the old church at Laverstocke in Hampshire, now a mortuary chapel of the Portal family.

On 10 October 1667 Parliament resumed with a determination to seek redress for the miscarriages of the war and to punish the culprits. As the most powerful man in the government, Clarendon was in everyone's sights. Burnet wrote: 'The Parliament were, upon their first opening, set on to destroy Lord Clarendon. And all persons who had heard him say anything that could bear an ill construction, were examined.'[4] Marvell, who spoke rarely in the House (by the standards of the time that was normal enough), made four speeches during October and November. The first was on 14 October, four days after Clarendon was impeached. 'There neuer appeared a fairer season for men to obtain what their own hearts could wish either as to redresse of any former grievances or the constituting of good order and justice for the future,'[5] Marvell had told Mayor Franke just before Parliament was due to open. Three weeks later he was confessing to him that 'really we are tired out with publick businesse'.[6] On 14 October he rose to intervene in the Clarendon debate in what is in some ways a puzzling speech. Marvell seemed not to have had the gift for plain, forceful speaking when on his feet in the Commons, and his speeches often appeared crabbed and difficult to follow. It was as if he hated having to come down on one side directly, preferring to offer qualifications and hesitations. In this intervention he seemed almost to be speaking up for Clarendon, as a result, perhaps, of some fear on his part that the faction clamouring for the Chancellor's impeachment might not actually be holding out a better alternative. The clear lines of Parliamentary opposition that came to be called the court and country parties were only emerging at this time, and Parliament did not have the sharply defined and whipped divisions and allegiances that have come to be the norm in the late twentieth century. Marvell's speech is missing from the official journals but two accounts survive, in the diary of the Derbyshire MP, John Milward, and in some manuscript notes collected by the Tewkesbury MP, Sir Henry Capel, and now preserved in the British Museum. Marvell rose after the Totnes MP, Sir John Maynard, had finished speaking:

> Mr Marvell. *The Raising and Destroying of Favourits and Creatures is the sport of Kings, not to be medled with by us. Kings in the Choice of their Ministers move in a Sphear distinct from us. It is said because the people rejoiced at his fall wee must thank the King. The people allso rejoiced at ye Restoration of the Duke of Buckingham the other day obnoxtious. Shall wee not thank ye King for that too? Its said wee hate him not, Would any man in this House be willing to have such a vote pass upon him? Wee are to thank the King for ye matter of his speech. This is not in perticuler any part of it and comes irregularly before us.*[7]

In his diary, John Milward reported that the whole morning was given over to speeches on this question of the right way to dispose of Clarendon 'and whether the King's laying him aside should be joined to the other acts of grace for which we were to give him the thanks of the House'.[8] The King had told both Houses of Parliament: 'I do assure you I will never again trust the late Lord Chancellor in any place of public employment.' That assurance seems to have been good enough for Marvell. In a parallel with his response to Cromwell, he seems to have fallen in naturally with the idea of the legitimacy of existing power, particularly when it was exercising its strength. A famous defender of the rights of dissenters, he was not himself a natural dissident. Perhaps as a result of this speech he was singled out three days later and placed on the committee inquiring into the miscarriages of the recent war.

On 26 October, Marvell spoke again, once more seeming to aim at a more just and particular indictment rather than have the House simply accede to a generalised clamour for Clarendon's scalp. In reply to a speech by Sir Richard Temple, the Warwickshire MP, who had bellowed: 'Let not this son of Zeruiah be too strong for king and parliament,'[9] Marvell called for fairness in the treatment of Clarendon:

> *Mr* Marvell *would have the faults hunt the persons: would not have a sudden impeachment by reason of the greatness of the person or danger of escape, lord Clarendon not being likely to ride away post.*[10]

That night Marvell reported to Hull's latest Mayor, Anthony Lambert: 'This morning seuerall members of our House did in their places moue the House to proceed to an impeachment against the earle of Clarinden, and layd very high crimes to his charge. The House proceeded in it with very much temper and the result at last was no further then to make a Committee to look out presidents against Tuesday morning (till when we adjournd) to report to the House what way formerly they had proceeded in capitall cases.'[11] On 31 October, Pett, the Superintendent of the Chatham Dockyard and another national scapegoat, was put in the Tower, and Marvell was one of those speaking up for him in Parliament. Once again, one assumes this came from a sense that proper justice ought to be done rather than for the House simply to indulge in revenge exacted on an easy target. The Clarendon business dragged on into November, with sessions so long and full that Marvell was forced to confess to Hull on 14 November: 'I lose my dinner to make sure of this Letter.'[12] He had just spoken again on 7 November in response to a claim by the Hindon MP, Sir Edward Seymour, who had brought in the impeachment, that Clarendon had allegedly said the King was unfit to govern. Marvell challenged Seymour to say where this information came from.[13] Difficulties arose between the Commons and Lords over the impeachment, the latter being unhappy with the Commons' call for Clarendon's impeachment, in Marvell's words, 'upon a generall charge of Treason'.[14] Like Marvell, the Lords wanted more specific charges to be brought. The Commons replied angrily that the Lords' refusal was 'an obstruction of the public justice in the proceedings of both houses of Parliament and in the president of evill and dangerous consequence'.[15]

But by the end of the month it was too late. Clarendon had fled. On 3 December Marvell reported to the Mayor that an order had been issued for the securing of all seaports to prevent Clarendon's escape, which, by that time, had actually happened. With what was presumably a dry Yorkshire irony, Marvell observed: 'I suppose he will not trouble you at Hull.'[16] The year ended with a gift, this time from the Brethren of Trinity House, of 'your towne liquor'.[17]

After the Christmas recess, Parliament met again on 6 February 1668, but so few MPs had bothered to turn up that the House was adjourned until the beginning of the following week when it resolved to fine future absentees £40. If they refused to pay they would be sent to the Tower until they agreed to pay the fine. One of Marvell's first acts in this session was to make another of those hot-headed speeches that contrast so oddly with his generally judicious and highly qualified approach to public business. He was clearly angered at the failure of grafting officials to secure proper intelligence during the Dutch War, believing that they lined their own pockets instead, and he contrasted intelligence operations with those of earlier English administrations. The object of his invective was Henry Bennett, Lord Arlington (one 'A' of the Cabal), Secretary of State:

> *Mr* Marvell, *reflecting on Lord* Arlington, somewhat transportedly said*: We have had Bristols and Cecils Secretaries, and by them knew the King of* Spain's *Junto, and letters of the Pope's cabinet; and now such a strange account of things! the money allowed for intelligence so small, the intelligence was accordingly – A libidinous desire in men, for places, makes them think themselves fit for them – The place of Secretary ill gotten, when bought with 10,000l. and a Barony* – He was called to explain himself but said, *The thing was so plain, it needed not.*[18]

The speech attracted some comment. Milward said it was 'a most sharp speech'[19] and said that it was directed at several members of the Council of State. Pepys referred to 'Great high words in the House' saying that reports of bad intelligence made many MPs 'bitter against my Lord Arlington' and that it was generally considered that 'the King paid too dear' for his intelligence in Arlington's case 'in giving him £10,000 and a barony for it'.[20] Arlington himself, in a letter to Sir William Temple, acknowledged that 'Mr Marvell hath struck hard at me.'[21] The evidence suggests that Marvell's anger was widely shared, but his manner of speaking ('somewhat transportedly') was sufficiently noteworthy to be recorded in Grey's Parliamentary reports. Curiously, on this and all the other occasions on which Marvell spoke in the House, he made no reference to the intervention in the course of his detailed letters to his constituents. He did, however, refer to the findings of the inquiry into the miscarriages of the war. The failure to guard the Medway with sufficient ships and the policy of paying the seamen with promissory notes or 'tickets' rather than hard cash were two mistakes identified by Marvell's committee. Referring to the latter issue in a speech on 22 February, Marvell said that the navy board might well be able to clear themselves from responsibility for the fiasco of the war 'yet it was requisite that they should be desired to inform the House where the fault was, for there is no question but that they are able to do it'.[22] Two days after his 'somewhat transported' speech, Marvell had been the first MP on his feet to propose consideration of the King's speech from the throne, almost certainly because it proposed measures of religious toleration. He returned to the theme on 13 March, when he spoke against a motion to renew the act against conventicles (unauthorised nonconformist meetings). He did so again on 30 March, but he was on the losing side and the act was renewed.

At this time Marvell was living 'att the Crowne over against the Greyhound Taverne neere Charing Crosse'.[23] He was working long hours in the House, sitting until five in the evening on 15 February and eight o'clock on 27 February. ''Tis nine at night and we are but just now risen,'[24] he complained two months later. At that period of the history of Parliament, this would be considered late. It is frustrating not to know more of the private life of the bachelor poet-politician at this time of his life. His letter to Sir John Trott about 'living to so little purpose' suggests that he may have had doubts about his aim in life. He may even have been lonely in his central London lodgings, although he had high-ranking friends such as Sir Jeremy Smith, a former Cromwellian and an admiral in the Dutch War. There is a glimpse in one of Marvell's letters of Smith, himself, and William Legge, Lieutenant-General of the Ordnance, relaxing after some piece of complicated business conducted by Marvell on behalf of Hull Corporation, the three of them sitting 'drinking a cup of sack'[25] and allegedly singing the praises of the burgesses of Hull. Smith was examined by the House at this time as part of the investigation into the conduct of the war, but Marvell was confident of his being cleared of any responsibility for the naval debacle: 'I doubt not but Sr Jeremy will come of with full reputation.'[26] Sir Jeremy later (13 October 1675) asked Marvell to witness his will and made him a trustee with three others, and Marvell would be at his bedside when he died. All four trustees were asked 'to take the Care and Tuition of my children'[27] and were each left 40 shillings. Those children would be added to Marvell's nephew, William Popple, to make up a group of young people for whom this childless man would have a special care.

For all his circle of distinguished acquaintances and his public profile – this was the period of his maximum exposure as a politician – Marvell was always reserved and prone to keep his own company. He was also very secretive, even in his chronicles to Hull. At the end of February he ended an account of recent Parliamentary proceedings with the tantalising declaration: 'Other things are of a privater nature.'[28] He would make a similar comment a year later: 'Let not my willingness to acquaint you with affairs be made too common or prejudiciall.'[29] Even some of what was enacted on the floor of the House of Commons or discussed in the lobbies was being turned into a mystery.

Marvell, it must be said, enjoyed the art of politicking and what would now be called lobbying. Early in 1669, he was working hard for the Trinity House Brethren, trying once more to frustrate the plans of Philip Frowde to build his lighthouse at Spurn Head, whose tolls would be a burden on Hull merchants, putting fees into Frowde's pocket rather than their own. From his Covent Garden lodgings Marvell elaborated the best tactics to use with this man: 'But I looke upon Frowd as the spring of that engine & haue been sometimes thinking whether, considering the block that you being so considerable a body may always put in his way, it were not fit to try whether he as an hungry and needy man might not be induced for some slight recompense to let fall his pretension . . .'[30] No Parliamentary Committee on Public Standards then existed to outlaw such financial inducements to favour constituency business in the House, and the lighthouse issue would consume a great deal of Marvell's attention during 1669. He wrote nothing and appears to have done little on the record during that year, though hinting darkly to Hull in September at 'some occasions of mine own & absence out of Towne',[31] which may have been no more than a sequestration at Highgate to read and write away from the press of business. Whether or not a bribe was actually paid to Frowde he was still pursuing a private bill to erect his lights and apparently getting the better of Marvell's attempts to deflect him. 'It is not necessary to make you a Cart of the flats & sands that we meet with at Court but in short Col: Frowd barrs us and he is always at the top and we at the botome,'[32] Marvell confessed to Trinity House on 18 September. The same month his name appears on a list of those who might be favourably inclined towards the Duke of York drawn up by Sir Thomas Osborne, later Lord Danby. Osborne's scheme was to construct a temporary alliance between the court and country parties, offering the latter some concessions on religious dissent in exchange for their agreeing to vote supplies to the King. The Duke of York's sympathisers were one of the factions he believed he could line up (though one might have expected Marvell to have been considered as part of Buckingham's camp). In the event, this coalition of interests did not come together and Osborne had to seek other means.[33]

Parliament had been prorogued for most of the year, from March until October. When it sat again on 19 October, the House, Marvell as a diligent attender pointing out, 'being but thin',[34] one of the first pieces of new business was the King's wish that Commissioners be appointed 'for making an Union of the two Kingdomes', England and Scotland. The House was also to be preoccupied this session with rumours of renewed religious and political dissent. The conventicles were alleged to be meeting again and 'other dangerous meetings' were taking place. The House agreed to investigate a rumour 'that Ludlow [the regicide who had escaped to Switzerland in 1660 after having been impeached] was in England' and 'that Commonwealths men flock about the town'.[35] Marvell, the former Cromwellian, reported in horror-struck tones that at these 'they talkt of New Modells of Government'. Five days later he reported new rumours 'that there was some great & euill designe on foot, & many old Army Common welths & Councill of States men & Outlaws & forainers about town'.[36] Those 'forainers' would undoubtedly be suspected of being papists.

Marvell's natural tendency was always to endorse the status quo, to respect the legitimacy of the prevailing power. He shrank from anything that smacked of revolutionary change. But as the next decade drew on he would become more and more disillusioned with King and court and more ready to countenance other political arrangements.

18

Arbitrary Malice

The terrible Bill against Conventicles is sent up to the Lords.[1]

Marvell's commitment to the notion of religious freedom and toleration – provided that this generosity was not extended to include Catholics – never wavered. It was this that made him, in the eighteenth and nineteenth centuries, when his poems were relatively neglected, a byword – and not just among nonconformists – for the defence of liberty. Marvell's notion of liberty was a very English one: passionate yet inseparable from a certain xenophobia. His hostility to Catholicism, it has already been argued, was only partly the result of religious prejudice, and was also connected to a fear of Catholicism as a conduit for subversive ideas and treasonable activity. England's enemies – whatever temporary alliances might have been formed at this time – were, according to this reading of events, found typically among the European Catholic monarchies. At the end of the twentieth century, fundamentalist Islam has often had the same effect on Western European polities, provoking mingled fear and prejudice, part racial, part political. If Marvell's phobia now seems unnatural there can be no doubt that his defence of nonconformity was deeply held and sincere. The epithet 'incorruptible patriot', attached to Marvell in the eighteenth century, underlines the rooted Englishness of his position. Against the court, with its corruption, dissolute behaviour and suspected crypto-Catholicism, Marvell opposed a sturdy Protestant patriotism, drawing strength from the country and founded in a love of his native soil. If this was an ideological construction, it was certainly a powerful one that continued to resonate long after his death. His father, the Reverend Andrew Marvell, had taught his son to be an independent-minded member of the Church of England. Marvell's anti-clericalism was his own development of this paternal temper.

On 14 February 1670 Parliament sat for the first time since its prorogation on 1 December with plenty of business to conduct. 'We haue kept to our selves these three dayes to so hard duty that you will excuse me if I be shorter then ordinary,'[2] wrote Marvell in one of his first letters of the new session to Hull. Since he entered the House a decade earlier the life of an MP had become more and more filled with activity. His letters increasingly reflect this fact, while at the same time suggesting, tantalisingly, that his workload might have had other undisclosed elements: discreet government activity, personal business affairs, intrigue, or, simply, the natural private preoccupations of a scholar-poet.

The Parliamentary session of 1670 was busy with the issue of suppressing the perceived threat of illicit nonconformist meetings, the conventicles; not only the Catholics posed a threat to the supremacy of Anglicanism. Suspicion of the King's foreign policy coloured the response of the House to many other issues. In May 1668 the peace of Aix-la-Chapelle had resulted in a 'Triple Alliance' between England, Holland and Sweden against France, but the following year the King's younger brother, James, Duke of York, acknowledged his conversion to Catholicism. Secretly, the King began negotiations with Louis XIV of France for an alliance based on a promise by Charles to declare himself a Catholic at an agreed time (which, in the end, he never did). The deal was secretly agreed in May 1670 by the Treaty of Dover, offering money and military aid to Charles in return for his declaration, which could be the opening for the establishment of Catholicism in England. Had this been publicly known, the anti-Catholics would have felt fully vindicated in their prejudice. The result of all these manoeuvrings was a continuing tension between the public and private policies of the King.

On 21 March, Marvell wrote to his nephew, William Popple, who was at his business address in Bordeaux. One of the longer surviving letters of Marvell, it is unusual in the extent and candour of its personal political opinion. The letters to Hull generally contained almost no personal judgements on politics, though the gaps in the archive could mean that some letters were destroyed precisely because of their possibly incriminating political content. Addressing his fond nephew as 'Dear Cousin',[3] Marvell began by explaining that he had 'writ twice to you at *Bourdeaux*', where Popple had another arm of his international trading business. The unfolding political chronicle began with a report of the mission to Scotland of Lord Lauderdale, the King's Commissioner for the Scottish Parliament. Lauderdale had done good work there for Charles, but Marvell clearly disapproved of his successes in not only 'giving the King absolute Power to dispose of all Things in religious Matters' in Scotland, but also in settling a militia in the country of 20,000 foot and horse 'to march into *England, Ireland*, or any Part of the King's Dominions, whenever his Person, Power, Authority, or Greatness was concerned'. These were precisely the sorts of powers that Marvell and the country opposition were determined the King should not be able to exercise in England. Lauderdale's third triumph was to empower Charles to start the machinery to bring about the union of England and Scotland, 'for which Service he was received, with extraordinary favour, by the King'. The opposition, Marvell reports, muttered that Lauderdale 'deserved an Halter rather than a Garter' for this work and asked itself if he could be impeached.

The habitual deference towards the King that marks Marvell's constituency correspondence (and that may, for all its formal eloquence, have been no more than politic) is noticeably absent from his letter to Will Popple. On the contrary, he was clearly annoyed by the attitude of the King who, before Christmas, had been voted £400,000 but now demanded even more. From the end of the session on 1 December to 14 February, when the House resumed, there had been 'great and numerous Caballing among the Courtiers', the upshot of which was that the King, 'being exceedingly necessitous for Money', addressed the House *'Stylo minaci & imperatorio'* (in an imperious and threatening manner) to warn that failure to agree to his supply would have all sorts of dread consequences. Because of a failure on the part of 'the Country Gentlemen' to get themselves to Westminster in sufficient numbers for the first session, the King won the votes that he needed. One of these ensured that 'The terrible Bill against Conventicles is sent up to the Lords', a measure for suppressing nonconformist meetings that Marvell described to Will as 'the Quintessence of arbitrary Malice'. With the sort of gossipy candour that is wholly absent from his official correspondence, Marvell confided to Will:

> *It is my opinion that* Lauderdale *at one Ear talks to the King of* Monmouth *[the Duke of Monmouth, James Scott, illegitimate son of Charles by Lucy Walters, and captain-general of the King's forces at this time] and* Buckingham *at the other of a new Queen. It is also my Opinion that the King was never since his coming in, nay, all Things considered, no King since the Conquest, so absolutely powerful at Home, as he is at present. Nor any Parliament, or Places, so certainly and constantly supplyed with men of the same Temper.*

Marvell was describing a Stuart despotism that made a mockery of Parliament and the role of an individual MP like himself. In a heartfelt cry to his nephew that marks something of a turning point in Marvell's politics he asked: 'In such a Conjuncture, dear *Will*, what Probability is there of my doing any Thing to the Purpose?' Marvell wanted to believe in constitutional monarchy and be a loyal servant of the state, but the abuse of power by the court was making it impossible for him to practise that loyalty with any conscience. His disillusion with power would reinforce his belief in the need for religious toleration, for the individual conscience to have some space to flourish and not to be ordered by the state in a polity where dissent was increasingly being outlawed. He concluded his letter with a Latin quotation, from the sombre words addressed by Aeneas to his son Ascanius just before Aeneas goes out to battle in the closing book of Virgil's *Aeneid*: '*Disce, puer, Virtutem ex me verumque Laborem,/Fortunam ex aliis*' (Learn from me, child, the meaning of true labour, and from others the meaning of fortune). Marvell had devoted his life to politics and had no other avocation apart from his writing, in an age when professional writers did not exist. Had it been worth it? Will was fortunate in having established a successful business career. He was not dependent on the vagaries of men of power. His uncle, however, must stick with it, increasingly conscious that this might be a labour in vain.

Marvell's parallel letters to Hull during this first session of 1670 deal with the matters that would naturally concern them – customs duties and taxes on wine – but when he comes to recount, in detail, the progress of the conventicles bill his account is descriptive rather than opinionative. The strong feelings on the issue expressed to Will are absent from the Hull chronicle. On the contrary, Marvell sounds like a supporter of the measure when he reports the activities of 'one Fox a teacher of some fanaticall people in Wiltshire'[4] who was said to have organised a conventicle at which some of these 'fanaticall' people 'had said they owned no King but that the King & the Duke his brother (they are words so odious as scarse to be written) were both bastards . . .' It was clear that it was the political as much as the religious freedom of the conventicles that affronted the government 'because seditious Sectaryes, under pretense of tender consciences do contrive insurrections at their meetings'. Soon, in his clash with the ultra-orthodox cleric Samuel Parker, Marvell would find himself arguing passionately in defence of that 'tender conscience' that the ruling party despised. The House, meanwhile, with the bit between its teeth, decided to extend the repressive measures to 'Popish recusants' as well as nonconformists. Marvell itemised in detail how the new act against conventicles, passed by 138 votes to 78, would work. Anyone over the age of sixteen attending a meeting 'under pretense of religion in other manner then allowd by the liturgy & practise of the Church of England' of more than five people, 'in an house field or place where no family inhabits', and who could be proved by the magistrates 'either by confession of the party or oath of witnesses or by notorious euidence or circumstance' to have done so, or simply being unable to deny the charge by calling witnesses, would be fined five shillings, doubled if they failed to pay the first time. There would be much sterner penalties for anyone preaching at such a meeting or hosting it. It was a witch-hunter's charter, but Marvell passed no comment to his electors, observing merely that he had gone into such detail 'that inconveniences might better and in time be prevented'. His inability to enter into frank political dialogue with his constituents is eloquent of the expectations they would have of their MP. He was in the House to perform services for the merchant aristocracy of Hull, not to exercise personal political judgement and discretion. He concluded his long newsletter with the words: 'I am now tired.' The letter that followed gave further proof of the growing pressure of Parliamentary business: 'We are this night upon the report of the City Bill; the crowd of business now toward our rising obliging us to sit both forenoon and afternoon, usually till nine a clock, which indeed is the occasion that I have the less vigor left at night, and cannot write so frequently to you'.[5] The work proved too much for some honourable members as the end of the session drew near, and by 7 April Marvell was reporting: 'Our house is now grown very thinne scarse more then an hundred for the most part.' On 11 April the House was finally adjourned until 24 October.

Once the recess had begun Marvell was free to write again to Will at Bordeaux. He had been using as postman Edward Nelthorpe, a banker who operated in partnership with his cousin Richard Thompson, both Yorkshiremen connected to Marvell and important players in the tortuous story of his final days. Nelthorpe's son, Robert, was Popple's clerk at Bordeaux. Once again, Marvell has more gossip for Will, in particular 'an extraordinary Thing done':

> *The King, about ten a Clock, took Boat, with* Lauderdale *only, and two ordinary Attendants, and rowed awhile as towards the Bridge, but soon turned back to the Parliament Stairs, and so went up into the House of Lords, and took his Seat. Almost all of them were amazed, but all seemed so; and the* Duke of York *especially was very much surprized. Being sat, he told them it was a Privilege he claimed from his Ancestors to be present at their Deliberations.*[6]

The King's tactic was to surprise and undermine the Duke of York's influence in the Lords. Marvell interpreted it as another sign of the times being out of joint: 'It is true that this has been done long ago,' he told Will, 'but it is now so old, that it is new, and so disused that at any other, but so bewitched a Time, as this, it would have been looked on as a high Usurpation, and Breach of Privilege.' By these high-handed acts and gestures, Charles was signalling to Parliament that he was not their creature and could do as he pleased. He was reported to have said that what quickly became established as his regular visits to the Lords were 'better than going to a Play'. On the London stage this year the plays of Dryden and Aphra Behn were being performed, the theatres – closed by the Puritans in 1642 – having now been fully restored. The King's next move was to persuade the Lords to send down a 'proviso' to the Commons 'that would have restored Him to all civil or eclesiastical Prerogatives which his Ancestors had enjoyed at any Time since the Conquest'. Marvell was horrified at this despotic impudence, telling Will: 'There was never so compendious a Piece of absolute universal Tyranny.' The Commons 'made them ashamed of it' however and the Lords withdrew the proviso. For Marvell this was a serious blow to the reputation of Parliament. 'We are all venal Cowards,' he wrote in despair. 'What Plots of State will go on in this Interval I know not.' The court intriguers would take advantage of Parliament not sitting from April until October to pursue their plotting and caballing. The King's favourite sister, Henriette, Duchess of Orleans, a Catholic like his brother, was reported to be in Canterbury during the French King's progress through Flanders. 'There will doubtless be Family Counsels then,' observed Marvell, who suspected, like many of his fellow countrymen, that the King was thinking of divorce because he had been given no heir. 'Some talk of a *French* Queen to be then invented for our King . . . The King disavows it; yet he has sayed in Publick, he knew not why a Woman might not be divorced for Barrenness, as a Man for Impotency.' Alarm at the slide towards royal arrogance if not despotism was inseparable from fears about secret treatying with Catholic powers.

Around this time, a poem called 'The Kinges Vowes' was circulating, anonymously, though it has been attributed tentatively to Marvell. Later additions have made dating and attribution still more complicated. As with so many of the doubtful poems in the Marvell canon there is a strong incentive to discard poems that are palpably not up to the standard of his best, but poor quality alone cannot justify exclusion. Some flavour of both content and poetic quality can be taken from the following excerpt:

I will have a fine Parliament allwayes to Friend,
That shall furnish me Treasure as fast as I spend;
But when they will not, they shall be att an end.

I will have as fine Bishops as were ere made with hands,
With consciences flexible to my Commands;
But if they displease me, I will have all their Lands . . .

I wholly will abandon State affaires,
And pass my Time with Parrasites and Players,
And Visit Nell when I shold be att Prayers.

Whether Marvell's growing disillusion with the King had reached the pitch where he would want to compose such a crude ballad is not clear. That such a view of the King as a rake and an unscrupulous manipulator of the constitution was circulating is not at all surprising.

Although Parliament was not sitting through the summer, Marvell was still saddled with the continuing business of the Spurn Head lighthouse and the egregious Philip Frowde, who evidently had not been successfully bribed. Marvell wrote to the Brethren of Trinity House about Frowde's endless manoeuvrings in some exasperation: 'as farre as I can observe the Gentleman a litle matter makes him much businesse and he seems to me one of those who thinke it the greatest point of wisdome to make the most scruples'.[7] In the middle of June Marvell described him angrily as 'so various & fickle in handling this businesse all along'[8] that he longed for them to find a way of bringing the business to an end. Perhaps out of gratitude for his heroic efforts with the insufferable Frowde, the Wardens of Trinity House now sent him a present of a Yorkshire salmon.

19

Our Mottly Parliament

Thus whilst the King of France with powerfull Armes
Frightens all Christendome with fresh Alarms,
Wee in our Glorious Bacchanals dispose
The humble fate of a Plebeian nose.[1]

On 24 October 1670 Parliament resumed after its long adjournment. It began, unsurprisingly, with a demand from the King for money. He told a House oblivious of the secret clauses of the Treaty of Dover that it was vital for British defences to be kept up to the mark, given the military build-up both of the King of France and of the United Provinces. The recent duties on wine had not generated the expected amount of revenue and, since 1660, the navy had been costing £500,000 a year. On top of this the King had many debts, and had to strengthen the navy, in part to be able to offer protection to the Mediterranean trade. His demand, in short, was for £800,000 and the paying off of all his debts before Christmas. Into Marvell's scrupulously neutral tone when reporting all this to Hull there enters just a shadow of irony.

The necessity of raising all this money compelled Parliament to propose various duties on drink and other commodities and they were not especially welcome to the Hull merchants. Duties on foreign imports such as tobacco were also proposed, a shilling per hundred was put on figs and prunes, five shillings on a barrel of foreign soap, and similar impositions on a host of goods such as nutmeg, cinnamon, mace and cloves. A little later in the session duties would be imposed on foreign imports, and an inventory made 'of all the French curiositys & trinkets of which our people are so new fangled'[2] so that punitive duties could be imposed on them. Marvell seems to have been surprised at the readiness of the House to agree to what would be seen in the country as fairly onerous taxes, simply in order to 'gratify his Majestyes utmost expectation'.[3] Nor, in reporting all this, had he lost his odd caution and secretiveness, warning the Corporation yet again to treat his letters as confidential: 'For I reckon your bench to be all but as one person: whereas others might chance either not to understand or to put an ill construction upon this openness of my writing & simplicity of my expression.' On reflection, he added: 'This perhaps is needlesse.' Given the prevailing caution surrounding accounts of the doings of Parliament – Arlington, for example, had ordered that the King's recent speeches requesting supply be not printed – the anonymous satires circulating in London may be better understood as a safety valve, letting off dissent and criticism.

As well as caution downright suppression featured in Marvell's Hull letters. On Monday 21 November he spoke in the House in defence of the dissenter Hayes, who had recently been arrested, but there is no mention of it – as was the case with all his previous speeches – in his correspondence.[4] He would not speak again in the House until 1677. With his nephew, however, he was always eloquent and Marvell's letter to Will Popple of 28 November is the nearest we have anywhere in his writing to an endearment, a personal tenderness. 'I need not tell you I am always thinking of you,'[5] wrote the fond bachelor uncle. His news was that the nonconformists had not been cowed by the Conventicle Act: 'To say Truth, they met in numerous open Assemblys, without any Dread of Government.' The trained bands in London or the local militia nonetheless 'harassed and abused' the dissenters, killing several Quakers. Marvell mentioned the two dissenters Hayes and Jekill who, during one of these clashes, had been picked out of the crowd at random and made an example of, but did not refer to his Parliamentary intervention on their behalf a week earlier. He reported, too, the recent case of the Old Bailey jury who had refused to be intimidated by a capricious and reactionary judge in the trial of the two Quakers William Penn and William Mead and who were committed to Newgate Prison for acquitting the two men. Their defiance has become legendary and today a memorial tablet in the Old Bailey records their courage. In Marvell's account there is little doubt of what he thought of the episode:

> *The Jury not finding them guilty, as the Recorder and Mayor would have had them, they were kept without Meat or Drink some three Days, till almost starved, but would not alter their Verdict; so fined and imprisoned. There is a Book out which relates all the Passages, which were very pertinent, of the Prisoners, but prodigiously barbarous by the Mayor and Recorder. The Recorder, among the rest, commended the* Spanish *Inquisition, saying it would never be well till we had something like it.*

Marvell's frank letter contains no trace of his former conventional loyalty to the monarch, who had been pressing the House hard for his money. 'The House was thin and obsequious,' he wrote, adding that when the supply was approved it was with little enthusiasm, 'few Affirmatives, rather a Silence as of men ashamed and unwilling'. With judges openly advocating the desirability of a Spanish Inquisition to root out dissent, and a Parliament in the King's pocket, these would indeed seem, to Marvell, dark days for English liberty. 'There is like to be a terrible Act of Conventicles,' he concluded.

Not merely did Marvell decline all general political opinions in his Hull letters, but he never sought any from his correspondents, so his letter to the Corporation on 17 December is unique in suddenly posing the question: 'What is your opinion at Hull of the bill from the Lords for general naturalization of all forainers that shall take the oaths of allegeance & Supremacy?'[6] In the surviving letters this was the first and last time he made such an inquiry. The session that came to an end at Christmas had been a long and gruelling one, as Marvell admitted to the York merchant Edward Thompson, to whom he wrote on the same day, saying he was 'tired out with sitting daily till nine a clock'.[7]

When the House returned in January 1671 there was nothing in the political situation to raise Marvell's spirits. 'The Court is at the highest Pitch of Want and Luxury, and the People full of Discontent,'[8] he reported to Will Popple. Ten years on from the high hopes of the Restoration, all he could see was corruption, extravagance and the erosion of civil liberty. Possibly around this time he wrote the satirical poem 'Further Advice to a Painter', which begins:

Painter once more thy Pencell reassume,
And draw me in one Scene London and Rome,
There holy Charles, here good Aurelius Sate,
Weeping to see their Sonns degenerate.

The present King's father, Charles I, is imagined looking down in dismay on his son's degenerate reign. The zoom lens then moves in on Parliament itself and its obnoxious (to Marvell) Speaker, Sir Edward Turner 'Whose life does scarce one Generous Action own'. Sir Thomas Clifford, Sir John Duncombe, and Ashley Cooper, the Treasury commissioners, are represented as 'This great triumvirate that can devide/The spoyls of England' and Secretary of State Arlington is painted as holding a drunken meeting of the Council of State: 'Our mighty Masters in a warme debate;/Capacious Bowles with Lusty wine repleat'. The poet mocks – and in general this poem does little more than mock, a weakness of the 'painter' genre, which often uses the instruction conceit to mask a lack of structural dynamic – 'the five recanters of the Hous/That aime at mountains and bring forth a Mous'. This was a reference to the five defectors from the country party whom Marvell had mentioned in a recent letter to Will: Sir Robert Howard, Sir Edward Seymour, Sir Richard Temple, Sir Robert Carr and Gervase Hollis (or possibly his son, Sir Frescheville).

The poem also contains an allusion ('The humble fate of a Plebeian nose') to an incident that took place just after the House was adjourned at the end of 1670 and figured largely in the debates of January 1671. Marvell describes, in a letter to Will Popple, an incident in the House in which Sir John Coventry, the Weymouth MP, moved that there be a tax on theatres. Sir John Birkenhead, MP for Wilton and a Royalist, had responded by observing that the theatres had been of great service to the King. Coventry replied with the sarcastic query – the allusion to the King's mistresses being unmistakable – as to whether he meant the male or female players, an inquiry which indicated the respect with which the King was held in some parts of the House. Marvell takes up the story of what happened next to Coventry:

> *On the very Tuesday night of the Adjournment twenty five of the* Duke of Monmouth*'s Troop, and some few Foot, layed in Wait from ten at Night till two in the Morning, by* Suffolk-Street, *and as he returned from the* Cock, *where he supped, to his own House, they threw him down, and with a Knife cut off almost all the End of his Nose; but Company coming made them fearful to finish it, so they marched off.*[9]

An anonymous poem on this incident, 'Upon the Cutting of Sir John Coventry's Nose', was at one time attributed to Marvell.[10] When the issue was first raised in the House the court party tried to brazen it out by deflecting blame on to Coventry for his original words, but the House resolved on introducing a bill banning the perpetrators for life and making the slitting of noses a felony without benefit of clergy. The incident illustrated the fact that the King and his courtiers could no longer take liberties with Parliament and was thus something of a benchmark, but it would have done little to lift Marvell's despondent mood in relation to public affairs. Nor did the firm action of the House dissuade courtiers from similar disorderly acts. The Duke of Monmouth and his friends were again in trouble a few weeks later in a scrap with the Watch during which a beadle was murdered. Marvell was appalled at the way the courtiers got away with this criminal behaviour. 'They have all got their Pardons, for *Monmouth's* Sake,' he told Will, 'but it is an Act of great Scandal.'[11]

Another scandal was the insidious growth of popery, with fresh and disturbing evidence from the Welsh Marches. It was alleged in the House that, 'notwithstanding his Mtys sincerity in the Protestant religion',[12] certain 'Eminent persons' were markedly off message. Reporting the debate to Hull, Marvell observed: 'One Gentleman particularly affirm'd that in Monmouth & Herefordshire there were more Popish Priests then Orthodox Ministers & that in six Hundreds of that Country, three were grown in a manner all Papists & whereas of late years there were not aboue 400 they were now grown to betwixt 4 & 5000.'[13] Accordingly: 'A Committee was orderd to inquire into the growth of Popery & to bring an Act in to prevent it.' There was also concern that in suppressing dissenters and papists there was a danger of forgetting another important group. As a prudent afterthought, therefore: 'The Jews were also added into the Question.'

Towards the end of February, a member of the House of Lords, Lord Lucas, made what Marvell called 'a fervent bold Speech against our Prodigality in giving and the weak Looseness of the Government'.[14] He was undeterred by the King's presence when he spoke. When copies of the speech were circulated some members of the Lords succeeded in having it declared a libel and it was burnt by the public hangman. In reporting this affair to Will Popple, Marvell was drawing attention yet again to the profligacy of the court and its lack of grip on affairs. He was disturbed that the King of France was then at Dunkirk, ostensibly for peaceful purposes, yet the navy was nowhere to be seen in spite of the fact that the King had recently been voted £800,000 for strengthening the navy. Marvell observed bitterly that there was no point in being worried. Louis would not lift a finger against England 'but leave us to dy a natural Death. For indeed never had poor Nation so many complicated, mortal, incurable, Diseases.' For his part, Marvell appeared to be about to go on another government mission to Ireland in connection with treasonable Catholic activity there. Though there is no concrete evidence that he actually went, it is significant that he was still considered trustworthy for such commissions. The opportunity to escape the corrupt odour of the English court would be no small part of the attraction of going to Ireland, he told Will: 'I think it will be my Lot to go on an honest fair Employment into *Ireland*. Some have smelt the Court of *Rome* at that Distance. There I hope I shall be out of the Smell of our.'[15]

Marvell's discreet mission to Ireland, had it taken place, might well have brought him into contact with the larger-than-life character Thomas Blood. An adventurer who in March 1663 had attempted to capture the Lord-Lieutenant of Ireland, James Butler, the Duke of Ormonde by seizing him in his own residence, Dublin Castle, Colonel Blood pulled off an even more daring stunt on 9 May 1671, when he tried to steal the Crown Jewels. A master of disguise and role-playing, Blood appeared on this occasion as a priest, but was caught in the Tower when the son of the Keeper, Edwards, whom he had befriended in order to gain access, returned to surprise him. When caught, he boasted: 'It was a bold attempt but it was for a crown.' His chutzpah seems to have endeared him to his captors and Evelyn reported in his diary that Blood refused to confess except to the King who, bemused by the Blood legend like everyone else, agreed 'being desirous of seeing so bold a ruffian'.[16] Far from being cast into a dungeon, Blood – who in the past, as a member of the Fifth Monarchy Men, had been suspected of being a double agent – somehow escaped punishment, got back the estates in Ireland that had been taken from him at the Restoration, and was seen at court. Marvell composed a short Latin poem, 'Bludius et Corona', which was similarly reluctant to see Blood as a dastardly criminal. It was translated into English in lines 178–85 of 'The Loyall Scot' and reveals a sympathy for the pretext of Blood's action (regaining wrongly confiscated lands), acknowledges his lack of real wickedness (evidenced by his failure to murder Edwards when surprised which would probably have guaranteed success) and takes the opportunity for a cruel anticlerical satire (his 'Lay pitty' conquered the 'Bishops Cruelty' that he might have been expected to have put on with the clerical disguise):

When daring Blood to have his rents regain'd
Upon the English Diadem distrain'd,
Hee chose the Cassock Circingle and Gown,
The fittest Mask for one that Robs a Crown.
But his Lay pitty underneath prevailed
And while hee spared the keepers life hee fail'd.
With the preists vestments had hee but put on
A Bishops Cruelty, the Crown had gone.[17]

In September 1671 an informer's report to Joseph Williamson, secretary to Secretary of State Arlington and an old acquaintance of Marvell's from Saumur in 1656, mentions, rather cryptically, 'Marvell with Bl from Bucks'.[18] Buckingham had been in France in the summer of 1670 trying – unsuccessfully as it turned out – to calm expatriate English fears about the sudden rapprochement between the King and Louis XIV. If 'Bl' is 'Blood' in the condensed informer's report then Marvell and he may have been obscurely mixed up with Buckingham's intelligence activities. In a letter to Thomas Rolt of the East India Company,[19] in August, Marvell returned to the Blood story. He calls him 'a most bold, and yet sober, Fellow'[20] and reveals that he shares the general attitude to Blood's escapade: 'He, being taken, astonished the King and Court, with the Generosity, and Wisdom of his Answers. He, and all his Accomplices, for his Sake, are discharged by the King, to the Wonder of all.'

Marvell may well have known Rolt during his period in Thurloe's office, Rolt having found favour with Cromwell. His letter appears to be advising Rolt about his personal affairs. The advice is of a kind that Marvell may well have had to learn for himself: 'stand upon your Guard; for in this World a good Cause signifys little, unless it be as well defended. A Man may starve at the Feast of good Conscience.' He offers Rolt a piece of his personal experience dating back to the European travels of his freer youth: 'My Fencing-master in *Spain*, after he had instructed me all he could, told me, I remember, there was yet one Secret, against which there was no Defence, and that was, to give the first Blow.' Marvell was almost exactly a year away from his encounter with Samuel Parker, whose 'Bishops Cruelty' he would be fencing with – verbally at any rate – under this rubric of the pre-emptive strike.

That encounter would be a distraction from the immediate political scene which, as he describes it to Rolt, consists of fawning courtiers acceding far too readily to the King's demands for money: 'that it is a Mercy they gave not away the whole Land, and Liberty, of *England*'. The King prorogued the Parliament until 16 April 1672, not a moment too soon, in Marvell's view: 'The House of Commons has run almost to the end of their Line, and are grown extreme chargeable to the King and odious to the People.' More than this: 'We truckle to *France* in all Things, to the Prejudice of our Alliance and Honour.'

During this year Marvell managed, however, to overcome his Francophobia sufficiently to enter a competition, with a putative prize of a thousand pistoles, to compose an inscription to be placed over the pediment of the newly completed Louvre in Paris. Half a dozen Latin distiches – none, unfortunately, prizewinners – appear under the title '*Inscribenda Luparae*' in the 1681 Folio of poems. Marvell appears to have been not the only poet who tried his luck, but all the entries from England were unsuccessful.

20

A Gracious Declaration

> *And accordingly he issued, on* March *the 15th 1672, His Gracious* Declaration of Indulgence, *of which I wish His Majesty and the Kingdom much joy, and, as far as my slender judgement can divine, dare augurate and presage mutual Felicity . . .*[1]

After the proroguing of Parliament in April 1671, Marvell, who had now reached the age of fifty, wrote no more letters to his constituents (at any rate none that have survived) until nearly three years later, at the start of 1674. The gaps in Marvell's correspondence have sometimes been attributed to nervousness on the part of recipients about their contents, though there is little evidence of even an approach to politically compromising frankness in those official letters that do survive. The loss of letters also resulted from more mundane treatment by posterity. William Skinner of Hull, who held a number of Marvell letters at the beginning of the eighteenth century, is said to have had so little interest in this trove that he 'gave them to the pastry-maid to put under pie-bottoms'.[2]

In the autumn of 1672 Marvell would publish his prose broadside against Samuel Parker, *The Rehearsal Transpros'd*, a defence of the King's policy of indulgence towards dissenters and Catholics, but there is no independent insight, through correspondence, into this important controversy. In the early part of 1672, however, before the King had issued the Declaration, Marvell's letters show that he was staying at a house at Winchendon, near Aylesbury, owned by Lord Wharton, the Opposition peer who shared Marvell's distaste for the Conventicle Act. It was to this address that several letters were sent by a Dr Benjamin Worsley to Marvell, who forwarded them to Lord Wharton, adding notes and sealing them with his personal seal, representing a stag. Marvell and Worsley were acting as matchmakers for Wharton's eldest son, who planned to marry a Mrs Cable from Honiton in Devon. Marvell had requested Worsley, who had friends in Devonshire, to conduct a few discreet inquiries about Mrs Cable, which he then passed on to the anxious father. In the end it was Mrs Cable who was unimpressed by young Wharton when he paid her a visit in Honiton and the match went no further. Marvell's presence in the house, and his role in this intimate matter, shows his close involvement with the leading Opposition figures.

It was possibly early in 1672 that Marvell – if he was the author, and the evidence both external and internal is slight – wrote the satirical poem, 'Nostradamus's Prophecy'. A manuscript version of the poem bearing the date 6 January 1672 has survived and, even if Marvell was not the author, it is interesting, if not poetically then politically, as a commentary on the immediate situation. It pretends to be a prophecy by the sixteenth-century Frenchman Michel de Notredame, better known as Nostradamus, some of whose prophecies were thought to have predicted the execution of Charles I and the Great Fire. The poem alludes not only to this but also to more immediate events and personalities, adverting to the sexual licence and corruption of the court and the alleged homosexuality of the King's first minister George Villiers, Duke of Buckingham:

When Sodomy is the Premier Ministers sport
And whoreing shall be the least sin att Court,
A Boy shall take his Sister for his Mate
And practise Incest between Seven and Eight.

It goes on to refer disparagingly to Lauderdale as 'an old Scotch Covenanter' now become 'The Champion of the English Hierarchye' and contains a very Marvellian tilt at the Bishops: 'When Bishops shall lay all Religion by/And strive by Law to 'stablish Tyrany'. Its closing couplet, which casts 'envious Eyes' on the Venetian republic as a better alternative to this corrupt English monarchy, may point to a shift taking place in

Marvell's thinking – again, if the poem is his – away from constitutional monarchism towards republicanism.

The decision of Charles to issue the Declaration of Indulgence heightened public fears about his covert motives. The Declaration claimed that he was entitled by his ecclesiastical prerogatives to suspend the laws against dissenters and to grant licences to them to open meeting-houses. Catholics would also be allowed freedom of worship in their own homes. These concessions worried those who disliked religious freedom and others also feared that the King might extend his claim to be able to suspend religious statutes to the suspension of other laws. And there was the question of the Duke of York. The King's brother was no longer seeking to conceal his Catholicism, his failure to take communion at Easter having been noticed. In spite of his numerous bastard offspring, the King had no legitimate heir. As John Dryden put it some years later in his satire *Absalom and Achitophel* (1681), referring to this period, Charles had 'Scatter'd his Maker's Image through the Land' by copulating prodigiously with various women, 'But since like slaves his bed they did ascend,/No True Succession could their seed attend'. The Duke of York was therefore the King's heir presumptive. The prospect of a Catholic king, bent on destroying Protestantism and establishing Romish power on English soil, alarmed many, who asked whether there was something more to the Declaration of Indulgence than met the eye. The alliance with Louis XIV had just resulted in an attack on Holland, a solid Protestant state. What was the King now planning with the Catholic ruler across the water? These fears and anxieties ensured that the twelfth session of the Cavalier Parliament that met in March 1673 would be a noisy and disputatious one, but for now Marvell would welcome the easing of the pressure on the dissenters, however little he relished the same spirit being shown towards the Catholics. The emergence in these years of the country and the court parties can suggest a neat modern division of party interest but the King was essentially a law unto himself. He was fond of intrigue and parleying with people of all sorts of political backgrounds. The flavour of this is caught by the memoirs of the Marquess of Halifax:

> *He lived with his ministers as he did with his mistresses; he used them, but he was not in love with them. He showed his judgement in this, that he*

cannot properly be said ever to have had a favourite, though some might look so at a distance . . . He had back stairs to convey informations to him, as well as for other uses; and though such informations are sometimes dangerous . . . yet in the main that humour of hearing everybody against anybody kept those about him more in awe than they would have been without it. I do not believe that ever he trusted any man or set of men so entirely as not to have some secrets in which they had no share; as this might make him less well served, so in some degree it might make him the less imposed upon.[3]

Such a secretive, crafty sensibility might well have been intrigued by – and made use of 'back stairs' for intrigue – the discreet and private figure of Andrew Marvell, who was about to emerge in print as the King's defender, at least in the matter of indulgence towards nonconformists.

Three months after the Declaration, in June, Marvell wrote to Will Popple offering an analysis of recent political events. To his customary circumspectness was added some consciousness of real risk, as he explained to Will: 'There was the other Day . . . a severe Proclamation issued out against all who shall vent false News, or discourse ill concerning Affairs of State. So that in writing to you I run the Risque of making a Breach in the Commandment.'[4] The political situation was deteriorating and suspicion was rife. 'Affairs begin to alter, and Men talk of a Peace with *Holland*,' Marvell wrote. He thought that this shift away from the alliance with France would happen 'before *Michaelmass*' (29 September), an opinion whose grounds could not be disclosed even to Will: 'for some Reasons not fit to write'. Marvell's sympathies were clearly with the Protestant Dutch: 'No Man can conceive the Condition of the State of *Holland*, in this Juncture, unless he can at the same Time conceive an Earthquake, an Hurricane, and the Deluge.' By contrast: '*France* is potent and subtle.' As if to underline the sense of impending crisis, a number of fires had broken out, at St Catherine's Dock, Bishopsgate and Southwark, recalling the Great Fire and the Catholic plotters whom many blamed for it. 'You may be sure all the old Talk is hereupon revived,' Marvell told Will.

Such affairs of state were much more interesting than Marvell's other duty, dealing yet again with the tiresome Philip Frowde and his lighthouse project. Throughout the year letters on the subject shuttled back and forth between the MP and the Trinity House Brethren. Marvell met Frowde by accident on 20 June and told him bluntly: 'I had been so unhappy in former discourses with him as to meet with such delays uncertaintys and repugnances that I was tired out of the businesse.'[5] It nonetheless dragged on and in late November Marvell dined at the other Trinity House in Deptford, to whom he was well known 'hauing obliged them much in our last Session of Parlt by opposing a new Act for Dover Peere',[6] in order to see if a common front between the two Houses could be effected.

At the end of September 1672 Marvell returned to London after a summer break to witness the reaction to his anonymous pamphlet *The Rehearsal Transpros'd: or Animadversions upon a late Book, Intituled A Preface Shewing What Grounds there are of Fears and Jealousies of Popery.* It did not bear his name and carried a cod-printer's declaration that it was published 'at the sign of the King's Indulgence, on the South-side of the *Lake Leman*'. This was to be Marvell's most famous prose work, particularly in the century after his death. In spite of the praise of Swift who wrote: 'we still read *Marvel*'s Answer to *Parker* with Pleasure, tho' the Book it answers be sunk long ago'[7] it is highly unlikely that 'we still read' it. In spite of the multiplicity of editions of Marvell's poems currently in print, *The Rehearsal*, together with its second part, published the following year, are the only prose works to have been published in modern scholarly editions; none of the prose, apart from a few excerpts, has found its way into a popular edition. Even for scholars, the rest of the prose writing still has to be read in the original editions or in nineteenth-century reprints. Marvell's prose satire is learned, witty, occasionally enlivened by flashes of vigorous language and vivid metaphor, but it lacks the immediacy, pace, rapid clarity and narrative invention of Swift. It is unlikely that it will ever achieve an appeal outside the ranks of dedicated Marvellians.

The book was written, as its title indicates, in response to a preface written by Samuel Parker, an up-and-coming thirty-two-year-old Anglican polemicist about whom few of his contemporaries could find a good word to say and who later became the Bishop of Oxford. The preface was attached to a theological work called *A Vindication of himself from the Presbyterian Charge of Popery* (1672) by Bishop John Bramhall, Archbishop of Armagh. Bramhall, a Yorkshireman born in Pontefract, had, according to his biographer, married a clergyman's widow who 'gave him a fortune and a library'.[8] He went to Ireland in 1633 as chaplain to Strafford, Charles I's trusted adviser, Sir Thomas Wentworth, and became Bishop of Derry in 1634 where he earned the nickname 'Bishop Bramble'. Although Marvell's quarrel was with the obnoxious Parker, the late Bishop Bramhall was an equal foe of toleration and suppleness of mind. As Bishop of Derry he opposed the use of the Irish Bible and Prayer Book because the native tongue of the Irish was 'a symbol of barbarism'. His virulence towards Catholicism was such that: 'It is said that he was so obnoxious to the papal powers that on crossing into Spain he found his portrait in the hands of innkeepers, with a view to his being seized by the Inquisition.'[9] When Marvell wrote his riposte, Bramhall was dead, but Samuel Parker was very much alive.

The apostate is often the fiercest opponent of his former co-religionists, a phenomenon paralleled in the sphere of political ideology; in the twentieth century one thinks of the virulence of many ex-communist Cold War ideologues. Samuel Parker, born in Northampton in 1640, though destined to become the scourge of nonconformity, was in his youth a very puritanical adolescent. At Wadham College, Oxford, encouraged by a Presbyterian tutor, he adopted a strict and self-denying religious discipline. With his companions he fasted and dined grimly on a thin broth made of oatmeal and water which earned them the nickname of the 'Grewellers'. The broth-eaters frequently went to a house of fervent religiosity in the Oxford parish of Holywell, kept by 'an old an crooked maid'[10] called Bess Hampton. The economic base on which her superstructure of piety rested was the taking in of washing. At the Restoration, Parker threw off this disguise and emerged as a career Anglican. Marvell accused him of subsequently attacking John Calvin and of having 'made a constant Pissing-place of his grave'[11] in his anxiety to distance himself from that brand of theology. After changing colleges to Trinity, Parker was ordained in 1664 and went to London to be the chaplain of a nobleman. From this vantage point he began to ingratiate himself, in Marvell's judgement spending 'a considerable time in creeping into all Corners and Companies, Horoscoping up and down concerning the duration of the Government'.[12] Having decided that 'the Episcopal Government would indure as long as this King lived', Parker decided to back the right horse and 'cast about how to be admitted into the Church of *England*'. Once this had been accomplished, Parker became chaplain to Archbishop Shelden at Lambeth Palace and in June 1670 was appointed Archdeacon of Canterbury. He then threw himself into religious controversy, defending royal absolutism and religious authority. In 1686 he would be appointed Bishop of Oxford by James II. Burnet described him as 'a covetous and ambitious man' who 'seemed to have no other sense of religion but as a political interest and a subject of party and faction. He seldom came to prayers or to any exercises of devotion, and was so lifted up with pride that he was become insufferable to all that came near him.'[13] An apocryphal story is told of his being asked what was the best body of divinity and replying: 'That which would help a man to keep a coach and six horses was certainly the best'.[14] Anthony Wood, in his *Athenae Oxoniensis*, was another, if slightly more sympathetic, contemporary, who thought that Parker laid himself open to Marvell's attack 'thro' a too loose and unwary handling of the debate'[15] but was chastened by the experience.

Parker's first book was *Tentamina de Deo* in 1665 but, after joining the Royal Society that year, he published his first noteworthy work in 1666, *A Free and Impartial Censure of the Platonick Philosophie*, which gave vent to his hatred of religious enthusiasm and his dislike of the 'common and mechanical sort of men'. He returned to this hatred of the lower orders the same year in *An Account of the Nature and Extent of the Divine Dominion and Goodnesse* where he expressed the concern that if the common people be 'suffered to run without restraint, they will break down all the banks of Law and Government'.[16] The earliest work that Marvell engaged with was the *Discourse of Ecclesiastical Politie*, whose subtitle more than adequately indicates its scope and the intellectual temper of its author: *wherein the authority of the Civil Magistrate over the Consciences of Subjects in matters of Religion is asserted; the Mischiefs and Inconveniences of Toleration are represented, and all Pretenses pleaded in behalf of Liberty of Conscience are fully answered.* The book was published in 1669 and its answers were replied to in 1671 by *A Defence and Continuation of the Ecclesiatical Politie.* It was the preface, however, issuing from Parker's period as rector of Ickham in Kent in 1672, that finally sent Marvell into action.

The drift of Parker's thinking in questions of ecclesiastical government was that, given the ungovernable variety of human beliefs, the 'Civil Magistrate' or head of government should be given total power in religious matters to prevent anarchy. There is an obvious analogy with the great seventeenth-century thinker Hobbes, who in *Leviathan* (1651), written in the immediate aftermath of civil war, advocated acceptance of the prevailing power as the only means to peace. Parker found the concept of freedom of conscience odious and believed instead in the virtue of absolute obedience. To him toleration was an evil and a threat to civil order. In the *Discourse* he claimed that the Church of England was being 'savagely worried by a Wild and Fanatique Rabble'[17] and attacked 'the wild and hair-brain'd Youths of the Town' who make atheism acceptable under the guise of liberty of conscience: ''Tis these Apes of Wit and Pedants of Gentility that would make Atheism the fashion forsooth.' He was contemptuous of the high moral ground claimed by the defenders of liberty of conscience, arguing that 'of all Villains the well-meaning Zealot is the most dangerous'. In spite of the aggressive spirit of Parker's polemic and its lurid terms, he tried to articulate in the *Discourse* either a disingenuous or a genuinely naive belief that he was a voice of moderation, reluctantly drawn into arguments of church discipline. 'The Author is a Person of such a tame and softly humour,' he wrote sweetly in the preface, 'and so cold a Complexion, that he thinks himself scarce capable of hot and passionate Impressions: and therefore if he has sometimes twisted Invectives with his Arguments, it proceeded not from Temper but from Choice; and if there be any Tart and Upbraiding expressions, they were not the Dictates of Anger or Passion, but of the Just and Pious Resentments of his Mind.'

With all his resources of elegant mockery, Marvell tore away this veil of pious cant, and both men clambered into the pit together in a tussle that the poet was foreordained to win.

21

Animadversions

For it is not impossible that a man by evil arts may have crept into the Church, thorow the Belfry or at the Windows. 'Tis not improbable that having so got in he should foul the Pulpit, and afterwards the Press with opinions destructive to Humane Society and the Christian Religion. That he should illustrate so corrupt Doctrines with as ill a conversation, and adorn the lasciviousness of his life with an equal petulancy of stile and language. In such a concurrence of misdemeanours what is to be done? [1]

In 1671, George Villiers, Duke of Buckingham, wrote a play called *The Rehearsal*. Buckingham, leader of the country party's opposition to Charles at a time when Marvell's sympathies were running in that direction, saw his play receive its first performance in London on 7 December 1671. The aim of this burlesque was to ridicule the current fashion for 'heroic' plays, a genre founded by the former Poet Laureate, William Davenant, nicknamed 'Bayes' because he wore the laureate's crown of bay leaves. When Davenant died in 1668 the mock title passed to his successor as Poet Laureate, John Dryden. As the Victorian critic, Henry Morley, introducing a selection of these plays which included *The Rehearsal*, put it: 'Bold rhodomontade was, on the stage, preferred to "good sense" upon poets, as a reaction against the strained ingenuities that had come in under Italian influence.'[2] When Marvell came to write his pamphlet, the recent success on the stage of Buckingham's play, which was printed in 1672, would still be reverberating; although popular in the eighteenth century, *The Rehearsal* is neither in print nor performed today. It is made up of a string of parodic passages mocking the heroic style, featuring a central character called Mr Bayes who takes two friends to see a rehearsal of his absurd new play. At one point Bayes, a self-confessed plagiarist, explains to his friends, Mr Smith and Mr Johnson, his method of composition:

> Bayes: . . . *I take a book in my hand, either at home or elsewhere, for that's all one, if there be any Wit in't, as there is no Book but has some, I Transverse it; that is, if it be Prose put it into Verse, (but that takes up some time), if it be Verse, put it into Prose.*
> Johns: *Methinks, Mr.* Bayes, *that putting Verse into Prose should be call'd Transprosing.*[3]

By equating Samuel Parker with the bombastic fool Bayes, whose embodiment on the stage would be fresh in many of his readers' minds, Marvell was being both witty and highly topical, and enjoying a further tilt at Dryden into the bargain. The implication is that Parker's attempts at wit, like those of Mr Bayes, are derivative and farcical. Marvell's earthy humour made what purported to be a contribution to theological controversy into an instant best-seller.

But he had a serious purpose in writing it. He wanted to defend the King's policy of indulgence towards nonconformists, which was coming under fire from many leading figures in the Church of England and even from some dissenters who saw it as a step towards popery. Samuel Parker was only the noisiest and most aggressive of the defenders of the Establishment. The MP Sir John Reresby later wrote in his *Memoirs* that the Declaration of Indulgence was 'the greatest blowe that ever was given, since the Kings restoration, to the Church of England'.[4] Leading figures in the Church of England, alarmed at the threat to their hegemony, began to campaign against the King's policy. The Bishop of London instructed his clergy to preach against popery such that, according to Burnet: 'The king complained to Sheldon [Gilbert Sheldon, Archbishop of Canterbury] of this preaching on controversy, as done on purpose to inflame the people, and to alienate them from him and his government.'[5] With opposition to his policy of toleration coming both from the Church and from Parliament, Charles took steps to make sure that the nonconformists, whose hatred of Catholicism was as potent as either, were on his side, and offered some of the leading nonconformists a yearly pension of £50 in order to secure their support, though the famous nonconformist minister Richard Baxter refused to take the King's money. A friend of Marvell, Baxter shared his retrospective scepticism about the value of the Civil War, writing in his autobiography, *Reliquiae Baxterianae:* 'I make no doubt that both parties were to blame, as it commonly falleth out in most wars and contentions, and I will not be he that will justify either of them.'[6] According to Wood, the physician and author Henry Stubbe, who wrote a response to Marvell's pamphlet, was well rewarded by the King for two pamphlets he wrote in 1672 and 1673 defending that other unpopular plank of royal policy, the Dutch War. Wood alleged that Stubbe received £200 from the royal purse. Although there is no suggestion that Marvell was rewarded financially for his polemic it would have been no less welcome to the King for the way in which it defended his policy, silenced its leading opponent, and presented Charles himself in a highly favourable light. Charles was not a lover of serious discourse but, if Burnet is to be believed, he took *The Rehearsal* to his bosom: 'the last King, that was not a great reader of books, read them [the two parts of *The Rehearsal*] over and over again'.[7]

As a theological treatise, however, *The Rehearsal Transpros'd* is of little value. It is almost entirely taken up with mockery and abuse of Parker – Wood's 'sportive and jeering buffoonry' – and says nothing of very much value on the substantive questions supposedly at issue. Marvell's technique, which was shared by his less talented and witty contemporaries, and which makes so much of their pamphleteering merely tedious to modern taste, was to answer relentlessly, and seemingly page by page, every point made by the opponent, quoting his words back at him at length and holding up passages to ridicule. The method is doggedly *ad hominem.* Reading the many responses to Marvell's pamphlet can be a gruelling exercise, in spite of their effort to be sportive and satirical. After prolonged exposure to all this 'wit', one begins to long for dullness.

Marvell opens his attack by calling Parker 'a lewd, wanton, and incontinent Scribler'[8] and swings directly into personal abuse. He mocks attempts in the recent past to suppress nonconformist meetings and conventicles, when effort would have been better directed instead to silencing the authors of windy, offensive pamphlets such as Parker: 'Two or three brawny Fellows in a Corner, with meer Ink and Elbow-grease, do more harm than an *hundred Systematical Divines* with their *sweaty Preaching.*'

He continues with a dig at Sir Roger L'Estrange, since 1662 the Surveyor of the Press, or chief government censor, and Sir John Birkenhead, the man authorised to search out unlicensed printers. Both men are referred to by their initials only in a passage satirising scribblers like Parker: 'Their ugly Printing-Letters, that look but like so many rotten-Teeth, How oft have they been pull'd out by B. and L. the Publick-Tooth-Drawers! and yet these rascally Operators of the Press have got a trick to fasten them again in a few minutes, that they grow as firm a Set, and as biting and talkative as ever.' Although, after several more pages in this vein, Marvell announces: 'Now, having had our Dance, let us advance to our more serious Counsels', the expectation is disappointed, for he continues to attack Parker's style rather than his substance. That style is 'luscious and effeminate' and the whole enterprise of Parker's preface, 'bedawb'd with Rhetorick', lacks proper decorum ('part Play-book and part Romance') when it is considered that he is writing a preface to the work of a bishop of the Church of England. Moreover, Parker exaggerates the greatness of Bishop Bramhall 'like a *St Christopher* in the Popish Churches, as big as ten Porters, and yet only imploy'd to sweat under the burden of an *Infant*'. Although appearing to concede the merits of Bramhall's advocacy of an ecumenical reconciliation between the churches ('though some that meddle in it do it chiefly in order to fetter men straiter under the formal bondage of fictitious Discipline'), Marvell believes that Bramhall would have been better employed in trying to unify Protestantism at home and abroad rather than in pursuing this idealistic goal. Disingenuously, it may be thought, Marvell now moves on to Parker and to allege that 'his only talent was railing'. The defence of Bramhall was mere camouflage, with Parker using him 'but for a Stalking-horse till he might come within shot of Forreign Divines and the Nonconformists'. Marvell calls him 'Buffoon-General to the Church of England' and singles out as an example of his lack of theological understanding or tact his attack on Calvin: 'I had always heard that Calvin was a good Scholar, and an honest Divine.' Marvell had perhaps heard this from his friend Richard Baxter. Parker, in fact, is 'a mad Priest, which of all sorts is the most incurable'.

Marvell's anticlericalism was always vigorous. Although he would later claim that, as far as the clergy were concerned, 'the memory of mine own extraction, and much more my sense of the Sanctity of their function ingage me particularly to esteem and honour them',[9] it was precisely from his 'own extraction' – his father's lack of eagerness to follow the rituals and rules of the Church of England – that he had learnt this coolness towards bishops and 'the brabbles and quarrels that have been unnecessarily sow'd by some of the clergy'.[10] Too many of the clergy, in Marvell's view, were bent on 'Preferment and Grandeur' and were, in an allusion to Ben Jonson's *Volpone*, 'the *Politick Would-be's* of the Clergy'. Ignoring Christian humility and meekness they became obsessed instead with 'Ceremony and Severity' and exhibit a strange ferocity:

> *That which astonishes me, and only raises my indignation is, that of all sorts of Men, this kind of Clergy should always be, and have been for the most precipitate, brutish, and sanguinary Counsels. The former Civil War cannot make them wise, nor his Majesties Happy Return, good natured; but they are still for running things up unto the same extreams. The softeness of the Universities where they have been bred, the gentleness of Christianity in which they have been nurtured, hath but exasperated their nature; and they seem to have contracted no* Idea *of wisdom, but what they learnt at School, the Pedantry of Whipping.*[11]

Certainly, Parker's clerical garb guarantees him no respect from Marvell who embarks on a mocking summary of Parker's curriculum vitae. In a sly hint that Parker may have been impotent, he writes: 'I do not hear for all this that he had ever practised upon the Honour of the Ladies, but that he preserved alwayes the Civility of a *Platonic Knight-Errant*.' Brushing aside Parker's intellectual credentials, Marvell concludes that very early on in his career: 'He lost all the little remains of his understanding, and his *Cerebellum* was so dryed up that there was no more brains in a walnut and both their Shells were alike thin and brittle.' In short: 'All that rationally can be gathered from what he saith, is, that the Man is mad.' In matters of Church discipline, Parker was more obsessed with rooting out dissent and enforcing authority than with saving souls. He 'made the process of Loyalty more difficult than that of Salvation'. Marvell demonstrates his own contrasting commitment to toleration by stating: 'I think it ought to be highly penal for any man to impose other conditions upon his Majesties good Subjects than the King expects or the Law requires.' Parker's own life, Marvell contends, is characterised by oppressive authoritarianism towards people with whom he disagrees, having 'fed all his life with Vipers instead of Lampreys'. He implies that some of his savagery towards dissenters may be the product of the unnatural reaction of an apostate towards his former associates. By contrast to Parker, Marvell praises the generosity and toleration of the King in bringing in the Act of Oblivion, which, like a truth and reconciliation commission, drew a line under the antagonisms of 'the late Combustions'. Unfortunately, the Church of England could not learn from this example: 'For, though I am sorry to speak it, yet it is a sad truth, that the Animosities and Obstinacy of some of the Clergy have in all Ages been the greatest Obstacle to the Clemency, Prudence and good Intentions of Princes, and the Establishment of their Affairs.' But perhaps the most damning indictment of Parker is provided by his own words, in the preface and in the *Discourse*, which Marvell (somewhat loosely) quotes back at him, showing that Parker believed in the absolute right of the monarch to lay down the law in matters of religion: 'The Government of Religion was vested in princes by an antecedent right to Christ.' One sentence in particular goes to the heart of the fundamental illiberalism of Parker's position: ''tis better to err with Authority than to be in the right against it: not only because the danger of a little error (and so it is if it be disputable) is outweighed by the importance of the great duty of Obedience'. Not merely free thought but morality must be sacrificed to the imperious demands of obedience, in Parker's eyes, when he writes: 'Princes may with less hazard give liberty to men's Vices and Debaucheries than their Consciences.' Marvell confessed to a concern at the low moral tone of much Restoration living, 'at such a time, when there is so general a depravation of Manners'. In spite of this reverence for absolutism, however, Parker does not, in Marvell's view, show sufficient respect for royal authorities because he 'thinks himself fit to be their Governour'.

When Marvell finally reaches a consideration of the preface itself he finds there 'scarce anything but slender trifling unworthy of a Logician, and beastly railing unbecoming any man, much more a Divine'. He accuses Parker of wild inconsistencies and impossible logic: 'In all his Writings he doth so confound terms, he leaps cross, he hath more doubles (nay triples and quadruples) than any Hare, so that he thinks himself secure of the Hunters.' Coming at last to the point of the preface, Marvell defends the King's policy of toleration against the oppressive conformity Parker would prefer him to practise, in a passage already quoted above, that salutes the King's Declaration as the augury of a period of 'mutual Felicity' between ruler and believer. In a brief intermission from raillery, Marvell also praises John Hales, his old friend from Eton days, as an exemplar of a more generous spirit in the Church of England, who suffered in the Civil War and exhibited 'the native simplicity of a Christian spirit'. But there is no escaping the essential formlessness of Marvell's polemical plan. He admits as much when he describes, about three-quarters of the way through the book, his random method of picking up on Parker's shortcomings: 'After this I walked a great way through bushes and brambles before I could find another Flower: but then I met with two upon one stalk.' This is, too often, how it strikes the reader: as a lazy way of proceeding, leafing through Parker's words in order to happen on some passage that can be held up to ridicule, before moving on to pluck off another dead-head. At the same time, however, the quotation demonstrates Marvell's habitually concrete and effective imagery, which is what, in the end, sustains the reader's interest.

In charging Parker with raising false fears about the threat posed by the return of popery, Marvell is on stronger ground, although this was a cause he would take up himself later in the decade. He regarded this argument against toleration as irresponsible: 'he is an Enemy to the State, whoever shall foment such discourses without any likelyhood or danger'. He reminds Parker of the role of the clergy in whipping up anti-Catholic feeling in the wake of the Declaration: 'For I suppose you cannot be ignorant that some of your superiors of your Robe did, upon the publishing that Declaration, give the Word, and deliver Orders through their Ecclesiastical Camp, to beat up the Pulpit-drums against Popery.'

In one of those rare autobiographical passages in his writing, Marvell reveals at one point that he used to play picquet with a clergyman whom he describes as 'a *Dignitary of Lincoln*' (possibly Francis Drope, prebendary of Lincoln, or William Reresby, prebendary of Brampton).[12] This clergyman was 'very well known and remembred in the Ordinaries' and seems to have cheated at the game by making some form of hand signal, an experience that did nothing to diminish Marvell's suspicion of the clergy. As a result of this, 'of all the money that ever I was cheated of in my life, none ever vexed me so, as what I lost by his occasion. And ever since, I have born a great grudge against their fingring of anything that belongs to me.' In order to press home this notion of clerical cupidity and crookedness, he then recounts the story of the notorious highwayman of the reign of Charles I who practised his profession near Hampton Court dressed up as a bishop. Marvell implies strongly that the principal motive for the hostility shown towards the Puritans by the Church of England was that they had deprived the clergy of their pre-Reformation luxury by obstructing 'that laziness and splendor which they injoyed under the Popes Supremacy, and the Gentry had (sacrilegiously) divided the *Abbey-Lands* [as at Nun Appleton], and other fat morsels of the Church at the Dissolution, and now was the time to be revenged on them'.

After accusing Parker in sum of 'making all Religion ridiculous', Marvell concludes by saying he wrote the pamphlet because he was 'offended at the presumption and arrogance' of Parker's style. He adds, however, one more interesting detail, confessing that Parker's habit of inveighing 'against the *Trading-part* of the Nation' was an added goad. Throughout his life, Marvell remained loyal to the commercial culture of Hull, with which he was connected by family ties, childhood memories, and professional responsibility. The fierce anticlericalism of *The Rehearsal* was intrinsic to his notion of English patriotism, to the defence of hard-working, anti-Establishment, provincial society to whom pompous and self-advancing prelates like Parker were an unwanted burden. The immediate battle, however, was not yet over. Parker would be unlikely to let this witty onslaught go unanswered. Lacking the self-knowledge to realise that it would do his reputation no good, he began to prepare an immediate riposte, but not before others had jumped into the fray. Marvell's goal of silencing Parker would not be attained for at least another year.

22

Rosemary and Bays

And if we take away some simpering phrases, and timorous introductions, your Collection will afford as good Precedents for Rebellion and King-Killing as any we meet with in the writings of J.M. in defence of the Rebellion and the Murther of the King.

Samuel Parker[1]

On 6 November 1672, with *The Rehearsal* having been well launched and his enemies sharpening their quills to reply, Marvell received one of his regular gifts from Hull, a 32-gallon barrel of the local autumn ale. Though Aubrey alluded to Marvell's alleged habit of solitary drinking 'to refresh his spirits, and exalt his Muse',[2] little activity on the part of his Muse was noticeable at this time. Several more verse satires were to come but nothing could for a moment compare with what he had already produced. His literary energies at this time were focused entirely on prose polemic. But, vigorous and scurrilous as the pamphlet wars could be, his clashes with Parker were not confined to the page. The two men had first met at Milton's house in London shortly after the Restoration – an acquaintanceship Parker would be keen to forget – but now, in the wake of Marvell's onslaught, they met in a London street. Parker, in the account of the incident first recounted by Thompson in 1776,[3] 'rudely attempted to take the wall' – as we might say 'elbowed him into the gutter', an even less savoury place in Restoration London than it would be today. Marvell, always ready to look after himself in a physical encounter, placed his foot and arm in such a way that Parker fell into the gutter. Leaning over him as he lay sprawled in the dirt, Marvell said 'with his usual pleasantry' to the clergyman: 'Lie there for a son of a whore.' Parker later complained to the Bishop of Rochester, who employed him as a chaplain at the time, about this treatment. The Bishop summoned Marvell, who asked politely why he had been called. The Bishop replied that it was his 'abusive usage' of his chaplain that had given offence, and in particular his 'foul language'. Unless Marvell made adequate satisfaction, the Bishop would prosecute and 'he would see justice done Dr Parker'. Marvell coolly replied that the Bishop's chaplain had been 'impudent' in demanding the wall from a member of the House of Commons. Besides, Marvell added wittily, 'he had only given him the reproachful name he had given himself'. Perplexed, the bishop demanded to know Marvell's meaning and the following dialogue ensued:

> *'Have you not, my lord Bishop, such a book which he hath lately written?'*
>
> *'Yes.'*
>
> *'Please to produce it. There, my lord, look over that page of the preface!'*
>
> *'Well, what of this?'*
>
> *'Why, my lord, does he not say he is "a true son of his mother the church of England"?'*
>
> *'Well, and what of that?'*
>
> *'Read further on, my lord: "The church of England has spawned two bastards, the Presbyterians and the Congregationals". Ergo, my lord, he expressly declares* that he is the son of a whore.'
>
> *'You are very witty, indeed, Mr Marvell but let me intreat you in future time to show more reverence to the cloth.'*

That Marvell declined to obey the Bishop's injunction is evident from his subsequent writings. Six printed replies to *The Rehearsal* appeared rapidly to provoke him further. The first of these was *Rosemary & Bayes: or Animadversions Upon a Treatise Called, The Rehearsal Transprosed. In a Letter to a Friend in the Country*. This short, twenty-two-page pamphlet was the first reply and must have been published within weeks of Marvell's work appearing, because it is dated 1672. The anonymous author was Henry Stubbe, described by Wood as 'the most noted Latinist and Grecian of his age . . . a singular mathematician, and thoroughly read in all poetical matters, councils, ecclesiastical and profane histories'.[4] Yet in spite of these accomplishments, Wood went on, Stubbe 'became a ridicule, and undervalued by sober and knowing scholars'. He was an intimate friend of the political philosopher Thomas Hobbes. His reply, 'written in haste' in the form of a letter to a friend in the country, reassures that person on its first page: 'Honoured Sir, Do not wonder that you so little understand the *Rehearsal Transpros'd*; I believe the *Author* himself never did.'[5] Stubbe's attempt at a riposte is, for the most part, footling and pedantic although he does not set out automatically to defend Parker and concedes: 'There are in it several Periods, which shew the Author to have had some Intervals of SENSE and WIT', though these are such as 'you may find in the Harrangues of Enthusiasts, and Madmen'. Stubbe claimed that Parker was not generally approved of: 'As to the Church of England few of them approved the Style of Mr Bayes, and fewer his Doctrines: He was in the Pulpit declaimed against as the young Leviathan.' But he feared that if the clergy were held up to ridicule and were '*inodiated*' civil peace would be threatened. Stubbe concluded by rejecting Marvell's analysis of the origins of the Civil War, arguing that no single cause could be adduced unless it were that 'the Lawyers (finding themselves too numerous, odious, burthensome and disrespected by the people) would indear themselves to the Nation, and make work for their profession, by seeming Assertions of the Laws, Rights and freedom of the Subject'.

Meanwhile, the government was considering its reaction to Marvell's talked-about work. On 23 January 1673, the Secretary of State, Henry Coventry, called in the Surveyor of the Press, Sir Roger L'Estrange, to find out how this unlicensed work had managed to escape the censor. L'Estrange, under examination, told Coventry that he 'neither knew, nor heard of'[6] *The Rehearsal* until the first impression had been distributed by the printer, whom he assumed to be Nathaniel Ponder. L'Estrange advised that 'if the Book were Questioned, there were those would Justify it' and a prosecution of the printer would very probably fail. Nonetheless, the Stationers' Company officials seized the sheets of a second impression at the printer, behaving with their customary selective zeal. Only about half of the pamphlet literature published between 1662 and 1679 was licensed, because L'Estrange was easily bribed and the Stationers' Company acted in a wholly arbitrary fashion. Strictly, all 'seditious' books (which included anything critical of Church or State) should have been licensed but the printer – probably, from the initials 'A.B.', Anne Brewster, widow of the printer for Cromwell's Council of State and later printer of Marvell's *Account of the Growth of Popery* – was one of a number who took advantage of the ineptness of the censors to evolve an efficient system of printing and distribution. Coventry's examination revealed that L'Estrange had been summoned by the Earl of Anglesey to his house in Drury Lane. On arrival, the Earl made clear that the book had met with approval in the very highest quarters. He told the censor:

> *Look you, Mr L'Estrange, there is a Book come out . . . [*The Rehearsal*] I presume you have seen it. I have spoken to his Majesty about it and the King says* he will not have it supprest, for Parker has done him wrong, and this man has done him Right.[7]

Thus informed by the Earl that 'the King will have the Book to passe', L'Estrange accepted instructions to license it, preserving his *amour-propre* by making some quibbles about one or two passages 'not fit to be Licensed'. No sooner had Anglesey agreed to this than L'Estrange primly asserted 'that he did not love to tamper with other mens Copyes, without the Privity and Allowance of the Author'. Anglesey replied with evident impatience that 'he could not say anything of the Author, but that such alterations might be made without him' and L'Estrange was sent away to license the book. The Clerk of the Stationers' Company now announced that he would not enter it. L'Estrange wrote and asked why, 'saying that he disliked the thing as much as anybody, but being over-ruled he expected the Company's officer should likewise conform'.[8] The clerk was adamant and the book was never entered on the Stationers' Register.

Events, however, were proceeding quickly and by the time Parker came to register his *Reproof to the Rehearsal Transprosed* in March 1673 with the Stationers' Company – it appeared in May – the political situation had changed significantly. The King had been forced to cancel his Declaration of Indulgence after the Commons had voted it down. Marvell had thus failed in his political aim and Parker was able to turn the tables on him, accusing the poet of being opposed to the will of

Parliament. Parker, taking his cue from Marvell, plunges directly *ad hominem*, rather than addressing the argument, into a tirade of personal abuse, in an attempt to demonstrate to the world, he says, that Marvell's literary accomplishments, foreign travels, linguistic skills and his 'being a cunning Gamester' fail to qualify him 'to discourse of Conscience and Ecclesiastical Policy'.[9] Marvell in fact is 'a Clown', 'a Buffoon' a 'Trifler', and 'as despicable a Scribbler as ever blotted paper'. Parker claims, however, to have a more serious purpose. What he calls 'my old War against Faction and Non-conformity' has been designed to expose 'that certain and inviolable confederacy that there has always been between Non-conformity and the Good old Cause'.

The history of polemic is generally written by the victors. Although the conventional assumption that Marvell won the argument is justified – for who is Parker to posterity compared with a major poet like Marvell? – it should not be overlooked that here and there, amid the ineffable splutter and bluster, Parker hits home. But, for the most part, Parker conducts himself like a pompous ass, rearing himself up in the opening pages to rebuke Marvell for 'acosting me in such a clownish and licentious way of writing, as you know to be unsuitable both to the Civility of my Education, and the Gravity of my Profession'. Trying to match his opponent for wit, he claims to have a further aim: 'to convince the world how little Wit is requisite to prove that you have none at all'. He claims, with some measure of justification, that Marvell makes no serious attempt in *The Rehearsal* to refute his thesis about the nature of ecclesiastical authority and the proper field of the individual conscience. He accuses his opponent of masking a lack of knowledge and a shortage of theological rigour under a cover of sportive mockery: 'it is in the nature of some Vermine to be nibbling though they have no Teeth'. Parker also correctly identifies Marvell's fervent anticlericalism: 'And if you can but get scent of anything that smells of a Priest, away you run with full Cry and open Mouth.'[10]

Parker follows Marvell's polemical method of The Tendentious Curriculum Vitae, mocking him, in passages already quoted, as 'an Hunger-starved Whelp of a Country Vicar' whose inherited distaste for church hierarchies makes him go for any clergyman 'with all the rage of a Phanatick Blood-Hound'. He refers to him as 'an Urchin', a 'boy' and a 'young man' as if he were dealing with a raw provincial youth, not a fifty-year-old MP. He blames Marvell's coarse language and scurrility on his 'first unhappy Education among Boat-Swains and Cabin-Boys, whose phrases you learn'd in your Childhood', that rough education being topped up by consorting with 'the Boys and Lackeys at Charing-Cross or in Lincoln's Inn Fields'. Parker hammers away in this fashion for over 500 pages before concluding:

> *So that if you must be scribling, betake your self to your own proper trade of Lampoons and Ballads, and be not so unadvised as to talk in publique of such matters as are above the reach of your understanding, you cannot touch* Sacred things *without* prophaning *them.*[11]

Parker may have stung Marvell when he refers to his 'juvenile Essays of Ballads, Poesies, Anagrams and Acrostics' (either Parker is misinformed or some interesting lost items of the Marvell canon are being alluded to here). Endorsing the view that Marvell's true poetic output belonged to the earlier part of his life, the passage goes on to refer to the poet's apparent desertion by his Muse: 'your Papers lying useless by you at this time when your Muse began to tire and set'.

Parker, though he would be silenced by the second part of Marvell's *Rehearsal* later in the year, made one more return to his opponent in a posthumously published work (he died, it is said, after a convulsive fit at being instructed by James II to admit nine more Catholic Fellows to Magdalen College, Oxford, where he was President in the 1680s). This was his *De Rebus sui Temporis Commentarium* (1726), published in an English translation the following year by Thomas Newlin as *Bishop Parker's History of His Own Time.* It contains the same blend of personal abuse and slander and alleges that Marvell was close to the Cabal, who met 'at a tavern at the sign of King Henry the Eighth, against the Temple . . . when they went abroad, they distinguish'd themselves by a green ribbon round their hats, as a badge of their society'.[12] Still nursing his resentment, he went on:

> *Amongst these lewd Revilers, the lewdest was one whose name was* Marvel. *As he had liv'd in all manner of wickedness from his youth, so being of a singular impudence and petulancy of nature, he exercised the province of a Satyrist, for the use of the faction, being not so much a*

> *Satyrist thro' quickness of wit, as sowerness of temper: of but indifferent parts, except it were in the talents of railing and malignity.*

Against the evidence that Marvell, at least until the mid-1670s, was not, in spite of his mounting disillusion, a serious opponent of the King (who had, after all, eased publication of *The Rehearsal*), Parker makes quite a specific allegation that has no other independent corroboration:

> *In all Parliaments he was an enemy to the King's affairs, being one of those Conspirators, who being sixty in number, of the remains of the Rebellion, had bound themselves by oath, from the beginning, to give all the trouble they could to the King, and especially never to vote for granting any taxes.*[13]

Parker alleges that Marvell, known to be one of this club of sixty, was treated by his fellow MPs 'with shame and disgrace', making it difficult for him to participate in debates 'for they were hardly ever suffer'd to speak without being hiss'd at; and our Poet could not speak without a sound basting'. Parker concluded that Marvell continuously represented the interests of this secret group of 'Sectaries' and that his defence of toleration and dissent was no more than a desire to advance the fortunes of his group. 'Whether the Conspirators aim'd at tyranny, *Marvel* himself was certainly a proper person to give testimony, who if he was not their Secretary, was yet admitted into their inmost counsels, for the sake of his ancient friendship with them.' In his earlier writings Parker had perfected this mode of slanderous insinuation, grounded perhaps in something more than gossip (he clearly knew something about Marvell and his background), but vitiated by the lurid tones of the conspiracy theorist. There is just sufficient mystery in some of Marvell's political dealings to allow for the possibility that his politics may have been more subtle and dark than they appear in his correspondence, but Parker is the most prejudiced witness of all, and one with obvious motives for wanting to allege the worst about his opponent.

Throughout 1673 replies appeared to *The Rehearsal*. Few of these were of great value in advancing an argument that even the two chief antagonists had allowed to dissolve into personal abuse. The poet Richard Leigh, a young Oxford graduate, published *The Transproser Rehears'd: or the*

Fifth Act of Mr Bayes's Play. It picks up the abusive tone of the controversy, rehashing many of Parker's gibes, and it may be no more than this pamphlet convention that is behind its insinuations of sexual oddity in Marvell. In a passage on 'his Personal Character' Leigh seems to be implying some anatomical sexual deficiency: 'Neither would I trumpet the Truth too loudly in your ears, because ('tis said) you are of a delicate Hearing, and a great enemy to noise; insomuch that you are disturb'd with the tooting of a sow-gelder's Horn.' A little later, Leigh adds: 'you may allow him to be an Allegorical Lover at least'.[14] And he concludes with a piece of doggerel that implies some unnatural acts between Marvell and Milton:

> *O marvellous Fate, O Fate full of marvel;*
> *That* Nol's Latin *Pay two* Clerks *should deserve ill!*
> *Hiring a* Gelding, *and* Milton *the* Stallion;
> *His* Latin *was gelt, and turn'd pure* Italian.

The anonymous *S'Too Him Bayes or Some Observations upon the Humour of Writing Rehearsal's Transpros'd* was also published at Oxford and is of even less value, adopting the same dreary blow-by-blow approach of dissecting Marvell's pamphlet and abusing him in similar terms to those employed by Parker. In a revealing comment that lays bare what was the real argument for many, the anonymous author writes: 'Thou art the imprudent'st Champion for Forein Jurisdiction or Toleration (chuse you which) that ever I knew.'[15] Edmund Hickeringill was another responder, who described himself as 'merrily disposed' in *Gregory, Father-Greybeard, with his Vizard Off: or, News from the Cabal in Some Reflexions Upon a Late Pamphlet Entituled the Rehearsal Transpros'd*. Like the others he indicts the anonymous author for his impudence and 'fashionable Drolling' but the new note is the attempt to link Marvell (who, of course, is not named but Hickeringill suggests his name through laboured puns) with a 'Cabal of wits' and a 'company in a coffee-house'. But his principal charge is that the author is a 'Fanatick' who has lost his reason in obsessive railing: 'Name but bayes, he cryes out (like that Hypocondriack that fancied he had Noah's flood in his belly, and if he piss'd should drown the world).'[16] And finally, the anonymous author of *A Common Place-Book Out of the Rehearsal Transpros'd Digested Under These Several Heads: viz His*

Logick, Chronology, Wit, Geography, Anatomy, History, Loyalty attempts to pick apart Marvell's logical errors and inconsistencies, while conceding that 'my Author has shewed a kind of Apothegmatical short Wit'.[17]

He is particularly angered by Marvell's censure of Archbishop Laud for helping to bring about the Civil War: 'Does it (think you) become the Son of a Vicar to prate thus of an Archbishop?' Marvell is dismissed, in terms that suggest the author was firmly in the orthodox church and court camp, as 'a little Fellow, who had formerly been a whiffling Clerk to a *Usurper*, and afterwards turn'd *Broker* for all *Phanatick Ware*'. He concludes with an interesting alternative analysis of the causes of the English Civil War: 'A wanton Pride of the People, bred out of Prosperity and long ease, infected with a touch of Levelling Principles, deriv'd over to their Politicks from the New Models of Church Government.'

The controversy was now nearly over. In the autumn Marvell would publish the Second Part of *The Rehearsal*, after which his critics would be silenced.

23

A Shoulder of Mutton

I intend by the end of the next week to betake my selfe some fiue miles of to injoy the spring & my privacy.[1]

On 3 May 1673, Marvell wrote to Sir Edward Harley at Brampton Bryan in Herefordshire to bring him up to date with metropolitan gossip and share his thoughts about the Parker controversy. Sir Edward, father of the rather more famous Robert Harley, 1st Earl of Oxford, had been Governor of Dunkirk in 1660–61 and had opposed its sale to the French. Although he had not been a supporter of Cromwell, he belonged to the country party in the Cavalier Parliament and opposed anti-nonconformist legislation, and would naturally be in sympathy with Marvell. In the letter, Marvell revealed that he had been on 'a sudden journy to Stanton-Harcourt',[2] the seat, near Oxford, of his friend Sir Philip Harcourt, the MP with whom Marvell was, in 1677, to be involved in an incident in the House of Commons which his enemies tried to exploit. Marvell recounted for Harley's benefit the appearance of *S'Too Him Bayes* which he thought was written 'by one Hodges'. Marvell was clearly well informed about the progress of the controversy and what was being planned by his opponents for he wrote: 'Gregory Gray-Beard is not yet out. Dr Parker will be out the next weeke.' In some way Marvell had managed to see the first 330 pages of Parker's work, enough to convince him that it was 'the rudest book, one or other, that ever was publisht (I may say), since the first invention of printing'. Although it handled him roughly, he told Harley, 'yet I am not at all amated [cast down] by it', but he did want to consult his friends about the best strategy for replying to Parker, and indeed whether it was advisable to do so at all. In the end, he concluded that it was right to reply but, with his customary circumspection and subtlety, he asked them to maintain the pretence for the time being that no answer was deserved by 'so scurrilous a book'. To Harley he disclosed his real intentions:

> *However I will for mine own private satisfaction forthwith draw up an answer that shall haue as much of spirit and solidity in it as my ability will afford & the age we liue in will indure. I am (if I may say it with reverence) drawn in, I hope by a good Providence, to intermeddle in a noble and high argument wch therefore by how much it is above my capacity I shall use the more industry not to disparage it.*[3]

But for the time being, Marvell declared, he would sequester himself some five miles off – presumably a reference to his retreat at Highgate – 'to injoy the spring & my privacy'. Should Harley wish to contact him, he was instructed to send his letter to Richard Thompson, the businessman with whom Marvell would later become involved in a complicated financial affair. The letter was to be left with Thompson 'at the Signe of the Golden Cock in Wooll-Church Market'.

The following month, Thomas Osborne, Earl of Danby, was appointed Lord Treasurer. Some time after this, possibly when Marvell had returned to London in the autumn to oversee publication of the second part of *The Rehearsal*, an incident is said to have occurred. In Marvell biography it has acquired the status of legend but it has no corroboration whatsoever except in tradition. 'A Life of Andrew Marvell,' wrote Grosart drily in 1872, 'would be as imperfect without it, as a history of King Alfred without the neatherd's cottage and the burnt cakes.'[4] It would be churlish to omit it here. Collating the various accounts,[5] the following playlet suggests itself:

The Incorruptible Member

The scene is the simple bachelor lodgings of Andrew Marvell, Member of Parliament for Hull, on the morning after the poet and politician has been honoured with an evening's entertainment by the King. Charmed by Marvell's easy manners, sound judgement, and keen wit, and delighted to have met the man who settled the hash of the egregious opponent of his policy of toleration, Samuel Parker, the King has despatched no less a figure than the Lord Treasurer, Danby, to visit Marvell. The encounter takes place in Marvell's second-floor rooms in a court near the Strand, probably in Maiden Lane, Covent Garden.

MARVELL: (*Looking up in surprise as DANBY rather abruptly bursts into the room from the dark and narrow staircase up which he had fumbled, but nonetheless greeting his visitor with a smile.*) My Lord, have you not mistaken your way?

DANBY: (*Bowing gracefully.*) No, not since I have found Mr Marvell. For my purpose is to bring a message from His Majesty, who wishes, on account of the high opinion he has formed of your merits, to do you some signal service.

MARVELL: (*With an ironic pleasantry.*) I think that His Majesty has it not in his power to serve me. (*Noticing Danby's consternation at this last remark.*) Forgive me, my Lord, but I know the nature of courts too well not to be sensible that whoever is distinguished by a Prince's favour is expected to vote in his interest.

DANBY: But, sir, His Majesty only desires to know whether there be any place at court you would accept.

MARVELL: I could accept nothing with honour, for either I must prove ungrateful to the King in voting against him, or false to my country in giving in to the measures of the court. Therefore, the only favour I beg of His Majesty is that he would esteem me as dutiful a subject as any he has, and one who acts more in his proper interest by *refusing* his offers than if he had accepted them.

(*DANBY goes to the door, but, turning back at the last minute, addresses MARVELL confidentially.*)

DANBY: His Majesty requests that you accept this sum of 1,000 guineas. (*Exit, the Lord Treasurer, having slipped the Treasury order for the amount into MARVELL's hand at the last moment. Looking down at the piece of paper in his hand, MARVELL rushes out on to the stair to recall DANBY who is now on his way back down to his waiting carriage.*)

MARVELL: My Lord! I request another moment.

DANBY: (*Having now re-entered the room.*) Very well, what is it?

MARVELL: Surely, my good Lord, you do not mean to treat me ludicrously by these munificent offers, which seem to interpret a poverty on my part? Pray, my Lord Treasurer, do these apartments wear in the least the air and mark of need? And as for my living, that is plentiful and good, which you shall have from the mouth of the servant. (*Turns to his servant boy.*) Jack, child, what had I for dinner yesterday?

JACK: Don't you remember, sir? You had the shoulder of mutton that you ordered me to bring from a woman in the market.

MARVELL: Very right, child. What have I for dinner today?

JACK: Don't you know, sir, that you bid me lay by the sweet blade-bone to broil?

MARVELL: 'Tis so, very right, child, go away. (*Turning to DANBY.*) My Lord, do you hear that? Andrew Marvell's dinner is provided. And when your Lordship makes honourable mention of my cook and my diet, I am sure His Majesty will be too tender in future, to attempt to bribe a man with golden apples who lives so well on the viands of his native country. There's your piece of paper back. I want it not. I knew the sort of kindness you intended. I live here to serve my constituents; the Ministry may seek men for their purpose; I am not one.

(*Exit DANBY for the last time, smiling at the wit and high principle of the poet he has left behind.*)

MARVELL: Jack, hasten along to my bookseller, Mr Nathaniel Ponder, at the sign of the Peacock in Chancery Lane near Fleet Street, and tell him that I must needs borrow a guinea of him.

(*Curtain.*)

The moral drawn by Marvell's eighteenth- and nineteenth-century biographers was that the poet was of unimpeachable principle. Like Diogenes in his barrel, informing Alexander the Great that the only favour the most powerful man in the world could perform for him was to stand out of his light, Marvell was beyond the reach of worldly suasion. 'No Roman virtue ever surpassed this temperance,' intoned Edward Thompson in 1776, 'nor can gold bribe a mind that is not debauched with luxury.'[6] Like the anecdote of his brandishing in triumph the half-crown that sufficed for his dinner 'at a great ordinary in the Strand', this story is part of a tradition of Puritan hagiography of Marvell. In his life of the poet in 1833, Hartley Coleridge sensibly described the latter story as:

'A piece of dry English humour mistaken for a stoical exhibition of virtue.'[7]

Life for Marvell at this time was perhaps not quite so easy and pleasant as these amusing tales imply. His polemic had made him enemies, including the 'J.G.' already mentioned (possibly John Gelson, who was known to have been acting as a spy for Secretary of State Williamson in Holland the previous year and who was the brother of the secretary to the Bishop of Oxford), who left a letter for Marvell at the house of a friend on 3 November. It was a death threat informing Marvell: 'If thou darest to Print or Publish any Lie or Libel against Doctor *Parker*, by the Eternal God I will cut thy Throat.'[8] Fearlessly, Marvell issued his final riposte to Parker, the second part of *The Rehearsal*, at the end of the year, stating boldly on the title page that it had been occasioned by two letters: the first being Parker's *Reproof* (said here to be 'by a nameles Author') and the second the letter of J.G. For the first time, Marvell appended his own name to the pamphlet. Six months after Parker defied him to 'do your worst. You know the Press is open'[9] Marvell answered the challenge.

The second part of *The Rehearsal* appeared with the sanction of the censors. It ran to a second edition, corrected by Marvell in a way that underlined and extended the attack on Parker, for example by augmenting the charge that Parker was suffering from venereal disease. The line of criticism does not differ in any significant way from the first part and once again is relentlessly personal in its abuse. Marvell mocks Parker's sense of injury and paranoia: 'And even so *the Author of the Ecclesiastical Polity*, ever since he crept up to be but the Weather-cock of a Steeple, he trembles and creaks at every puff of Wind that blows him about, as if the *Church of* England *were falling and the State totter'd.*' He claims that Parker's attacks on the nonconformists may not have had the effect he intended for: 'he hath done more service to their cause by writing against it, than all their own Authors that ever writ for them'. Marvell has left almost no record of his thoughts on the art of writing, which makes an early passage in this second part of special interest. 'Those that take upon themselves to be Writers,' he points out, 'are moved to it either by Ambition or Charity: imagining that they shall do therein something to make themselves famous, or that they can communicate something that may be delightful and profitable to mankind.' But writing is 'an envious and dangerous imployment' given the fact that the writer appears to assume that he or she has some superior gift to bestow on the humble reader and, by doing so, appears to suggest that the reader is ignorant:

> *So that not to Write at all is much the safer course of life: but if a mans Fate or* Genius *prompt him otherwise, 'tis necessary that he be copious in matter, solid in reason, methodical in the order of his work; and that the subject be well chosen, the season well fix'd, and, to be short, that his whole production be matur'd to see the light by a just course of time and judicious deliberation . . . For indeed whoseover he be that comes in Print whereas he might have sate at home in quiet, does either make a Treat, or send a Chalenge to all Readers; in which cases, the first, it concerns him to have no scarcity of Provisions, and in the other to be compleatly Arm'd: for if any thing be amiss on either part, men are subject to scorn the weakness of the Attaque, or laugh at the meanness of the Entertainment.*[10]

Parker, Marvell strongly implies, has ignored this sensible and workmanlike aesthetic and by writing 'an Invective' has taken the greatest risk. Rather disingenuously for the author of several biting satires, the poet argues that the importance of preserving a person's reputation is so great a civic good that satire, however lofty its professed aims, may be undesirable: 'For 'tis better that evil men should be left in an undisputed possession of their repute, how unjustly soever they may have acquired it, then that the Exchange and Credit of mankind should be universally shaken, wherein the best too will suffer and be involved.' The target of 'Clarindon's House-Warming', had these words reached him in his French exile (he had only another year to live), would no doubt have permitted himself a bitter laugh at this doubtful argument. Parker, Marvell says, has chosen personal invective in preference to the celebration of virtue. Writing these words, did he reflect on the way he himself had abandoned his lyric delicacy in favour of coarser satire and prose polemic? There may have been a suppressed personal charge in his observation that 'whereas those that treat of innocent and benign argument are represented by the *Muses*, they that make it their business to set out others ill-favouredly do pass for *Satyres*, and themselves are sure to be personated with prick-ears, wrinkled horns, and cloven feet'. In this second engagement with Parker, Marvell is expressing genuine doubts about whether it is a valid proceeding to protract personal invective, but he is goaded to it by the injustice of Parker's attack which makes what he does 'not only excusable but necessary'. Higher moral standards are rightly demanded of clergymen, which would not matter in any other trade or profession: 'No Mans Shooe wrings him the more because of the Heterodoxy, or the tipling of his Shooe-maker.' Marvell concedes that he too has 'imperfections' and 'though I carry always some ill Nature about me, yet it is I hope no more than is in this world necessary for a Preservative'. In what could be no more than a rhetorical strategy but which nonetheless seems to carry a note of personal feeling and is consistent with what we know about his love of privacy and apartness, Marvell says that he was reluctantly tempted to this encounter 'from that modest retiredness to which I had all my life time hitherto been addicted'.

Marvell then proceeds to unpick Parker's arguments, to mock his personal history as the son of 'whining Phanaticks' and his sanctimonious period with the Grewellers and to declare that 'it hath been this for the odiousest task that ever I undertook'. Taking care to stress that his support for the cause of toleration does not mean that he himself is a nonconformist ('I am come not long since from swearing religiously to own that Supremacy'), Marvell at last addresses the substantive argument: 'I do most certainly believe that the Supream Magistrate hath some Power, but not all Power in matters of Religion . . . I do not believe that Princes have Power to bind their subjects to that Religion that they apprehend most advantageous.' He denies that he is an enemy of the Church of England or resentful of its ecclesiastical wealth, which is 'all but too little', but he is angered by the vulgar displays of wealth of certain prelates such as Parker, whom he accuses of sauntering 'about City and Countrey whither your gilt Coach and extravagance will carry you . . . This is the great bane and scandal of the Church.' Marvell is fundamentally opposed to law-abiding people being turned into enemies of the state simply by virtue of their religious beliefs. He concedes that 'The Power of the Magistrate does most certainly issue from the Divine Authority' and that kings 'as they derive the Right of Succession from their Ancestors, so they inherit from that ancient an illustrious extraction, a Generosity that runs in the Blood above the allay of the rest of mankind'. Their special eminence relieves them from 'the Gripes of Avarice and Twinges of Ambition', disposing them in consequence 'to an universal Benignity'. No apologist for hereditary monarchy could wish for more than this and Charles's delight with *The Rehearsal* is not hard to comprehend. Nonetheless, Marvell counsels kings to practise magnanimity and, in one of those characteristic concrete and vivid images he deploys frequently in both parts of *The Rehearsal*, he compares the ruler to a shepherd who has an obvious interest in keeping good care of his flock: rulers cannot prosper 'if by continual terrour they amaze, shatter, and hare their People, driving them into Woods, & running them upon Precipices'. In short, while defending the divine right of hereditary kingship, Marvell was arguing that the monarchy had duties towards its subjects, one of which was to practise toleration. Advocating a moderate reformism, Marvell extends the virtue of toleration to the sensible allowance of the need for constructive and gradualist change, but avoiding the 'Schisms, Heresies, and Rebellions, which are indeed crimes of the highest nature'. Societies do change and are in need of modernisation: 'And therefore the true wisdom of all Ages hath been to review at fit periods those errours, defects or excesses, that have insensibly crept on into the Publick Administration; to brush the dust off the Wheels, and oyl them again, or if it be found advisable to chuse a set of new ones.' Against Parker's virulent contempt for the herd, Marvell defends 'the Common People' as possessing innate good sense, observing shrewdly: 'Yet neither do they want the use of Reason, and perhaps their aggregated Judgment discerns most truly the errours of Government, forasmuch as they are first to be sure that smart under them.'

Marvell argues again that the Civil War was provoked by the people being forced into religious conformity, which led to 'those dismal effects, which, if they cannot be forgotten, ought to be alwayes deplored, alwayes avoided'. Marvell had no nostalgia for the Civil War. He defended toleration and the individual conscience and pragmatism in government and deplored the oppressive temper of men like Parker who could openly declare that vice was preferable to disobedience. By the time Marvell laid down his pen, Parker was finished. The experience, Wood would later write, 'took down somewhat of his high spirit' and he 'judged it more prudent to lay down the cudgels, than to enter the lists again with an untowardly combatant so hugely well-vers'd and experienc'd in the then, but newly, refin'd art (tho' much in mode and fashion almost ever since) of sportive and jeering buffoonry'.[11]

Marvell, too, though the acknowledged victor, must have felt some relief also in putting this controversy to rest. The hints thrown out in the second part of *The Rehearsal* about the toll taken on a poetic sensibility by these engagements with satire and angry polemic point to Marvell's sense that certain costs were being incurred by his mode of life and the activities into which it inevitably drew him.

24

Tinkling Rhyme

Thou singst with so much gravity and ease;
And above humane flight dost soar aloft.
'On Mr Milton's Paradise Lost'

Though he may have been the victor over the enemies of toleration in a pamphlet war, Marvell could draw little comfort from the political situation at the start of 1674. Early in 1673 the King had been forced to withdraw the Declaration of Indulgence as the price of getting the supply he needed from Parliament. Parker claimed that Marvell voted with fellow MPs for the withdrawal but in fact there is no record. He could have done so as a Parliamentary tactic designed to achieve legislative action to guarantee toleration rather than continuing to rely on royal prerogative. Meanwhile, a Test Act had been passed, forcing all holders of public office to swear that they rejected the Catholic doctrine of transubstantiation and to furnish a certificate proving that they had recently taken Anglican communion. This attempt to flush out Catholics from public positions resulted in Clifford, a member of the now disintegrating Cabal, deciding to resign rather than renounce his Catholicism publicly. James, Duke of York, also resigned, and announced his intention to marry a Catholic, Mary of Modena, raising the prospect of a Catholic successor to Charles. In a mounting atmosphere of mistrust and fear, opinion in Parliament began to shift towards the reliably Protestant Dutch, with whom the country was still officially at war. Dutch propaganda was active and there existed at this time a fifth column, described by its historian as 'a strange story of spies and secret agents, smugglers, and conspirators, which at times reads more like historical fiction than sober fact'.[1] Marvell, a man 'of singular desert for the State to make use of', was once again involved in this clandestine work, operating under the alias of 'Mr George'.

The fifth column was based in The Hague where William of Orange plotted to turn English opinion against France with the aid of his confidential secretary, the Huguenot refugee du Moulin. The latter dealt with all the intelligence coming from England from around the autumn of 1672. At the London end of this spy network were men operating understandably under false names. One key figure, William Medley, was a former Fifth Monarchy Man who had signed the manifesto of the plotters against Cromwell in 1657, *A Standard Set Up*, and had been thrown into the Tower for two years. A former colleague of Medley's turned informer and identified him as 'Mr Freeman'. Another plotter was William Carr, more mercenary than ideologue, who was engaged in sending Dutch propaganda pamphlets to Arlington. In May 1674, Carr had an interview with Sir Joseph Williamson, Secretary of State, in Rotterdam, where he spilt some of the beans, including the following from Williamson's unpublished journal in the state papers:

> *There were certain young gentlemen relations to Parliament men, that had managed all this matter here [in Holland], during the last session of Parliament [i.e. January–February 1674]. They have come over twice or thrice. Once came over a Parliament man under the name of Mr George by du Moulin's order, was but one night at The Hague, and having spoken with the Prince returned. Carr saw him, was a thick, short man, as Carr judged much like Marvell, but he could not say it was he, though he knows, as he says, Marvell very well.*[2]

At the start of 1674, increasingly disillusioned with the political scene, Marvell had decided to act. In some later papers of du Moulin, dated 22 June 1674, Marvell's name appears, this time assigned the alias 'Mr Thomas', and in a letter to du Moulin from London of 30 June 'Mr Thomas' is said to have been 'in the country, and will not return for some time'. Marvell was also said to have been involved in causing an argument among the spies. In 1673 a man called Abraham van den

Bempde was arrested on suspicion of being involved in espionage. He was a friend of Marvell's as is clear from the dedication by Cooke of his edition of Marvell's works to van den Bempde's son John, who lived at Scarborough, referring to 'that inviolable Friendship betwixt your Father and Mr Marvell'.[3] The evidence that Marvell was engaged in espionage at the start of 1674 is thus compelling. His involvement in this sort of activity would be consistent with his growing association with the country party, now headed by the Earl of Shaftesbury. As a lifelong anti-Catholic, during 1673 and 1674 Marvell would have had an interest in supporting a policy designed to break the Anglo–French alliance. Given that his country was officially at war with the Dutch and in alliance with the French, his activity was both dangerous and treasonable. The fact, however, that on 3 February 1674 he was appointed for the only time in his Parliamentary career to draw up reasons for a conference with the Lords about an address for peace[4] indicates that there may have been some permeability between the legitimate and illegitimate streams of knowledge on foreign affairs at this critical moment.

By 1674 the King's secret Catholic policy was in tatters. Denied money by Parliament unless he did so, he made peace with the Dutch by signing the Treaty of Westminster in February. The Cabal was now dissolved and the King's new chief adviser was Danby, whose putative visit to Marvell's garret has already been described. The bribes and inducements used from now on by Danby to build up the court party in the Commons deepened Marvell's disillusion with the court and heightened his fears about popery and arbitrary government. On 26 April, he wrote to Edmund Popple claiming that Arlington, architect of the secret Treaty of Dover, had been appointed Lord Chamberlain after a bribe of £10,000 had been paid on his behalf.[5]

In July a second edition of Milton's *Paradise Lost* appeared. First published in 1667, the new edition was prefaced by two poems, one in Latin by Samuel Barrow and one by Marvell, signed merely 'A.M.'. Milton was now free from the odium attached to his name at the Restoration and had been the recipient of recent praise from Marvell in the second part of *The Rehearsal*, where Marvell was keen to rebut Parker's charge that Milton somehow had a hand in its first part. 'For by chance,' Marvell wrote, 'I had not seen him of two years before; but after I undertook writing, I did more carefully avoid either visiting or sending to him, least

I should anyway involve him in my consequences.'[6] He then continued – somewhat outrageously – boldly to rewrite Milton's republican and regicidal past: 'J.M. was, and is, a man of great Learning and Sharpness of wit as any man. It was his misfortune, living in a tumultuous time, to be toss'd on the wrong side, and he writ *Flagrante bello* certain dangerous Treatises.' Safely sanitised, Milton is now living a quiet life: 'At His Majesties happy Return, J.M. did partake, even as you yourself did for all your huffing,' Marvell reminds Parker, 'of his Regal Clemency and has ever since expiated himself in a retired silence.' Marvell reveals that it was at Milton's London home after the Restoration that he first accidentally met Parker who at that time 'frequented *J.M.* incessantly and haunted his house day by day', although Milton is 'too generous to remember' what the two men talked about on these occasions. Marvell himself, though meeting Parker four or five times, 'never contracted any friendship or confidence with you'.

Written in the early summer of 1674, 'On Mr Milton's Paradise Lost' opens with a confession by Marvell that 'When I beheld the Poet blind, yet bold,/In slender Book his vast Design unfold,' he had misgivings that Milton would 'ruine' the sacred scriptural truths 'to Fable and old Song'. Marvell's residual Puritanism made him uneasy at the turning of sacred matter into material for poetry. As he read on, however, he became 'less severe', although a new anxiety arose that Milton would prove the victim of his own success in making the whole thing seem too easy. Some lesser talent might even be given the idea of putting the story of creation on to the Restoration stage as an entertainment. Dryden – tilted at here as 'the *Town-Bays*' – actually did write an opera, inspired by *Paradise Lost*, called *The Fall of Angels and Man in Innocence*, but it was never performed in spite of having been licensed on 17 April 1674. Marvell's final judgement, however, was that Milton had got it exactly right:

At once delight and horrour on us seize,
Thou singst with so much gravity and ease;
And above humane flight dost soar aloft,
With Plume so strong, so equal, and so soft.

Milton's astonishing achievement, Marvell suggests, constitutes a gift from heaven, a compensation for his loss of sight in the form of an inner vision. The closing lines of the poem allude briefly to Milton's refusal of rhyme in favour of blank verse. A note by Milton on the verse of his epic – attached, like Marvell's poem, to this second edition only – says categorically that rhyme is 'no necessary adjunct or true ornament of poem or good verse . . . but the invention of a barbarous age, to set off wretched matter and lame metre'.[7] Milton believes that rhyme is 'to all judicious ears, trivial and of no musical delight' compared with the real marks of poetic craftsmanship which do not depend on 'the jingling sound of like endings'. Marvell, who wrote all his poetry in rhyme, generally in rhyming couplets, alludes – with a gentle, self-mocking irony – to his fashionable fondness for that 'tinkling Rhime' which the severe Milton abhors: 'I too transported by the *Mode* offend.'

Towards the end of April, Marvell wrote to Edmund Popple in Hull to say that he was coming to the city, though not until Will had returned from Paris to accompany him. The erection of a lighthouse at the mouth of the Humber was a more local issue than the intrigues of foreign powers, but one that demanded his attention. In a letter to the Trinity Brethren in October, Marvell displays once again his subtlety in public affairs by pointing out that the wardens could no longer oppose the weight of opinion in favour of a lighthouse, advising them to avoid loss of face by using new evidence of a sandbank having formed at the mouth of the Humber to justify their U-turn. This would enable them to be seen to be 'retracting or rectifying with more honour' their former objections and 'serve for a just pretense to the variance of our judgements'.[8] Marvell's other correspondence in the autumn of 1674, especially several letters to Henry and Edward Thompson, reveals his anxiety about the political situation and impatience with 'the hurry and foolery of the Town'.[9] Aware of the intrigues conducted on all sides, he told Henry Thompson on 5 November, the anniversary of the gunpowder plot: 'Things stand as I feare but ticklish and insincere betwixt us and Holland.'[10] To Henry's brother, Edward Thompson, he reported the following month the case of the 'Popish Priest', Father Alexander Burnet, who had been condemned to be hanged, drawn and quartered. ''Tis the most criticall thing since this Kings reigne whether he shall be executed or not. Few days will tell us.'[11] In the event, Burnet was merely banished, but the incident was the latest evidence of official paranoia about clandestine Catholic influence on the state. In the same letter Marvell reveals in passing his estimate of the legal profession, which he held in much the same estimation as the clergy: 'As to what you say of dealing with his sollicitors [those of Sir John Hewley, who disputed Henry Thompson's electoral victory over him at York] that race of men you know are not easy to discourage a cause wch brings them grist, and they will claw any mans humour as long as he feeds them with mony.' Nothing in the public climate could have contributed to a softening of Marvell's satirical temper and around this time he wrote several satires that can probably be attributed to him with reason.

On 29 October 1674, the King attended a City of London banquet at which the new Lord Mayor, Sir Robert Viner, a prominent goldsmith, was installed. On 18 December the aldermen presented him with the Freedom of the City in a golden box valued at £1,000. The poem 'Upon his Majesties being made free of the Citty' satirises the event by representing the King as a feckless and idle apprentice who should not have been honoured by a company of hardworking citizens and merchants. The sheer awfulness of the verse is explained in part by its probable intended use as one of the rough songs sung at the Lord Mayor's table during the annual festivities in the City:

He spends all his Days
In runing to Plays,
When in his Shop he shou'd be poreing;
And wastes all his Nights
In his constant Delights
Of Revelling, Drinking and Whoreing.

More particularly, the poem makes the direct accusation that Charles 'still doth advance/The Government of France/With a Wife of Religion Italian'. If this poem is by Marvell it gives a truer picture of his view of the monarchy and its trustworthiness at the end of 1674 than the pious declarations of loyalty in works like *The Rehearsal*. Sir Robert Viner, before being made Lord Mayor, had presented to the King on his birthday on 29 May 1672 a white marble equestrian statue of his monarch, which he had erected in Stocks Market, the site of the present-day Mansion House, though the statue was later removed to Newby Hall, Ripon, in 1734. The statue was in fact a recycled figure of the King of Poland,

John Sobieski, altered to represent Charles. The poem is thought to have been written in the autumn of 1674, after the statue had been covered up for a period of alterations. The poet represents the statue ironically as the tribute of a conquered people to their new master: the City of London wholly defeated by the profligacy of the King. The statue is considered ridiculous and its location in a marketplace appropriate for a King 'Who the Parliament buys and revenues does sell.' In an allusion to the retouching, the poet suggests: ''tis such a king as no chisel can mend'. Nevertheless 'though the whole world cannot shew such another,/Yet we'd better by far have him than his brother.'

Another possible Marvell poem of late 1674 or early 1675 is 'Britannia and Rawleigh', a poem cast in the form of a dialogue between Britannia and Sir Walter Raleigh. Britannia recounts to Raleigh her abhorrence of the contemporary English court: 'A Colony of French Possess the Court;/Pimps, Priests, Buffoones i'th privy chamber sport.' She tells how she has reminded the King of past precedent when England stood up to foreign powers like Spain in Elizabethan times, but the dangerous advisers are leading the King astray: 'I'th sacred ear Tyrranick Arts they Croak,/Pervert his mind, his good Intencions Choak.' In spite of Raleigh's urging to try to bring the King to his senses and dismiss his corrupt courtiers, Britannia protests: 'Rawleigh, noe more; too long in vain I've try'd/The Stuart from the Tyrant to devide.' Instead she will reject monarchy in favour of republicanism on the Venetian model – a motion that those who accept the attribution of this poem to Marvell believe he also made in the four years of life that remained to him: 'To the serene Venetian state I'le goe/From her sage mouth fam'd Principles to know.'

That Marvell's disillusion was affecting his private disposition as well as his public interventions as a politician and anonymous satirist is clear from a letter he wrote to Sir Henry Thompson at the start of 1675. It hints, not for the first time, at his sense of isolation, of solitary uselessness. Thompson's reluctance to trouble the poet, Marvell says, is 'the cruellest piece of your Ciuility: to me especially who haue no imployment but idlenesse and who am so oblivious that I should forget mine own name did I not see it sometimes in a friends superscription'.[12] Marvell was now fifty-three, with no wife or family or settled property. He had published little except some occasional verses and anonymous satires.

His best-known work was *The Rehearsal.* He was a career politician, mocked by his more patrician colleagues in the House for being dependent on a salary from his provincial electors. His future was to sit in the House and serve Hull – he was just about to take up his pen and thank the burgesses for their annual gift of a barrel of ale – in spite of a deep and growing disillusionment with contemporary politics. Resignation in disgust was not an option, for what alternative career did he have? The most effective role for a writer in politics is to diagnose and to warn. Marvell's growing sense that the country was being at best lied to, at worst betrayed, would culminate, three years later, in the publication of his pamphlet *An Account of the Growth of Popery.* Surrounded by these public men with their estates and fine houses and their large families, Marvell had only his meagre lodgings in central London and the fierce integrity that would become the stuff of his legend in later centuries to sustain him. As the news came of the calling of another Parliament in April 1675, after a long proroguing, he would be girding himself up for the thirteenth session of the Cavalier Parliament. He did not expect much from it, but he would not abandon his commitment. 'I shall not faile to obeye your commands,'[13] he promised the Hull Corporation stoically.

25

The Late Embezzlements

Then, England, Rejoyce, thy Redemption draws nigh;
Thy oppression togeather with Kingship shall dye.[1]

When Parliament resumed on 13 April 1675, members filing into their seats found in their places a mock speech from the throne written by an anonymous hand. It is now considered to be by Marvell, the irony more mordant, the regard for the King more scant than ever before. *His Majesty's Most Gracious Speech to Both Houses of Parliament* begins with the King explaining that, though he had always assumed winter to be the best time for Parliamentary business, he has been assured by the Lord Treasurer 'the spring was the best season for sallads and subsidies'.[2] The thirteenth session of the Pensionary Parliament was plainly to be no different from the others: the King would seek money from Parliament and the latter would seek from the King something in return in the shape of constitutional guarantees about civil liberty and religious freedom. 'I hope therefore,' the mock speech continued, 'that April will not prove so unnatural a month, as not to afford some kind showers on my parched exchequer.' There is a plain, Swiftian directness in this short satire of a kind that the long-winded pamphlets often lost sight of in the thicket of their elaborate invectives. Asking the Parliament for more supply, the King declares: 'The nation hates you already for giving so much, and I'll hate you too, if you do not give me more. So that if you stick not to me, you must not have a friend in England.' The essential irresponsibility and triviality of mind that Marvell sees in Charles, as well as his gullibility in relation to his scheming ministers, are the main constituents of this satire. 'I have made a considerable retrenchment upon my expenses in candles and charcoal,' the King is made to say, 'and do not intend to stop there, but will, with your help, look into the late embezzlements of my dripping-pans and kitchen stuff . . . for, I would have the world to know, I am not a man to be cheated.'

Marvell's official view of the first day's proceedings was contained in a more sober letter to the Hull Corporation that night, which reports that the King actually said that he had summoned Parliament 'that he might know what further he could do towards the securing of their Religion and Property and to establish a durable Correspondence betwixt him and his People'.[3] He also pledged that he would 'always maintaine the Religion and the Church of England as now established'. The fact that he felt it necessary to make this assurance indicates how widespread were the fears that he was inclined towards Catholicism. In the first week of the new Parliament measures were discussed, and reported by Marvell with evident approval, for the more effective harrying of 'Romish Priests' and for their 'speedyer conviction'.[4] In particular there was a clause proposed 'to distinguish between Papists and Protestant Dissenters' so that certain obvious inconveniences of a policy of toleration could be removed. A week later Marvell was appointed as teller for the bill disqualifying officials from sitting in the House.

On 24 April an unusually vehement tone enters into Marvell's routine letter to Mayor Hoare at Hull. He reports the case of Sir Robert Viner (whom he had several months earlier satirised in *The Statue in Stocks-Market*), who was now in deep financial trouble. As a way out of his difficulties, Viner was trying to get his stepdaughter married to Peregrine, the son of Lord Treasurer Danby, a move described by Marvell as 'a detestable and most ignominious story',[5] not least because she appeared already to be married. But the explanation for Marvell's anger is a little more complicated. Two of Marvell's distant relatives, Richard Thompson and Edward Nelthorpe, ran a merchant bank together in the City and were also engaged in the wine and silk trade, lead mines and Irish manufacturing, 'omitting nothing within the compass of our ingenuity'[6] as their later bankruptcy statement put it. For a mixture of political and commercial reasons Thompson, Nelthorpe & Co – who may also have been the holders of Marvell's modest savings – were enemies of the Establishment figure of Sir Robert Viner. A month before Parliament opened a heated dispute had arisen between the Lord Mayor Viner and the Common Council of the City over the appointment of a judge to the Sheriff's Court. Two leading members of the Common Council opposing Viner were Nelthorpe and Thompson, which may explain why Marvell thundered against Viner's alleged 'late enterprising to subvert in all manners the Libertyes of the City'. For his part, Viner saw the actions of Nelthorpe and Thompson as a crude attempt to undermine his political position by having him arrested for debt, though in fact it was soon to be the two merchant bankers who were in difficulty. Within a year they went bankrupt and into hiding from their creditors. Marvell helped by taking lodgings for them in his own name in Great Russell Street. He was always ready to perform a good turn to Yorkshire businessmen and relatives, especially when, as in this case, they had been of assistance to his favourite nephew Will in his activities as a wine importer. Marvell's act in sheltering these bankrupts in Bloomsbury would later have far more interesting reverberations, though.

Marvell's routine dispatches to Hull during this session refer repeatedly to the progress of the anti-Catholic legislation and the new Test aimed at exposing covert Catholic tendencies and confining office-holding to Anglicans. He signs off one letter in June by noting: 'The Pope hath given a Cardinalls Hat to Father Howard, the Queen's Almoner.'[7] Clearly there could be no let-up in the vigilance against Popery. During this early summer, Marvell may have been approached to write a life of his old friend, John Milton, who had died in November. On 18 May, John Aubrey wrote to Anthony Wood, claiming: 'Mr Marvell has pmised me to write *minutes* for you of Mr Jo: Milton who lyes buryed in St Giles Cripplegate ch: – I shall tell you where.'[8] Nothing seems to have come of this, though at one time there was speculation that Marvell may have been the author of an anonymous early life of Milton now attributed either to Cyriack Skinner or to Milton's nephew John Phillips.

During the summer, Danby, at his own expense, arranged for the erection of a bronze equestrian statue at Charing Cross, cast by a sculptor called Le Sueur in 1633. The Civil War broke out before it could be erected and Parliament sold it contemptuously to a brazier called Rivet who, after the King's execution, made a profitable sideline in bronze-handled knives and forks that he persuaded ardent Royalists to buy, under the impression that they were purchasing implements made from the very material used to portray the Royal Martyr. In fact, Rivet had kept the statue intact, producing it after the Restoration and eventually selling it to Danby. The poem 'The Statue at Charing Cross', attributed to Marvell, mocks the statue as a thing put up 'to comfort the hearts of the poor Cavaleer' and asks: 'Does the Treasurer think men so Loyally tame/When their Pensions are stopt to be fool'd with a sight?' It advises that the face of Charles I should be arranged to face away from Whitehall lest: 'Tho of Brass, yet with grief it would melt him away,/To behold every day such a Court, such a son.' Underlying the poem is the conviction that Danby was principally employed in buying votes and bribing support, which it is hard to deny. Abortive moves were made to impeach Danby in April – an allusion is made to this in a poem of doubtful attribution, 'A Ballad call'd the Chequer Inn' – but Danby survived to go on bribing.

The poem 'A Dialogue between the Two Horses', written probably in the autumn of this year, has, like most of these late satires, been attributed only with difficulty to Marvell. The possibility must be faced that none of these later satires could have been written by Marvell and certainly none adorn his poetic reputation, though that cannot in itself stand as an argument against his authorship. Critics have been uneasy with the attribution of the 'Dialogue' because of its marked republicanism and its lack of Marvell's customary tenderness towards Charles, but it is clear that in the last three or four years of his life Marvell had begun to shed the last vestiges of instinctive loyalism towards the ruling power and to view the consequences of 'His Majesty's happy restoration' in a more jaundiced way.

The two horses in question are the ones in Stocks Market and Charing Cross, supporting Charles I in bronze and Charles II in white marble. After an introduction that muses on precedents in classical literature for animals and inanimate oracles giving speech (though deriding parallel examples from Catholic shrines), the poem fancies a dialogue between the two steeds. They share a mutual dismay at the state of affairs where 'Church and state bow down to a whore' and where the King's brother, the Duke of York, becomes a Catholic in order to 'that Church defy/For which his own Father a Martyr did dye'. In spite of the King's greed for revenue the country is impoverished and 'Our worm-eaten Navy be laid up at Chatham'. Invited to comment on the bronze horse's 'Royall Rider' – Charles I – the white horse offers a rather more stringent view of Charles I than Marvell once offered in the 'Horatian Ode'. The indictment suggests once again that the Civil War ('too good to have been fought for') could have been avoided if it were indeed no more than a dispute about Church ceremonial ('He that dyes for Ceremonies dyes like a fool') aggravated by Laud:

Thy Priest-ridden King turn'd desperate Fighter
For the Surplice, Lawn-Sleeves, the Cross and the mitre,
Till at last on a Scaffold he was left in the lurch
By Knaves who cry'd themselves up for the Church,
Arch-Bishops and Bishops, Arch-Deacons and Deans.

Charles II's mount declares that he prefers Cromwell to either of these kings, notwithstanding his despotic tendencies, because at least the country was not a laughing-stock: 'Tho' his Government did a Tyrants resemble,/Hee made England great and it's enemies tremble.' Marvell – if the poem is truly his – is thus revising his earlier poetic estimates of Cromwell as much as those of Charles I, for in the poems of the 1650s he came closer to glorifying rather than expressing doubts about Cromwell's autocracy. Faced with the prospect of the Duke of York, the white horse cries out: 'A Tudor a Tudor! wee've had Stuarts enough;/None ever Reign'd like old Besse in the Ruffe.' His last word is: 'A Commonwealth a Common-wealth wee proclaim to the Nacion;/The Gods have repented the King's Restoration.' Although this poem cannot be mentioned in the same breath as the great 'Ode', its politics are quite without ambiguity and would fit the outlook of a fundamentally democratic, anticlerical politician, looking out with dismay at the contemporary political scene of duplicity, jobbery, bribery and corruption.

Marvell mentioned the Charing Cross statue in a letter to Will Popple on 24 July. In addition to its jaundiced view of the political world, the letter betrays Marvell's desire to find some calm, reflective time to address his nephew away from the increasingly unsympathetic atmosphere of Westminster:

> *Being resolved now to sequester myself one whole Day at* Highgate, *I shall write four whole Sides (if my Spirit will hold out) in Answer to your kind Letter, and to attone for my so long unaffected Silence.*[9]

The letter mirrors the attitude to the King found in the contemporary satires. Marvell does not dress up the reasons for this Parliament being called: 'It seemed necessary for the King's Affairs, who always, but now more, wants Mony, the Parliament should meet.' He describes to Will the emergence in this session of an 'Episcopal Cavalier Party' as the dominant influence on the King and reports the erection of the statue at Charing Cross 'for more Pageantry'. Further ideas were being discussed to cement public loyalty to the monarch, including digging up the body of Charles I 'to make a perfect resurrection of Loyalty, and to be reinterred with great Magnificence'. He reports both the attempts to impeach the King's favourite minister Lauderdale and the general disorder of the House. One day it erupted into chaos on the floor of the Commons with 'every Man's Hand on his Hilt'. In a concluding remark to Will, Marvell seems to be trying to express some wish for his nephew to be emancipated from the press of business and to find something more worthwhile as a focus of his energies, projecting on to him, perhaps, some of his own anxieties about the futility of his life as a politician in this 'odiously ridiculous' Parliament: 'O when will you have arrived at what is necessary? Make other serviceable Instruments that you may not be a Drudge, but govern all your Understanding.'

'The times are something critical,'[10] Marvell wrote to Hull on 21 October, explaining why he was once again counselling the Corporation to be cautious about circulating too much of what he told them in confidence, 'beside that I am naturally and now more by my Age inclined to keep my thoughts private'. Marvell's reserve, his caution, his lack, in Aubrey's words, of 'a generall acquaintance', may have conspired to bring about a certain increase in withdrawal, perhaps even a renewed anxiety about his personal safety in an unscrupulous political culture, where means could be found for most of the ends politicians sought. There would be plenty of reasons to want this lethal satirist silenced, but withdrawal would hardly be conducive to effectiveness as a practical politician in the House of Commons. If he felt, at fifty-four, he was getting old, the spectacle of his friend Jeremy Smith's approach to death that autumn would have been chastening. On 13 October, Marvell witnessed Smith's will, having already been appointed a trustee on 12 June with three others, all of whom received forty shillings. This would result in his having to take some responsibility for the funeral and settling the estate.

At the end of the month, during a brief adjournment of the House, Marvell went over to Sir Jeremy's house at Clapham and spent the night at his deathbed. On the night of 3 November his 'very cordiall friend' died. In a letter to Mayor Shires of Hull the next day Marvell wrote: 'I was yesternight againe with Sr Jer: and saw him expire at eleuen a clock at night dying very peacably and with perfect understanding memory and speeche to the last gaspe.'[11] The death of a good man at such a moment was peculiarly affecting, 'such breaches being in these times very difficult to be repaired'. Marvell was worried at this time that there might be some sort of surveillance of his letters – a possibility hinted at in some of his correspondence with Hull. He warned the Mayor: 'it seemes therefore that there is some sentinell set both upon you and me. And to know it therefore is a sufficient caution.' In this fraught, threatening atmosphere the King himself was not free from a sense of menace. Marvell reported to Sir Henry Thompson in York: 'I heare that two ugly distichs haue been pasted up at the Kings Bedchamber doore. I am sorry that they should haue so much effect as to make the King distrust his Safety and walk with guards.'[12] This was a reference to some rather ungrammatical doggerel found pinned to the King's bedchamber door on 27 November: 'in vaine for help to your old friends you call, when you like pittied them they must fall[*sic*]'.[13] The growing political tension had evidently generated a sense of danger among all those in public life. Marvell's early biographers frequently alluded to the threats he faced during this time. 'He was often in such danger,' wrote Thomas Cooke, 'that he was forced to have his letters directed to him in another name, to prevent any discovery that way.'[14] Thompson likewise claimed: 'He was frequently threatened with murder, and way-laid in his passing to and from Highgate, where he was fond of lodging.'[15] Marvell would have been an attractive target – he was an irritant to the court and the suspected author of offensive satires – as well as being an easy one. Living in isolation, frequently alone, he could easily have been picked off by some hired assassin. Both Cooke and Thompson, keen to portray Marvell as a martyr in the cause of religious freedom and conscience, no doubt exaggerated his 'life of perpetual danger' and his 'fear of losing his life by treachery' but the likelihood is that he would have had to exercise caution at this period in his political life.

On 22 November the King prorogued Parliament for fifteen months until 15 February 1677. The Member for Hull, however, was not idle, for early in the new year he would once again enter the field of religious controversy. He had not yet done with the Church of England hierarchy and its more disputatious members.

26

Divines in Mode

As the arts of glass coaches and perriwigs illustrate this Age, so by their trade of Creed-making, then first invented, we may esteem the wisdom of Constantine's and Constantius his empire.[1]

Parliament had been prorogued as a result of a secret agreement between the King and Louis XIV which meant that Charles received £100,000 a year from the King of France. He had his money and therefore had no need of Parliament. Danby was not party to this agreement and continued to wage war against Catholics and dissenters by strengthening the power of the Anglican establishment. In so doing he was accused of reopening the wounds of the Civil War and at the very least provoking conflict between the liberals and the hardliners within the Church of England. Marvell's interpretation of these events – or those of which he would have been aware – was that the power of Parliament to resist popery and absolutism was being weakened by Lord Treasurer Danby's regime of bribery and corruption.

The publication, in 1676, of a book called *Animadversions Upon a Late Pamphlet Entitled The Naked Truth*, written by the Reverend Francis Turner, Master of St John's College, Cambridge, gave Marvell his opening for a new polemic in defence of toleration. The object of Turner's 'animadversions' was a work published by the Bishop of Hereford, Herbert Croft, in the spring of 1675. *The Naked Truth. Or, the true state of the Primitive Church* was Croft's attempt to argue that the enforcement of conformity in the Church of England by penalties and persecution was not the way forward. Croft was a vigorous opponent of Catholicism and, according to Burnet (who was one of several who responded in print to *The Naked Truth*), he was not a diplomat: 'Croft was a warm, devout man, but of no discretion in his conduct: so he lost ground quickly. He used much freedom with the King: but it was in the wrong place, not in private, but in the pulpit.'[2] Anthony Wood observed that 'the appearance of this book' – which came out first as a privately printed appeal to Parliament and which was then taken up by a bookseller – 'at such a time was like a comet'.[3] Croft, like Marvell, had an early, but in his case rather more substantial, flirtation with Catholicism. The son of Sir Herbert Croft, of Croft Castle in Herefordshire, Croft had been educated by Jesuits and had attended the English College in Rome in 1626 under the assumed name of James Harley. Converted to Anglicanism in the 1630s and later a chaplain to Charles I, his fortunes naturally dipped during the Civil War. After the taking of Hereford, the Parliamentary commander, Colonel Birch, had to restrain a guard of musketeers from seizing him. Famously, he preached at the Roundheads as they entered his cathedral when he was still only Dean, the pulpit from which he did so still on display at Hereford in the south-east transept. After the Restoration, however, he was made Bishop of Hereford where, in one of the most touching of English church monuments, in Hereford Cathedral, he can be seen holding hands with his lifelong friend Dean George Benson, who is buried beside him. A Latin inscription reads: '*In Vita conjuncti In Morte non divisi*' (Together in life, undivided in death).

For Marvell the controversy was to some degree a reprise of the engagement with Samuel Parker. The aim was to advance the cause of religious toleration, to administer some satirical sideswipes to the stuffier and more conservative parts of the Anglican establishment and to have some sport with an ill-matched opponent. As with *The Rehearsal*, Marvell went to the contemporary theatre for a title. Sir George Etherege's *The Man of Mode* had just received its first performance at court. In the play, Sir Fopling Flutter, 'the prince of fops', is the eponymous man of mode, though it is a minor character, Mr Smirke, chaplain to Lady Biggot, whose name provides Marvell's title. His subtitle advertises the work as being 'certain annotations' on the *Animadversions*. He calls Bishop Croft 'judicious, learned, a sincere Protestant' and his book 'of that kind that no Christian scarce can peruse it without wishing himself had been the author'.[4] Marvell sums up the initial reaction of the clergy to Croft's pamphlet:

> *Not only the churches but the coffee-houses rung against it. They itinerated like excise-spyes from one house to another, and some of the morning and evening chaplains burnt their lips with perpetual discoursing it out of reputation, and loading the Author, whoever he were, with all contempt, malice and obloquy.*[5]

Marvell sensed that Turner, like Samuel Parker before him, was a bully in clerical garb, and leapt to the defence of Croft. Because of the rancour of the punitive tendency in the Church of England, Croft had been shown no mercy over his pleas for toleration. In Marvell's view, Turner's reply to Croft – 'a lasting pillar of infamy' – had been executed 'not according to the ordinary rules of civility, or in the sober way of arguing controversie, but with the utmost extremity of jeere disdain, and indignation'. Worst of all for Turner, he 'took up an unfortunate resolution that he would be witty'. In truth he was a pompous fool like Parker, 'huff'd up in all his ecclesiastical fluster'. His style was crushingly pedantic, 'so wretchedly does he hunt over hedge and ditch for an university quibble'. This put Marvell in mind of his own schooling at Hull Grammar School – another of those fugitive autobiographical touches – where the pupils were taught to scan Latin verses prior to any understanding of what the words might mean: 'For as I remember this "scanning" was a liberal art that we learn'd at grammar-school: and to scan verses as he does the Author's prose, before we did, or were obliged to understand them.'[6] Marvell also criticised the Act against printing without a licence because it allows clergy to attack 'men's private reputations', having easier access to publication. He adds: 'It is something strange that to publish a good book is a sin and an ill one a vertue; and that while one comes out with Authority, the other may not have a dispensation.' He accuses the Church of England writers of wanting to exercise a monopoly ('these single representers') on Church questions and of using that privilege not to attack wickedness but to entrench their own position: 'to render those peccadilloes against God as few and inconsiderable as may be, but to make the sins against themselves as many as possible, and these to be all hainous and unpardonable'. The Act works 'by ingaging men's minds under spiritual bondage, to lead them canonically into temporal slavery'. This introductory passage is charged both with Marvell's liberal attachment to freedom of speech and with his fervent anticlericalism. It is also done with his usual vigour of expression and vividly apt similes: he observes that 'calumny is like London dirt, with which though a man may be spattered in an instant, yet it requires much time pains and fuller's-earth to scoure it out again'. And again, when he finally begins to get down to the matter of Turner's book, he censures him for imputing all sorts of things to Croft which are not there in his argument: 'So men with vicious eyes see spiders weave from the brim of their own beavers.'

As with Marvell's previous polemics, the lively engagement with the opponent is of more interest than the sequential argument, which is as difficult to summarise as ever. He epitomises Croft's original argument thus: 'That nothing hath caused more mischiefe in the Church, then the establishing new and many Articles of faith, and requiring men to assent to them with divine faith.' Forcing impositions on dissenters, in Croft's own words, 'hath caused furious wars and lamentable bloodshed among Christians'. This is the essence of Marvell's ecclesiastical politics: that the state should not impose too much in matters of faith. Its secular counterpart is his view that the constitutional monarch should not exact too much from the citizen. In both contexts the freedom of individual conscience is paramount, it being argued that nothing is gained by the religious or secular authorities seeking more control than is strictly necessary. This current of thought places Marvell firmly in the mainstream of the English liberal tradition, marred only by the occasional excesses of his xenophobic anti-popery, the English tradition often losing its way when travelling on a passport. It justifies his posthumous reputation as a defender of civil and religious liberty at home. All such arguments, however, are lost on individuals like Turner, whom Marvell mockingly describes as 'the Animadverter' in allusion to the title of his attack on Croft: 'But like some cattle, the Animadverter may browze upon the leaves, or peel the barke, but he has not teeth for the solid, nor can hurt the tree but by accident.' For Marvell, simple Christian faith is enough 'without the chicanrey and conveyancing of humane extentions'. Scripture, rather than Church discipline, is his guide for Christians and should be the guide for men like Turner:

> *but these are the Divines in Mode, who, being by their dignities and preferments plump'd up beyond humane proportion, do, whether for their pride or ignorance, neither understand themselves or others (men of nonsense) much less do they speak of God, which ought to be their study, with any tolerable decorum. These are the great Animadverters of the times, the church-respondents in the pew, men that seem to be members only of Chelsy Colledge, – nothing but broken windows, bare walls and rotten timber.*[7]

After declaring that 'I do not reckon much upon a Church historical, devilish beliefe. Unless a thing be in the express words of Scripture, there are some of the laity to whom a Council cannot demonstrate, sneezing powder cannot demonstrate, no earthly power can do it,' Marvell lays down his pen. Abandoning his original intention of examining each of Turner's arguments one by one he declares (somewhat to the relief of the reader): 'I am weary of such stuffe . . .'

Appended to the work, however, is *A Short Historical Essay Touching General Councils, Creeds and Imposition in Religion*, which develops the original argument of Croft – that the essential truths of primitive Christianity have been obscured by the machinations of the later ecclesiastical politicians – by offering an historical account of the development of religious 'creed-making' at councils of theologians summoned to deliberate on what they regarded as vital questions of faith. It demonstrates the extraordinary depth of Marvell's knowledge both of scripture and of Church history and is unusual in its logical arrangement and flow. His understanding convinces him that it is undesirable for the civil power to involve itself in policing questions of religious belief. His jaundiced account of the councils of the early Church makes him reflect: 'a man would scarse think he were reading an history of bishops, but a legend of divels'.[8] In a discussion of the Arian heresies, Marvell observes pointedly on the fact that: 'Whereas truth for the most part lyes in the middle, but men ordinarily look for it in the extremities.' He mocks the emergence of bishops in early Christianity, falling over themselves in their profusion and their self-importance, obsessed with detecting heresy at every turn, 'when every hare that crossed their way homeward was a schismatic or an heretick, and if their horse stumbled with one of them, he incurred an anathema'. As well as preferring the *via media,* Marvell confesses to an instinctive sympathy for the underdog: 'Only I will confess that as in reading a particular history at adventure a man finds himself inclinable to favour the weaker party, especially if the conqueror appear insolent'. As a child, Marvell had witnessed his father's clashes with the 'insolent' church hierarchy and remained a lifelong opponent of their arbitrary exercise of power. In censuring the manufacture of creeds and the accompanying invention of heresies, he argues, in a way that would have endeared him to the nonconformists, for the primacy of individual conscience over episcopal jurisdiction: 'It is not as in secular matters where the States of a kingdom are deputed by their fellow subjects to transact for them, so in spiritual.' And again: 'The soul is too precious to be let out at interest upon any humane security, that does or may fail; but it is only safe when under God's custody in its own cabinet.'

Marvell accuses the bishops of having their own material reasons for wanting to impose creeds and of being worldly and ambitious. The orthodox bishops in the reign of Constantius were 'obstinate for power, but flexible in faith', losing sight of the essential truth of Christianity in the heat of ecclesiastical power politics: 'And all this mischief sprung from the making of Creeds, with which the bishops, as it were at Tilting, aim'd to hit one another in the eye, and throw the opposite Party out of the saddle.' In Marvell's reading of early Christianity, the bishops were overeager in the matter of persecution, exhibiting a 'wolfishness' towards their flocks. They then progressed from 'a spiritual kind of dominion' to a desire to wield civil power: 'A bishop now grew terrible.' In a sharp reminder to his readers of the applicability of these arguments to the 1676 context, Marvell connects the earthquakes in the reign of Valens, which were seen as full of portent, to recent natural phenomena in England:

> *All which put together, could not but make me reflect upon the late earthquakes, great by how much more unusual, here in England, thorow so many counties since Christmas, at the same time when the Clergy, some of them, were so busy in their cabals, to promote this (I would give it a modester name then) persecution, which is now on foot against the Dissenters . . .*[9]

Marvell quickly notes, however, that he is 'not neither one of the most credulous nickers or applyers of natural events to humain transactions'. In the 1650s he had made use of the pathetic fallacy in his Cromwell poems, but the growing scientific spirit of the age was making its impression on him and rendering him sceptical about seeing natural phenomena as judgements of God. Continuing to underline the parallels with present events, he accuses the bishops of making Christians more 'distressed' under their rule than they were during the early era of persecutions, and of fomenting political discord by ecclesiastical means: 'turning makebates between prince and people, instilling dangers of which themselves were the authors'. The result of this activity was that 'most princes began to look on their subjects as enemies'. The political mischief created by the bishops has forced recent English monarchs into more repressive behaviour than they would otherwise have adopted. Charles II they have thus 'induced to more severities, then all the reigns since the Conquest will contain if summ'd up together'. There is a very real danger of a revival of 'the former persecutions'. Marvell's remedy for these maladies is that the Church hierarchy should 'inspect the morals of the Clergy' and recommend more use of the Bible: ''Tis a very good book, and if a man read it carefully, it will make him wiser.' In addition the bishops 'ought to disintangle from the world'; they should not 'take up the ministry as a trade' but lead good, exemplary lives and leave off theological niceties and the imposition of rules. In short the desideratum was: 'That they do not come into the pulpit too full of fustian or logick. A good life is a clergyman's best syllogism, and the quaintest oratory.'

Unsurprisingly, the Church of England hierarchy took great offence at this. The Bishop of London demanded that the Privy Council take action and the Earl of Anglesey, the Lord Privy Seal, unsuccessfully petitioned the Lord Chancellor to throw Marvell's bookseller, Nathaniel Ponder, into jail for having printed the book without a licence. Even the Presbyterians were unhappy at Marvell's strictures on the Council of Nice. But Bishop Croft was delighted and wrote to tell Marvell of his satisfaction at his having 'set forth Mr Smirk in soe trim & proper a dresse'.[10] Croft offered his thanks for the 'humane civility & christian charity shewed to ye author of naked truth soe bespattrd wth ye dirty language of foule mouthed beasts whoe though he feared much his own weaknesse yet by gods undeserved grace is soe strengthned as not at all to be dejected or much concerned wth such snarling currs though sett on by many spightefull hands & hearts of a high stamp but as base alloy'. Faintly amused at Croft's strong language, Marvell wrote back to say rather extravagantly that he had in fact 'given you ye highest provocation' by the inadequacy of his work on Croft's behalf. In a reference to Croft's 'christian magnanimity' (which in fact seems rather lacking from the quoted remarks), it is possible to detect some irony on Marvell's part. In a letter to Will Popple enclosing copies of the correspondence with Croft, Marvell refers to Croft as 'ye foole', which suggests that he saw him as a rather pathetic figure. His role for Marvell was as a pretext for an attack on his favourite targets.

While the controversy was breaking out in the wake of publication of *Mr Smirke*, Marvell was spending June in the country – possibly in Highgate or perhaps farther afield. 'To make the Town new to me I haue been airing my selfe for near three weeks in the Country,'[11] he wrote to Sir Edward Harley, Croft's fellow Herefordshire man, who had probably apprised the Bishop of the identity of his friendly pamphleteer, on 1 July. The letter also refers in passing to a 'debauch' at Epsom involving the poet Rochester, who was an admirer of Marvell's satirical poetry but who lived rather more loosely. Marvell tells Harley of a number of pamphlets that have come out in response to the *Naked Truth* controversy. One is called *The Catholic Naked Truth* ('by a Papist') and another is by Bishop Burnet. By referring to Croft's work as 'the poore mans book' Marvell continues to regard him as someone in some sense to be pitied, perhaps for his naivety in thinking that such a book would not provoke a furious reaction. Again in ironic mood, Marvell pretends in the letter that he is not the author and writes of himself in the third person:

> *the book said to be Marvels makes what shift it can in the world but the Author walks negligently up & down as unconcerned. The Divines of our Church say it is not in the merry part so good as the Rehearsall Transpros'd, that it runns dreggs: the Essay they confesse is writ well enough to the purpose he intended it but that was a very ill purpose. The Bp of London's Chaplain said it had not answerd expectation.*[12]

Christopher, later Viscount Hatton, was one of many who knew that Marvell was the author. Writing to his brother on 23 May, Hatton expressed the hope that: 'Andrew Marvel will likewise be made an example for his insolence in calling Dr Turner, Chaplain to His Royal Highness, Chaplaine to Sir Fobling Busy, as he terms him in his scurrilous satyrical answer to his Animadversions on Naked Truth.'[13] To Harley, Marvell reported that the leading Presbyterian, William Bates, objected to his interpretation of the Council of Nice, making him speculate as to whether there was some ulterior motive for Dr Bates's animosity: 'But some years agoe I heard that he said Marvell was an Intelligencer to the King of France. 'Twas about the same time that the Doctor was in pension to another Monarch.' In sardonic conclusion about all this sniping at his work Marvell asks Harley rhetorically: 'Who would write?' But if this indicated some weariness with polemic, events would force him back into print the following year. Besides, it is possible to detect more than a little relish in his account of the reactions to his work. *Mr Smirke* was not written by someone who did not take pleasure in the art of satirical flyting.

27

This Sickly Time

I desire, that, during this king's reign, we may apply ourselves to preserve the people in the Protestant Religion, not only in the profession of it, but that men may live up to it, in morality and virtue of religion, and then you establish men against the temptation of Popery and a prince that may be popishly affected.[1]

The continued suspension of Parliament throughout 1676 meant that Marvell wrote no letters to the Hull Corporation containing reports of Parliamentary business. After the stir of the *Mr Smirke* publication in the early summer, we hear nothing from him again until the autumn. On 28 November he wrote from London – mentioning that he had been 'out of Town till this night' – to George Acklam, one of the Trinity House Brethren. Though he could be of little benefit to the town as an MP during the prorogation, there was plenty of business to conduct on behalf of Trinity House, in this instance the pursuit of a timber importer called Clipsham who was refusing to pay the duty of primage on a cargo of fir deals rightly due to Trinity House. Marvell advised them on this matter, although he wished they could have avoided getting themselves into a position of having to contemplate litigation. He had little respect for lawyers, particularly provincial practitioners, and observed to his brother-in-law on the Clipsham case: 'Country Counsell like ill Tinkers make work for those at London.'[2] Throughout the following year Marvell would pursue this case with an impressive doggedness and attention to detail.

In an extravagant signing off to his letter to Trinity House, Marvell stressed the 'great obligation' the Brethren laid upon him by allowing him to serve them in their affairs, 'which I shall preferre to my own upon all occasions'.[3] He also thanked them for their 'kind present of Ale lately sent me'. It had apparently been tampered with or carelessly handled, as Marvell explained to another correspondent, Edward Thompson the York merchant. The barrel was in short measure by about six inches as a result of the ale porters being either 'carelesse or thirsty'.[4] A little less conventionally and with more real feeling, Marvell added to the Corporation that: 'I am heartily glad to read in this sickly time the hands of so many my old & good friends'. Disillusioned with public life, Marvell was taking increased consolation from his personal friendships. A letter to his brother-in-law Edmund Popple a few weeks later signed off with an unusual personal touch: 'Remember to all friends & Katy beside'.[5] Katy may well have been Catherine Alured, whose daughter Mary married Edmund and Mary's son, Will Popple. Marvell's other friends at this time included Sir Thomas Allin, the naval commander and comptroller of the navy in the 1670s, with whom Marvell dined in December.[6]

At the start of 1677 the signs were that Parliament would be recalled soon. Marvell decided to write to William Foxley, Mayor of Hull, in anticipation of the event, pointing out his situation of 'not having in the intervalls of Parliament any frequent or proper occasion of writing to you' and his wish, in the absence of serious Parliamentary business, not 'to interrupt you with unnecessary letters'.[7] He made the point that the infrequent sessions of Parliament had not been helpful to anyone, least of all a provincial corporation seeking to promote private bills, but he was ready to do what he could by 'giving you account that I am here in Town in good health, God be praised, and vigour, ready to take that Station in the House of Commons which I obtain by your favour and hath so many years continued'. Rather self-righteously he added that he would strive to do his duty 'and in the more generall concerns of the nation shall God willing maintaine the same incorrupt mind and cleare Conscience, free from Faction or any self-ends, which I haue by his Grace hitherto preserved'.

On 15 February he was at last able to report that the fifteen-month prorogation had come to an end. Marvell's summary of the King's opening remarks to the session showed that it was to be business as usual:

He was pleas'd in a most weighty and gracious manner to profer on his part all things that might tend to the securing of the true Protestant Religion, the Libertyes and Propriety of the Subject and the Safety of the Nation: mentioning also his Debts & the necessity of building shipps.[8]

Parliament immediately plunged into a procedural quagmire to determine 'whether we act under a Prorogation or an Adjournment',[9] which affected whether resumed Bills could be judged now to be receiving their first or second readings. There was also the need to issue by-election writs, thirty-two seats having become vacant.

Behind this fussy concern with procedure the old enmities and conflicts were being revived. Shaftesbury and Buckingham were sent to the Tower 'for their High Contempt of the House' because they had the temerity to challenge the legitimacy of the proroguing. Marvell reported: 'To day I heare they are made close Prisoners.'[10] The session was, unsurprisingly after such a long intermission, a busy and hard-working one, which took its toll on MPs. 'I am in much weariness,' Marvell protested on 8 March, and on 17 March he pleaded to Mayor Foxley: 'I must beg your excuse for paper penn writing & euery thing. For really I haue by ill chance neither eat nor drunke from yesterday at noone till six a clock to night that the house rose.'[11] He was taking a keen interest in what was happening in Parliament and was particularly concerned at the Bill 'for securing the Protestant Religion, by educating the Children of the Royal Family therein' which was first introduced on 20 March. The old fears that the Royal Family was far too close to Catholicism – the King's brother was a declared Catholic and there were suspicions about the King himself – were sharpened by an anxiety that a Catholic could succeed to the throne if Protestants did not take action to ensure the King's heirs were brought up free from the taint of popery. It was an issue on which Marvell could not remain silent. In the debate on 27 March he rose to make his longest ever speech in Parliament, though once again his report to Hull made absolutely no mention of his intervention.

In the debate of the first reading Secretary of State Williamson, attempting to disarm objections that such a Bill was offensive to the King by in effect treating him with suspicion, had argued that it was necessary only 'should the misfortune befall the kingdom of a prince of the Romish religion'.[12] When the Bill came in for a second reading on 27 March it was greeted at first with a silence in the House, which Secretary

Williamson said was a token of its seriousness. Speakers immediately rose, however, to argue that it was a threat to royal prerogative and was handing power to the bishops. 'It is now a thesis amongst some churchmen, that the king is not king but by their magical unction,' said one MP, Mr Mallet. Marvell was the fourth speaker in the debate but, notwithstanding his abhorrence of Catholicism, he opposed the second reading. 'It is an ill thing, and let us be rid of it as soon as we can,' he told the House, adding: 'I am sorry the matter has occasioned so much mirth. I think there was never so solemn and sad an occasion as this bill before you.' He then proceeded to explain why he thought its introduction 'unseasonable'. He objected to its shockingly unadorned reference to the contingency of the 'death' of the King: 'It might have had a more modest word to have disguised it from the imagination (demise?).' Again attacking the injudicious drafting, he highlighted the reference to the eventuality 'that possibly the crown may devolve on a Popish government'. Marvell urged that this was something 'which ought not to be supposed easily and readily'. For one thing it was outrageous to suggest that the King was in any danger of meeting his death, and indeed the law made it treasonable 'to imagine the death of the king that is'. In an outburst of fervent loyalism, the putative author of 'The Statue in Stocks-Market' and 'A Dialogue between the Two Horses' declared: 'God be thanked for the king's age and constitution of body! The king is not in a declining age; and if we intermeddle in things of this consequence we are not to look into it so early, as if it was the king's last will and testament.' As for the raising of the spectre of a 'Popish successor', Marvell 'would not precipitate that evil, no, not in a supposition'. The king has world enough and time: 'Whilst there is time there is life, and whilst life, time for information, and the nearer the prospect is to the crown, information of judgement will be much easier.' Don't talk about it loosely now, he seems to be saying, for, when the true seriousness of the succession stares people in the face the fact will steady people's minds.

Marvell then went on to call the bill 'a great invasion on prerogative: to whom ever God shall dispose the kingdom, it is entire to the king'. He objected to the bishops being given power by the bill and suggested it would be just as appropriate or inappropriate for the power to be given to a delegation from the College of Physicians (a frivolous comparison that earned him a rebuke in committee the following day from the Speaker who 'cast a severe reflection'[13] on it). The fact is that 'this power is not fit to be lodged in any sort of persons whatsoever. Whatever prince God gives us, we must trust him. Let us not, in prevention of things remote, take that immoderate care in this bill.' Marvell said that instead: 'We may apply ourselves to preserve the people in the Protestant Religion.' If people lived good and virtuous lives as Protestants, he argued, that would be the best safeguard for the future of the religion. 'If we do not practise upon ourselves, all these Oaths and Tests are of no use; they are but phantoms.' He concluded: 'Whether this bill will prevent Popery, or not, this will secure the promotion of the bishops; it will make them certain.' In the contest between his anticlericalism, combined with a dislike for tests of allegiance on the individual, and his detestation of popery, the former triumphed. In a speech whose erudition – a learned reference to the Patriarch of Antioch – and elaborate metaphors obstructed its clarity and flow, Marvell had discharged himself rather uncomfortably. Before sitting down he confessed to the House: 'I am not used to speak here, and therefore I speak with abruptness.' The experience had not been an easy one for him. Although the bill was committed by 127 votes to 88 – and Marvell was appointed to the committee – it seems to have died of neglect and was not taken further. Two days later, however, Marvell was again on his feet, this time defending himself against the charge that he had been acting in a disorderly manner towards another Member of the House.

The incident was seized upon by Marvell's enemies in the House who tried to get him committed to the Tower for it. What seems to have happened is that, on approaching his place in the chamber, Marvell tripped over the feet of another MP, his old friend Sir Philip Harcourt. In putting out his hands to steady himself he appeared – to the hostile witnesses of the court party – to have landed 'a box on the ear' to Sir Philip. Evidently they complained to the Speaker, who had just reprimanded Marvell for his conduct in the earlier debate and now instigated, on 29 March, a debate about the incident because: 'I saw a box on the ear given, and it was my duty to inform the house of it.'[14]

With consummate lack of tact, Marvell rose to defend himself:

> *What passed was through great acquaintance and familiarity betwixt us. I neither gave him an affront, nor intended him any. But the Speaker*

> *cast a severe reflection on me yesterday, when I was out of the house, and I hope that, as the Speaker keeps us in order, he will keep himself in order for the future.*

Sir Job Charlton, MP for Ludlow, goaded by this impertinence, spluttered his indignation on behalf of the Speaker: 'You in the Chair, and a stroke struck! Marvell deserves for his reflection on you, Mr Speaker, to be called in question. You cannot do right to the house, unless you question it; I move to have Marvell sent to the Tower.' The Speaker then claimed to have seen a blow struck and a retaliation but Sir Philip Harcourt insisted: 'Marvell had some kind of a stumble, and mine was only a thrust; and the thing was accidental.' Secretary Williamson said that he could not excuse Marvell, 'who made a very severe reflection on the Speaker', and asked that Marvell withdraw so that the house could consider what should be done. Colonel Sandys was outraged that, instead of apologising, Marvell had made some disrespectful remarks to the Speaker: 'A strange confidence, if not an impudence!' Marvell then tried again to defuse the situation by saying that he was 'content to be a sacrifice' by withdrawing because he had such respect for the House. He added that he had simply seen an empty seat 'and going to sit in it, my friend put me by, in a jocular manner, and what I did was of the same nature. So much familiarity has ever been between us that there was no heat in the thing. I am sorry I gave offence to the house.' No doubt reflecting inwardly that his Commons interventions seemed to be rather incompetent and his habitual silence and reserve were well worth returning to, he added: 'I seldom speak to the house, and if I commit an error, in the manner of my speech, being not so well-tuned, I hope it is not an offence.' But the Speaker seemed reluctant to let the matter drop, insisting that he had seen a blow struck. With MPs becoming impatient at the issue being strung out, Sir Thomas Meres, the MP for Lincoln, rose to pronounce the last word: 'By our long sitting together we lose, by our familiarity and acquaintance, the decencies of the house. I have seen 500 in the house, and people very orderly; not so much as to read a letter, or set up a foot. Once could scarce know any body in the house, but him that spoke. I would have the Speaker declare that order ought to be kept; but as to that gentlemen [Marvell] to rest satisfied.' With that the matter does indeed seem to have rested.

Less than three weeks later Parliament was adjourned for an Easter recess from 17 April until 21 May, on which day there was an eclipse of the sun. On 10 May Marvell received the sum of £40 14s in Parliamentary wages but the frequent adjournments throughout the summer left him plenty of time for his own pursuits. 'I am much out of Towne,' he wrote to Sir Edward Harley on 7 August. He was making use of his leisure to write, probably in seclusion at Highgate, his most serious work, *An Account of the Growth of Popery*, which would appear, anonymously, at Christmas. In parallel with this mounting concern at the perceived Catholic threat, Marvell was anxious about the revival of attempts to suppress dissent. In Scotland, he reported to Sir Edward, the field conventicles were rife: 'And the proceedings against them as violent. Even poor herd-boys are fined shillings and sixpences.'[15] His reports of the popular hostility to the decision of the Bishop of Argyle ('who is also Parson of Glasgow') to limit the way in which the burial of a nonconformist minister's child was conducted in Glasgow leave little doubt about what he thought of these attempts to suppress dissent. In addition to these serious matters his letters to Hull were often padded out with gossipy detail, such as his report in July about what had transpired at the London sessions. A Frenchman had been indicted for the rape of a ten-year-old girl and another man 'for buggery of a Mare'.[16] Another case involved an indictment of a woman 'for beastliness with a Dog for wch she is condemned & will be executed'. Marvell added: 'I wish I had something better left to take of the ill relish of such horrid wickedness at the end of my Letter.'

Just before Christmas, Marvell was instructed by the Hull Corporation to pay a visit to James, Duke of Monmouth, the illegitimate son of the King. They asked him to procure six pieces of gold 'with a little silke purse'[17] and to present them to the Duke, who was the High Steward of Hull, 'as his annuall honorary from the town'. Monmouth had been involved in the incident of the slitting of Sir John Coventry's nose in 1670 and the murder of a beadle the following year, and therefore would be unlikely to prove an attractive figure to Marvell – but he was later put forward by Shaftesbury as a substitute for the Duke of York to succeed the King to the throne. Marvell's correspondence shows him making several visits to the Duke at the end of 1677, ostensibly on the Hull business, but it is possible that he may have discussed other things.[18]

On 27 December 1677, Marvell acknowledged a present of ale from

Trinity House. This time it was a full measure. 'I acknowledge all your favors and thanke you particularly for your Ale which came up in very good condition and is excellent Liquor,' he wrote. A similar gift was expected from the Corporation but had not yet arrived at his lodgings in Maiden Lane, Covent Garden. From that address he wrote to the Mayor to express his fear 'that there is a probability of a warre with France'.[19] Such an eventuality, he suggested, would have at least one desirable consequence: 'that by prohibiting their wines we were obliged to drinke so good Liquour'.[20]

28

No Popery

And as we are thus happy in the constitution of our State, so are we yet more blessed in that of our Church; being free from that Romish yoak, which so great a part of Christendom do yet draw and labour under.[1]

Early in 1678, Shaftesbury was released from the Tower, where he had languished for a year after his ill-judged attempt to challenge the legitimacy of the resumed Parliament the previous February. This was not an easy time for the opposition. The King and his minister, Danby, while not always pursuing the same policies, had nonetheless gradually fortified the position of the government by a combination of secret dealings with the French King and bribery of potential opponents. The notorious Titus Oates conspiracy, alleging a popish plot, would not be announced until the autumn. The opposition, whatever intimations it might have of the King's secret deals with Louis XIV, lacked clear evidence. Public opinion, however, was anti-French and vigorously anti-Catholic. The marriage of the Duke of York's daughter Mary to William of Orange was a popular move seen as strengthening Protestantism. By the end of the year a treaty with the Dutch would be signed, ostensibly placing England against France, but Charles continued his covert links with Louis, trying to secure more money from him in exchange for maintaining English neutrality. Opposition members like Marvell, who feared an international Catholic conspiracy, looked on in alarm at these machinations.

His new-year letter to Hull, referring to 'the probability of a warre with France', reflected the general mood of the opposition MPs. Not that the high-minded like Marvell were, in their personal dealings, averse to proposing a little inducement. In a letter written from his Covent Garden lodgings to the Trinity House Brethren on 8 January 1678, Marvell suggested to them, in regard to a Mr Fisher who had been of service to Trinity House in the matter of the timber importer Clipsham who was trying to avoid his dues: 'I thinke if you incouraged him sometime or other with a little vessell of your Ale it would be very well placed.'[2] The accounts of Trinity House for the year show that money was spent on 'two barrells of ale sent to Coll Gilby & Mr Marvell', a further 'tenne gynneys' that was 'Given to Mr Marvell for a gratuity for all his labour & paines & writeing letters in the business' and a further £2 11s 4d 'Spent now at Mr Marvell's comeing downe with Coll Gilby & him upon a treate'.[3] The Trinity House Warden, Thomas Coates, wrote from London to his fellows on 5 February to report on Marvell's shyness in accepting these gifts:

> *Accordinge to your order I waited on Mr Marvell att Westminster yesterday to whome I presented your reall respects with the testimony thereof your kinde token, which att the first he very modestly refused untill I did assure him if he did not accept itt the House would demonstrate their gratitude some way equivolent to itt. Then hee received itt desireinge me returne you his hearty thankes protestinge (and I doe beleive him) hee never expected such recompence for any service or kindnes hee had donne or could doe the House and would be ready to serve and assist them.*[4]

So grateful was Marvell for this significant addition to his Parliamentary income that he wrote soon afterwards, with just a hint of sanctimoniousness, to the Wardens saying: 'I find my self very much surprised lately by a Token which you were pleased to send me by Mr Coates. And truly I was very unwilling to have accepted having always desired rather to doe those offices of friendship where I could have no prospect of other gratification then the goodness of the Action.'[5] When this eloquent asseveration was over, Marvell pocketed the money.

Having just been elected a younger Warden of the Trinity House in London at Deptford, Marvell found himself, in the spring of 1678, caught in a conflict of interest. He was obliged to tell the Hull House: 'I am under some constraint, not hauing liberty being a member of this Trinity House to impart their resolutions to you upon this affaire and yet being desirous to doe you all reasonable service.'[6] This new appointment is testimony to Marvell's lifelong interest in mercantile and maritime business.

On the wider international stage, Marvell was apprehensive about the behaviour of the French, whose army was in Flanders. Reporting to the Hull Corporation on a range of trade sanctions against the French, and describing the French troop movements, he again predicted: 'So that all things compared it lookes like warre.'[7] If that were to be the case, he was confident that any extra expenses demanded by the King for the conduct of the war would be 'chearfully supplyed by all his good Subjects'.[8] Three days later, however, the House voted to confine such supply 'to the use of the French war in the strictest termes'[9] – knowing the propensities of the King in the matter of supply. One consequence of these war preparations was that more urgent business was laid aside, in particular measures to tackle 'the danger from the Growth of Popery'.[10] Nonetheless, a committee was established 'to consider of the dangers by the Growth of Popery and the Remedyes for the same'.[11] The House also received 'seuerall particulars in Monmouth and Herefordshire about Masses Priests &c: and other things too open and visible in those Countyes'.[12] Nothwithstanding the strength of Marvell's animus towards the Catholics he could still manage to maintain an equilibrium of sorts. In a letter to Hull on 30 April, after recounting some lurid details of the activities of the 'Popishly affected' in the Welsh Marches, he nonetheless entered the caveat that they could just be rumour: 'I write these things unwillingly as being of ill Report & whch therefore although fit to be communicated to persons of your prudence yet it may be prudent to keep within a narrow compasse.'[13] Throughout the early spring war seemed imminent but then the possibility of a peace between Holland and France began to emerge. In one of his last letters to his constituents, Marvell reported on the apparent moves towards peace and its likely acceptance by the Spanish Emperor 'so that all the late Alarum vanishes'.[14]

If the prospect of war had receded, the forward march of popery was certainly not, in Marvell's estimation, being halted. On 10 June he wrote to Will Popple a cleverly ironic letter that made it pretty clear that he was the author of an anonymous pamphlet that had been circulating for at least six months:

There came out, about Christmass last, here a large Book concerning the

> Growth of Popery and Arbitrary Government. *There have been great Rewards offered in private, and considerable in the Gazette, to any who could inform of the Author or Printer, but not yet discovered. Three or four printed Books since have described, as near as it was proper to go, the Man being a Member of Parliament, Mr* Marvell *to have been the Author; but if he had, surely he should not have escaped being questioned in Parliament, or some other Place.*[15]

Marvell's early biographers were in little doubt that this work was the triumph of their English patriot. 'He sets, in a true light, the miseries of a nation under a papal, and the blessings of a protestant administration,'[16] wrote Cooke. In the view of Thompson it was 'the means of discovering the Popish Plot, and other diabolical intrigues of the Jesuits'.[17] Marvell's conspiracy theory may now strike us as excessive but the historical evidence, much of which would have been unavailable to him, bears out at least some of his contention that Parliament was being hoodwinked by the King, who was engaged in covert dialogue with a foreign power of a kind that was profoundly undemocratic and unconstitutional. The full title of the work indicates its scope and its historical specificity: *An Account of the Growth of Popery, and Arbitrary Government in England: More Particularly from the Long Prorogation of November, 1675, Ending the 15 February 1676 [1677 n.s.], till the Last Meeting of Parliament the 16th of July 1677.* The 1678 edition, published after his death and naming him as the author, adds that it was 'Recommended to the Reading of all *English* Protestants'.

The perceived threat from the Catholic European powers rather than the nature of the Catholic religion itself was the primary motor of Marvell's animosity. He was capable of admitting the sincerity of individual Catholics and even of acknowledging their disabilities in the state, but this anonymous work begins badly with a highly prejudicial attack on Catholicism that does Marvell little credit. It is in fact one of the canonical texts in the long history of English anti-Catholicism. With the overemphatic rhetoric of a fundamentalist preacher thumping the lectern in a corrugated iron mission hut, he inveighs against Catholicism in the usual terms. Catholicism, he argues, combines the worst abominations of Judaism, Islam ('Plain Turkery') and paganism, with some 'peculiar absurdities of its own in which those were deficient'.[18] The whole package, which has no claim to be considered a religion at all, is 'carried on, by the bold imposture of priests under the name of Christianity' and constitutes a 'last and insolent attempt upon the credulity of mankind'. In particular, by confining its use of scripture to the language of Latin it deprives 'the poor people' of direct access to the word of God. It practises 'idolatry' in its worship of saints and angels, and it builds its foundation on 'incredible Miracles and palpable fables'. Its central enormity is the Mass, conducted:

> *in an unknown tongue, and intangled with such Vestments, Consecrations, Exorcisms, Whisperings, Sprinklings, Censing and phantasticall Rites, Gesticulations, and Removals, so unbecoming a Christian Office, that it represents rather the pranks and ceremonies of Juglers and Conjurers.*[19]

But the ultimate provocation to the good sense of an English Protestant is the doctrine of transubstantiation: 'that Transubstantial solacism . . . a new and antiscriptural Belief, compiled of Terrours to the Phancy, Contradictions to Sense, and Impositions on the Understanding'. In exchange for blind loyalty to this ceremonial nonsense, the Catholic powers have 'discharged the people from all other services and dependence', in sharp contrast to the English constitutional position where the citizen is not dictated to by a theocracy. The scandal of indulgences makes the Pope 'clerk of the spiritual market' in which 'the worse Christians men are, the better customers'. Absolute power and infallibility is granted to the Pope, who 'does persecute those to death who dare worship the Author of their Religion instead of his pretended Viceregent'. Finally, the celibate Catholic priests – and this is an interesting observation from the unmarried Marvell – 'by remaining unmarried, either frustrate human nature if they live chastly, or, if otherwise adulterate it'.

Marvell contrasts this 'gross superstition' with the English way. In contrast to the states of Catholic Europe, skewed towards absolutism and insensitive to individual civil liberties, he argues, 'here the subjects retain their proportion in the Legislature; the very meanest commoner of England is represented in Parliament, and is a party to those laws by which the Prince is sworn to govern himself and his people'.

Marvell then claims in regard to the King (he must have been aware of the ironic cast of these words as he framed them, for the whole tenor of the pamphlet is to contradict this comforting assertion in reality): 'His very Prerogative is no more than what the Law has determined.' The English King is 'the onely intelligent ruler over a rational People'. These fine words on the constitutional position of the King as dutiful and answerable servant of his people bear little relation to the reality Marvell's pamphlet sets out to describe. He adds that there is absolutely no question of England going back to the unfortunate 'Romish perswasion' of its past, because for Anglicans their doctrine is 'true to the principles of the first institution' of Christianity. One look at the state of things in Europe will teach England how fortunate she is in avoiding the enslavements of the Continent and will bolster her Euroscepticism.

Although Marvell was a member of the Parliamentary committee that examined the evidence of the causes of the Great Fire, and which reached a sceptical conclusion, he now asserts baldly that it was a deliberate act of foreign papists 'acted by Hubert, hired by Pieddelou, two Frenchmen'. With an interesting dash of pragmatism, Marvell concludes that there is little prospect of the English returning to their original religion, 'the Protestant Religion being so interwoven as it is with their secular interest'. Reclaiming the Church lands confiscated after the Reformation now would 'make a general earthquake over the nation'. In spite of all these points, there are still those in England, Marvell contends in terms that would make his old friend, Milton, turn in his grave, who would wish to 'introduce a French slavery' by converting England back to Catholicism:

> *For, as to matter of government, if to murther the King be, as certainly it is, a fact so horrid, how much more hainous is it to assassinate the Kingdom? and as none will deny, that to alter our Monarchy into a Commonwealth were treason, so by the same fundamental rule, the crime is no less to make that Monarchy absolute.*[20]

After these preliminaries, Marvell proceeds to the real matter of his pamphlet, which is not just to inveigh against Catholicism but to offer 'a naked narrative' of recent events, quoting documents, many of which would not be in the public domain, in order to expose the conspiracy working against the government of the land. Vitiated like all conspiracy theories by its lack of specific evidence and its shadowy gesturing at possible culprits, the remainder of the pamphlet is nonetheless characterised by a more level and coherent tone than his earlier ribaldries and satires such as *Mr Smirke.* The urgency of his self-appointed task seems to have sobered and controlled his prose. The thesis had already been stated plainly in the opening pages:

> *There has now for divers years a design been carried on to change the lawful Government of England into an absolute Tyranny, and to convert the established Protestant Religion into downright Popery: than both which, nothing can be more destructive or contrary to the interest and happiness, to the constitution and being of the king and kingdom.*[21]

In fact Marvell goes a little further back in history to the beginning of the decade in search of evidence of the conspiracy. The proroguings of Parliament in the 1670s (which did actually tend to happen when the King was being supplied with covert funds from France) are seen as opportunities for the conspirators 'to give demonstrations of their fidelity to the French King'. He attacks, surprisingly in view of the effort he put into defending it in *The Rehearsal,* the Declaration of Indulgence in 1672 as a bid by the 'hellish conspiracy' to 'defraud the nation of all that religion which they has so dearly purchased . . . it was the masterpiece therefore of boldness and contrivance in those conspirators to issue the declaration'. Not for the first time in his political career, Marvell thus radically revised his stance. In spite of a backhanded tribute to the crypto-Catholics like Clifford who 'honourably forsook their places rather than their consciences' in 1673, when the Test Act was introduced in the wake of the repeal of the Declaration, Marvell is contemptuous of the Duke of York, who married a Catholic, Mary of Modena. 'Such marriages,' he declared, 'have always increased Popery, and incouraged priests and jesuits to pervert His Majesty's subjects.' Claiming that the conspirators made overtures to 'the old Cavalier party' to boost their strength, Marvell accused them of an intent 'to have raised a Civil War'.

Coming closer to the present – the long prorogation of 22 November 1675 to 15 February 1677 which he called 'this vast space' in which the conspirators flourished – Marvell, in default of harder evidence, notes that it is 'very remarkable' that five judges were replaced during this period: 'What French counsel, what standing forces, what parliamentary bribes, what national oaths, and all the other machinations of wicked men have not yet been able to effect, may be more compendiously acted by twelve judges in scarlet.' He then turned his attention to his fellow MPs, observing that it was 'too notorious to be concealed, that near a third part of the House have beneficial offices under his Majesty'. A further third were 'hungry and out of office' and therefore angling for the same sort of favour. In spite of having been elected to oppose the court party, these country MPs 'when they come up, if they can speak in the House, they make a faint attack or two upon some great minister of State'. Fortunately, there remain among the final third some who are 'constant, invariable, indeed Englishmen' who can be counted upon to behave decently. But, in truth, Parliament presents a sorry picture: 'It is less difficult to conceive how fire was first brought to light in the world than how any good thing could ever be produced out of an House of Commons so constituted.' There is a fatally complacent conviviality among these Parliamentary time-servers, in Marvell's picture: 'They live together not like Parliament men, but like so many goodfellows met together in a publick house to make merry. And which is yet worse, by being so thoroughly acquainted, they understand their number and party, so that the use of so publick a counsel is frustrated, there is no place for deliberation, no perswading by reason, but they can see one another's votes through both throats and cravats before they hear them.' Only the four lords, including Shaftesbury, who challenged the prorogation and were sent to the Tower for doing so earn Marvell's unqualified praise in this Parliament. As he reviews in detail the events of 1677, Marvell sees the hand of the conspirators in everything: 'For all things betwixt France and England moved with that punctual regularity, that it was like the harmony of the spheres, so consonant with themselves, although we cannot hear the musick.'

Marvell ends by claiming to have 'laid open' the conspiracy if the country will care to examine the evidence: 'yet men sit by, like idle spectators, and still give money towards their own tragedy'. The pamphlet, he claims, was written 'with no other intent than of meer fidelity and service to his Majesty', when he knew full well that if there was any conspiracy the King was at the heart of it. Far from welcoming its publication, however, the government set on foot immediately a hunt for the author. The *London Gazette* for 21–25 March 1678 carried an advertisement offering a reward of £50 for anyone who could find 'the Printer, Publisher, Author, or Hander to the Press' of this and other 'Seditious, and Scandalous Libels against the Proceedings of Both Houses of Parliament'.[22] The person who found the actual 'Hander of it to the Press' could expect a reward of £100.

It was not until after Marvell's death in the summer of 1678 that Sir Roger L'Estrange confidently identified the poet as the author in a letter to Secretary of State Williamson.

29

A Death in Bloomsbury

Some suspect that he was poysoned by the Jesuites, but I cannot be positive.[1]

John Aubrey

Was Andrew Marvell gay? That he was unmarried and lived the life of a frequently solitary bachelor in modest lodgings where he kept a supply of wine to 'refresh his spirits, and exalt his muse', in Aubrey's phrase, can hardly be brought forward in evidence. Being in or out of the state of marriage is not decisive in settling questions of sexual orientation. Marvell's secretiveness, the complex ambiguity that surrounds so many of his thoughts and actions, and that lies at the root of his poetics, makes it difficult to produce confident assertions about that most private of areas in a life, a person's sexuality. What we have can best be described as a certain body of insinuation, some of which has already been hinted at above: the faint trace of incipient paedophilia in 'Young Love', the rough allusions of his enemies in the pamphlet wars of the 1670s both to his putative sexual impotence and to a similarly attributed habit of sodomy with the author of *Paradise Lost.* The distinguished critic Sir William Empson – with a possible irony given that he was one of the few Marvell scholars to have been convinced of the evidence that Marvell had a wife – thought he detected the whiff of unnatural sex in Marvell's descriptions of the brawny and perspiring mower in 'Damon the Mower'. 'I think he fell in love with the Mower,'[2] Empson opined, and again: 'I do not know that any other poet has praised the smell of a farm hand.'

One particular passage in the poem 'The Loyall Scot' has disturbed a number of critics, including both Empson and Elsie Duncan-Jones, the latter pointing out that the youthfulness of the naval hero Captain Archibald Douglas, who refused to desert his ship as it was consumed with flames, is 'rather uncomfortably'[3] stressed. Empson, in another essay, thinks that: 'The case is so bad as to excite grave suspicion against the subconsciousness of the poet.'[4] Traces of homoeroticism in the portrayal of Douglas might be detected in the two lines in 'The Loyall Scot' that originally appeared as part of 'Last instructions to a Painter': 'Not so brave Douglass, on whose Lovely Chin/The Early down but newly did begin,/And modest beauty yet his sex did vail,/Whilst Envious virgins hope hee is a Male.' The poem goes on to note that 'His shady locks Curl back themselves to seek/Nor other Courtship knew but to his Cheek' – a dash of narcissicism now entering the picture of adolescent loveliness. In the later lines, the youthful sexual innocence of Douglas modulates into a picture of his death by fire, in which the description is unnaturally prolonged and mixed in with what could be sexual feeling: 'Like a glad lover the fierce Flames hee meets/And tries his first Imbraces in their sheets . . . His burning Locks Adorn his face divine.' Empson recoils: 'I find this disgusting, and all too likely to well up from the worst perversion, that of Gilles de Rais, the craving to gloat over the torturing of a tender innocent.'[5]

Marvell's is not a poetry of personality. He does not follow a confessional aesthetic. His characteristic poetic motion is to proceed by examining alternatives and holding them in balance, dramatising conflicts in search of an equipoise, using a deliberate ambiguity. In poems like 'Young Love' or 'The Loyall Scot' he may be doing no more than playing with hints and shades of feeling for poetic effect. Or he may not. What is certain is that no reliable evidence for his actual conduct in life can be derived from these sources. If he was a closet homosexual (and it is difficult to imagine any other kind at that historical epoch, particularly among Members of Parliament already coping with an array of vigorous enemies keen to pounce on any imagined misdemeanours), leaving his lodgings at night to seek illicit pleasure with young men in the smoky taverns and alleyways of Covent Garden and the City, there is no evidence for it.

Marvell's last surviving letter was written on 6 July 1678, to the Corporation that had employed him as its Parliamentary representative for nearly twenty years. It was a typical combination of Parliamentary bulletin and selective concentration on the matters that would interest the Hull merchants most: an 'Additional Impost upon Wines'.[6] The House was thinning out, as the meagre number of votes on either side of the divison on this issue attested. 'Things tend toward an end of the Session,' Marvell explained. Nine days later the House was prorogued and by the end of the month the MP was in Hull, attending a formal meeting of the Court of the Corporation. According to the minutes for 29 July: 'the Court and Mr Marvell held severall discourses about the Towns affaires'.[7] An audit book notes that the local worthies spent £3 8s 4d on a municipal lunch or 'collation' 'to give Coll Gilbe & Squier Marvell Burgesses of Plement for this towne a treatment for meate & wines'.[8] Two days later, France and Holland signed a peace treaty at Nijmegen. The Cavalier Parliament in which Marvell had sat since 1661 had only six months to go before being finally dissolved.

After completing his round of municipal duties, and no doubt having visited his family and friends in Hull, Marvell returned to London. Somewhere between leaving Hull on 9 August and arriving in the capital, he contracted a fever, traditionally described as a tertian ague but possibly malarial, which brought him down very low. Although his lodgings were in Maiden Lane, Covent Garden, his sickbed was on the north side of Great Russell Street in Bloomsbury (the site now occupied in part by the forecourt of the British Museum). A doctor was summoned and his intervention seems to have made matters worse. He later recounted his treatment to another doctor, Richard Morton, who published in 1692 a Latin treatise describing it as an example of what can happen when the wrong drugs, particularly opiates, are administered at the wrong time. Morton's account, written by a man who shared Marvell's religious and political opinions, affords posterity an unusually detailed account of the poet's medical treatment.[9] On arrival at Great Russell Street, the 'conceited doctor', as Morton calls him, instead of prescribing an ounce of quinine as a cure for the intermittent fits produced by the ague, bled and sweated the patient in a way that Morton strongly disapproved. He had Marvell almost buried in stiflingly thick blankets under the impression that the heavy sweat would counteract the cold shivers which generally accompany the onset of the ague fit. As to the bleeding, Morton considered that it was extremely unwise to bleed a man aged fifty-seven.

On Friday 16 August, Marvell died in a coma brought on by these medical attentions. Immediately, in that overheated atmosphere which preceded the discovery of the Titus Oates plot, speculation grew that he had been poisoned – 'by the Jesuites', according to Aubrey, who later crossed out in his manuscript the qualifying 'but I cannot be positive'. The popular name for the quinine that might have saved him had it been applied was 'Jesuit's powder', so called because it was introduced to Europe by Jesuit missionaries.

Marvell's presence in Great Russell Street, rather than in Maiden Lane, can be explained by the fact that in June 1677 he had taken out a lease on a property in this rapidly developing part of London, in order to be of service to the two young Hull-born bankers, Richard Thompson and Edward Nelthorpe, whose merchant bank, Nelthorpe & Co, had collapsed in 1676 after a run on the bank by creditors starting in the autumn of 1675. Two other partners were John Farrington and Edmund Page. Fleeing from their creditors, Thompson and Nelthorpe took refuge in the house in Great Russell Street that Marvell had leased in the name of his housekeeper, Mary Palmer, from a John Morris. Nelthorpe was known to his neighbours only as 'Mr White'. The Bloomsbury household contained at various times the two bankrupts, Mary Palmer, Thompson's wife, Dorothy, and a servant. Marvell himself remained in Maiden Lane, where he kept his papers and valuables, but he was presumably a regular visitor to Great Russell Street. In sheltering from the law two bankrupts who owed people money, Marvell might be considered to have been in an ethically dubious position. It is unlikely, however, that he would have seen it in this light. Doing favours to the Hull business community and to people related to him by birth was quite proper as far as Marvell was concerned. The fact that his relatives had clashed with Sir Robert Viner and were ardent anti-Royalists would have increased his sense of their being a deserving case. As well as upsetting the City establishment, the bankrupts had also clashed with the East India Company. Although they had suffered heavy shipping losses in the period leading up to their business collapse in March 1676, they may also have been the victims of a vendetta in the City when their offer to pay compensation, or a 'composition', to their creditors was rejected by a minority of those creditors after lobbying by the Lord Mayor.[10] Marvell may have considered that the balance needed tilting a little in their direction. He may also have invested what few savings he had in the bank, again for patriotic reasons as a man of Hull, and therefore could have been an interested party as a creditor himself. In what would now be considered a highly dubious conflict of interest, he actually sat on the Commons committee appointed to consider a bill introduced on 4 February 1678 'for the better Discovery of the Estates of Richard Thompson, Edward Nelthrop, and others, Bankrupts'. In their own published account of what happened, *The Case of Richard Thompson and Company: With Relation to their Creditors* (1678), the two claimed that they had become 'in the compass of one Year the sad Objects of common Obloquy, or Pity'.

Marvell had first become directly involved with the affairs of the bankrupts when his name appeared on a bond for repayment of £500 on 9 June 1677.[11] Edward Nelthorpe had taken the money to Charles Wallis, a London goldsmith, presumably hoping to keep the cash out of the hands of any creditors and trusting Marvell to take good care of the bond. Three days later the two principal bankrupts disappeared into the obscurity of a Great Russell Street lodging leased in someone else's name (though Thompson spent some time in hiding at the home of his brother-in-law Major Braman in Chichester in the early part of 1678). The *London Gazette* published in January 1678 an advertisement offering a reward for any information about the whereabouts of the four partners. John Farrington gave himself up and was imprisoned in the King's Bench prison but was apparently allowed to come and go into the City as he pleased. Edward Nelthorpe died a month later than the poet, on 18 September, and Thompson assumed management of the house, paying Mary Palmer her housekeeper's salary of £10 a year. The survivors then began a lawsuit that dragged on until 1684. Records of it have survived, in which Mary Palmer asserted that, far from being Marvell's housekeeper, she was in fact his wife and had been secretly married to him since 1667. When the first edition of Marvell's poems was published in 1681 the title page was followed by a short note 'To The Reader':

> *These are to Certifie every Ingenious Reader, that all these Poems, as also the other things in this Book contained, are Printed according to the exact Copies of my late dear Husband, under his own Hand-Writing, being found since his Death among his other Papers, Witness my Hand this 15*th *day of* October, *1680.*
>
> Mary Marvell

According to Mary Palmer/Marvell's deposition, now in the Public Record Office, Farrington approached her a day or two after Marvell's death and asked her for the keys of the Maiden Lane lodgings. Without her having the chance to inspect what was there, Farrington carried off various hampers, trunks and financial bonds and bills, including – Mary Palmer was convinced – the bill for £500 referred to above which she was anxious to acquire. In the usual interpretation of her motives, she was ready to pretend she was the poet's widow in order to secure it. A little later than Farrington, she herself called at Maiden Lane and found nothing more than 'a few Books & papers of small value'.[12] That negligible heap of things would have included the manuscript of 'To his Coy Mistress'. Farrington rejected entirely this version of events, claiming that he had never had the keys, but the records show that he began to take an interest in Marvell's estate, filing a legal request, a caveat, in the name of Marvell's sister in Hull, Mrs Blaydes, to prevent anyone taking out administration of the estate without his knowledge. He accused Mary Palmer, in one deposition, of pretending to have been Marvell's wife immediately after his death and of putting on a tearful act in order to inveigle money for the funeral out of his relatives in Hull. She also offered, 'by insinuating & crafty speeches', to be of service to Farrington, who thought her 'an ill woman' whose aim was to defraud Farrington of Nelthorpe's estate as well as getting her hands on Marvell's money.

In the end she was granted administration of Marvell's estate, jointly with John Greene, in September 1679, a year after the poet's death. The £500 was now pursued by Mary Palmer for herself and Farrington for the Nelthorpe estate. Inevitably, litigation ensued, in the course of which the other litigants began to question, apparently for the first time, Mary Palmer's claim to be Marvell's wife. Farrington argued that Mary Palmer was a housekeeper who never even shared a table with Marvell and who was his social and intellectual inferior: 'Nor is it prbable that the said Andrew Marvell who was a Member of the house of Comons for many years together & a very learned man would undervalue himselfe to intermarry with so mean a pson as shee the said Mary then was being the widdow of a Tennis Court Keeper in or near the City of Westm who died in a mean condicon.' Mary Palmer ingeniously replied that it was precisely this difference of condition that led Marvell as 'a Parliamt man and a Learned man' to disguise the marriage and that she played along with the concealment by eating separately in the servant's quarters. She went further by asserting that the marriage took place on 13 May 1667 at the Church of the Holy Trinity in the Little Minories and defied anyone to consult the marriage register – a document that no longer exists. The case finally came to court on 15 November 1682 – well after the publication of the volume of poems – but more than a year would elapse before the second hearing at which the Court of Chancery finally decided, in June 1684, that the bond was part of the estate of Nelthorpe. When she died in November 1687 her entry in the burial register of St Giles-in-the-Fields read Mary Palmer, not Mary Marvell.

If Marvell's marriage is not categorically disproved by this evidence, it is certainly extremely difficult to sustain belief in it after a reading of his substantial correspondence and an examination of the records of his life. Nowhere does he reveal himself as anything other than a single man, enjoying the company of friends but living alone in a solitary, reserved existence. If Mary Palmer was his wife it would need to have been an arrangement of the kind she describes, being kept like a Victorian mistress, unacknowledged, unknown to any of his family, business associates, or acquaintances in the political world. Given Marvell's ability to hold various worlds in suspension, his secretiveness, his reserve, it cannot be said to be utterly implausible, but the truth will never be known.

Two days after he died, Marvell was buried in St Giles-in-the-Fields. Anthony Wood said that he was told by the sexton that Marvell was interred under the pews 'in the south isle by the pulpit'.[13] Two days later, two of the Hull Trinity House Brethren, Thomas Coates and Edward Hodgson, wrote to Marvell's friend Dr Robert Witty to say that their messenger, unable to find Marvell at his Covent Garden lodgings, made inquiries and discovered that he was dead 'for which we are all very sorry and as unhappy in our loss of so faithful a friend to our society'.[14] The Corporation voted £50 towards the funeral expenses and for a monument at St Giles that no longer exists (if it ever did), the church having been rebuilt in the eighteenth century. Legend has it either that the monument was destroyed in 1682 during the reaction against the Whigs or that the rector refused to allow the erection of a monument to such a man as Marvell. In St Giles Church today there is only the epitaph of 1764, the words thought to have been composed by his nephew Will Popple, with their echo of Eliot's famous 'tough reasonableness beneath the slight lyric grace' in the reference to his 'joining the most peculiar graces of wit & learning with a singular penetration, & strength of judgement'. It stresses his Parliamentary service as 'a true patriot' and judges him finally to be: 'a strenuous asserter of the constitution, laws & liberties of England', the character his reputation would now assume until the recovery of his full poetic reputation in the early twentieth century.

30

The Island's Watchful Sentinel

But whether Fate or Art untwin'd his thread,
Remains in doubt. Fames lasting Register
Shall leave his Name enroll'd as great as theirs,
Who in Philippi for their Country fell.[1]

Shortly after Marvell's death the above anonymous lines were written, although they were not published until 1697 in the collection *Poems on Affairs of State.* As well as hinting darkly at the possibility that Marvell did not die a natural death, they are the first foundation stone of the Marvell legend. For the next two centuries or more, Marvell would be regarded as his admiring contemporaries largely saw him: an incorruptible English patriot on the Roman model, a defender of English liberties against the threat from Europe, an island hero rather than a poet. Like all such legends a grain of truth was combined with rather more exaggeration. Marvell was indeed a courageous advocate of religious toleration, notwithstanding his deep prejudice against European Catholicism. A certain kind of English liberal outlook, about which it is no doubt easy to be complacent, finds its best expression in some of Marvell's writings and official correspondence: the belief that the citizen has rights and freedoms that should not be surrendered lightly; that the balance of power between the metropolitan elites and provincial society always needs a little rectification in favour of the latter; that the power wielded by monarchical, civil, and ecclesiastical authorities must always be monitored with vigilance by the active citizen and required to justify any encroachment on the liberties of the individual. Although his Parliamentary interventions were few and not always entirely happy, Marvell seems to have been consistent in his principles. The same anonymous poet calls him 'this Islands watchful Centinel'. The purity of the legend, however, has to be considered a little diluted when one examines the various instances recorded above of slightly questionable behaviour or partiality to questionable friends and associates, or the rewriting of history and the revision of his personal place within it. Even if one does not go so far as the distinguished Marvell critic Sir Frank Kermode, who judged passages in his political poetry 'odious',[2] one might hesitate to elevate Marvell to sainthood. In one of many internal contradictions in this complex man – that between principle and a principle of pragmatism – there was sometimes too much of a readiness to adopt a new position on practical grounds, forgetting former objections and beliefs. Sitting generally on the fence, Marvell could sometimes leap off it with surprising agility. Equally, the peculiarly English stamp of his Yorkshire-rooted patriotism did indeed occasionally carry a xenophobic undertow, but he was a poet steeped in European literary culture, and in particular that of the Latin language. An accomplished linguist, an eager reader, a keen and knowledgeable traveller, Marvell cannot in any sense be compressed into the mould of a late twentieth-century 'Euro sceptic' or Little Englander.

The Marvell legend continued to be burnished after his death. *An Account of the Growth of Popery* and the verse satires attributed to him were frequently reprinted throughout the eighteenth century. In the year of his death a posthumous work, *Remarks upon a Late Disingenuous Discourse,* written by 'A Protestant' but from Marvell's hand, appeared. A defence of John Howe, former chaplain to Cromwell, who had written a tract on predestination, it was probably the last thing on which Marvell had been working when he died. It is a characteristic attack on otiose theological debate, on 'those peevish questions which have overgrown Christianity' with 'endless disputes concerning the unsearchable things of God'.[3] In it he confesses that he 'cannot boast of any extraordinary faculty for disputation' but nonetheless comes to the defence of Howe as he came to the defence of Herbert Croft, condemning the pamphlet written by Howe's antagonist Thomas Danson for 'its street adages, Its odd ends of Latine, Its broken shreds of poets, and Its musty lumber of schoolmen'. The new critical prose of the late seventeenth century, influenced by the scientists, was making this old-fashioned, fussy discourse increasingly irrelevant. Had Marvell survived to write more prose he may well have developed a leaner, more tightly argued style. The signs of its beginning are present in his very late works. Summing up his task in this minor pamphlet, Marvell explained his own sense of his mission, in terms that would apply to his previous engagements in *The Rehearsal* and *Mr Smirke*:

> *As for myself, I expect in this litigious age, that some or other will sue me for having trespassed thus far on theological ground: but I have this for my plea, that I stepped over on no other reason than (which any man legally may do) to hinder one divine from offering violence to another.*[4]

With those words, Marvell's career as a prose polemicist ended.

Marvell's enemies as well as his panegyrists were active in the years after his death. John Dryden, whom Marvell had done much to provoke, made in the preface to his poem 'Religio Laici' an indirect allusion to an earlier Elizabethan pamphleteer: 'And *Martin Mar-Prelate* (the *Marvel* of those times) was the first Presbyterian Scribler, who sanctify'd Libels and Scurrility to the use of the Good Old Cause.'[5] In the contest between Whig and Tory, Marvell was inevitably conscripted into the former's ranks and his reputation became embroiled in their quarrels.

Apart from those brief biographical sketches by his contemporaries – John Aubrey, Gilbert Burnet, Anthony Wood, Samuel Parker[6] – the first attempt at a biography of Marvell was the short *Life of Andrew Marvell* attached to the first collected edition of his works published in 1726, nearly fifty years after his death, by Thomas Cooke, who claimed to have had the benefit of privileged conversations with the poet's surviving relatives, or as he put it, 'the Ladies his Nieces'.[7] Cooke – nicknamed 'Hesiod Cooke' after he translated the poet – was a man of Grub Street who died in poverty in Lambeth, his daughter being forced on to the streets. Cooke made no bones about representing Marvell as a Whig hero: 'My design in this is to draw a pattern for all free-born Englishmen in the life of a worthy patriot.' He sketched out the first draft of the Marvell legend by painting him as combining poverty and high principle, and living dangerously because of the threat he posed to the rich and powerful. Another fifty years later, a large three-volume edition of Marvell's works, retailing at three guineas a set with a subscribers' list that included Edmund Burke and John Wilkes MP, 'the friend of liberty', was edited by Captain Edward Thompson and dedicated to the Mayor and Aldermen of Hull. It too contained a floridly characterised *Life of That Most Excellent Citizen and Uncorrupted Member of Parliament, Andrew Marvell* that recapitulated the anecdotes of Cooke to confirm the developing image of one 'who was so far from being venal that he could not be bribed by the King into silence, when he scarce knew how to procure a dinner'.[8] The lyric poetry did not seem to be at the centre of this enterprise, which was closely involved with the agenda of the eighteenth-century Whigs.

In the nineteenth century Marvell's lyric poetry slowly began to emerge from behind the shadow of his political work. In 1819, Thomas Campbell printed 'The Bermudas', 'Young Love' and 'The Nymph complaining for the death of her Faun' in his 'Specimens of the British Poets' and two years later Charles Lamb mentioned Marvell's 'witty delicacy'.[9] The critic William Hazlitt praised Marvell several times, observing in 1825: 'Marvell is a writer almost forgotten: but undeservedly so. His poetical reputation seems to have sunk with his political party . . . His verses leave an echo on the ear, and find one in the heart.'[10] Other nineteenth-century poets and critics expressing their admiration in passing included Leigh Hunt, Ralph Waldo Emerson, John Clare (who paid him the compliment of passing off one of his own poems as being by Marvell), Edgar Allan Poe, John Greenleaf Whittier, James Russell Lowell, Matthew Arnold (who called the 'Horatian Ode' 'beautiful and vigorous') and Tennyson who loved to quote long passages from Marvell.

The first book-length, separately published life of Marvell was written by John Dove and appeared in 1832. In the same year, confusingly, Hartley Coleridge published a life of Marvell in a series called *The Worthies of Yorkshire and Lancashire* whose text seems indistinguishable from Dove's. In 1872 Alexander Grosart published a four-volume edition of Marvell's *Complete Works in Verse and Prose*, the last volume of which is still in use by scholars for those works which have not found a modern scholarly edition. He too attached an *Essay on the Life and Writings of Marvell*, which was an advance on all previous attempts and remained the standard account of his life until the start of the twentieth century when Augustine Birrell's

Andrew Marvell appeared in 1905 in the *English Men of Letters* series. Birrell was an MP and there is great emphasis in this biography on Marvell's Parliamentary career. Birrell observed: 'A more elusive, non-recorded character is hardly to be found . . . the man Andrew Marvell remains undiscovered.'[11] This seems to have been the verdict of the twentieth century, even when the critical rediscovery of Marvell accelerated with breakneck speed in the wake of T.S. Eliot's 1921 essay on the poet. This was also in spite of the appearance in 1928 of the major critical biography by French scholar Pierre Legouis: *André Marvell: Poète, Puritain, Patriote.* Written in French, the book was published in an edition of only 500 copies so many libraries do not have a copy, yet it has remained the standard biography of Marvell even though Legouis insisted that it was as much about the writing as the life ('*la biographie n'occupe pas ici la première place*'). In 1965 he produced an abridged English version, shorn of its valuable footnotes, but nonetheless updated.

In 1978, the next landmark in Marvell biography was the staging of an exhibition at the British Library to commemorate the tercentenary of Marvell's death. The catalogue of the exhibition by Hilton Kelliher, deceptively slight as its format was, represented an important advance on Legouis and was accompanied in the same year by a study of Marvell's life and writings by John Dixon Hunt. Two decades later there is no life of Marvell in print and there has arguably (given Legouis's insistence that his book was not a biography solely) never been a full biography of Marvell in the modern sense, concentrating primarily on the life and incorporating all the findings of recent biographical scholarship. In the belief that the time is right to attempt this, the present biography has worked from the premise that Marvell – however elusive and private his personality – can be known and better known than ever before. Given the cumulative work of scholars in recent decades, the old assumption that not enough was known about the poet can no longer be sustained. We have a clear outline of his life. We have his voice in public affairs. We have plentiful evidence of how he was seen by others. Above all we have the unique voice of the poetry itself: delicate, enigmatic, yet passionate as the man himself.

Marvell, since the full recovery of his reputation earlier in the twentieth century, has become one of the best-loved English poets. His life, even at its most tantalisingly elusive, remains fascinating both in itself and in the way it opens a fresh perspective on one of the most interesting periods in English history. Marvell was at the centre of that historical moment as he is at the centre of the development of English poetry in the seventeenth century. Like his contemporaries we may feel that we know him and we do not know him at the same time yet we cannot resist – nor cannot think that we would ever want to resist – the spell of his poetic voice.

Notes

Abbreviations

Aubrey: *Aubrey's Brief Lives* (1949) edited by Oliver Lawson Dick.
Burnet: *History of His Own Time* (1687; 1833 edition in six volumes). Oxford. Vol. I, p477.
Cooke: 'The Life of Andrew Marvell Esq' from *The Works of Andrew Marvell, Esq* (1726; 1772 edition), edited by Thomas Cooke, Vol. I.
Grosart: *The Works of Andrew Marvell Esq.* (1872; four Volumes). Vol. IV contains all prose cited other than *The Rehearsal* and the letters.
DNB: *The Dictionary of National Biography.*
Kelliher: *Andrew Marvell: Poet and Politician, 1621–78* (1978) by Hilton Kelliher. Catalogue of a British Library exhibition to commemorate the tercentenary of his death, 14 July–1 October 1678.
L.: *The Poems and Letters of Andrew Marvell: Volume II. Letters* (1971). Edited by H.M. Margoliouth. Third edition revised by Pierre Legouis with the collaboration of E.E. Duncan-Jones. Oxford.
Legouis 1928: *André Marvell: poète, puritain, patriote, 1621–1678* (1928). Paris and London.
Legouis 1965: *Andrew Marvell: Poet. Puritan. Patriot* (1965; second edition 1968). Oxford.
Leishman: *The Art of Marvell's Poetry* (1966; second edition 1968) by J.B. Leishman.
P.: *The Poems and Letters of Andrew Marvell: Volume I. Poems* (1971) edited by H.M. Margoliouth. Third edition revised by Pierre Legouis with the collaboration of E.E. Duncan-Jones. Oxford. All quotations in the present work are from this edition.
The Rehearsal: *The Rehearsal Transpros'd and The Rehearsal Transpros'd the Second Part* (1971), edited by D.I.B. Smith. Oxford.
Thompson: *The Works of Andrew Marvell Esq . . . With a New Life of the Author* (1776) by Captain Edward Thompson.
Wood: *Athenae Oxoniensis: An Exact History of All the Writers and Bishops Who Have Had Their Education in the University of Oxford* (1813 edition edited by Philip Bliss in four volumes), IV.

Prologue

1 See Tom Paulin, *The Day Star of Liberty: William Hazlitt's Radical Style* (1998), p57.

Chapter 1: By the Tide of Humber

1 Samuel Parker, *A Reproof to the Rehearsal Transpros'd, in a Discourse to its Author by the Author of the Ecclesiastical Politie* (1673), p270.
2 Joseph Hall, *Virgidemiarum*, Book VI (1598), satire I.v. 65–6: 'A starved tenement, such as I guesse/Stands straggling in the wastes of Holdernesse'. Cited Legouis (1928), p3n. Legouis describes 'La campagne environnante, plate et triste', p6.
3 A.S. Ellis, *Notes and Queries*, 17 April 1880, p319. Describes three manuscript wills, with notes by a local antiquary, William Cole.
4 The evidence is presented by L.N. Wall 'Andrew Marvell of Meldreth', *Notes and Queries*, September 1958, pp399–400.
5 *The Rehearsal*, p133.
6 *The Rehearsal*, pp203–4.
7 Thomas Fuller, *The Worthies of England*, ed. John Freeman (1952), p58.
8 Quoted by Kelliher, p27.
9 Samuel Parker, *A Reproof*, p77.
10 L.N. Wall, *Notes and Queries*, March 1958, p111.
11 Norman James Miller, *Winestead and Its Lords: the History of a Holderness Village* (1933), Hull, p169.
12 John Lawson, *A Town Grammar School Through Six Centuries* (1963), Hull, p83.
13 *Mr Smirke or The Divine in Mode* (1676), Grosart, Vol. IV, p15.
14 Samuel Parker, *A Reproof*, p227.
15 *The Rehearsal*, p41.
16 L.2.
17 Wood, pp230–2.
18 John Cook, *The History of God's House of Hull Commonly Called the Charterhouse* (1882), p148.
19 Thomas Gent, *History of Hull* (1735), p39.
20 Grosart, pxxx.
21 T. Tindall Wildridge, *The Hull Letters* (1886), p164.
22 John Cook, op. cit., p148.
23 Thomas Gent, op. cit., p141.
24 See Hartley Coleridge, *The Life of Andrew Marvell* (1835), pp4–5.

Chapter 2: Cringes and Genuflexions

1 Edward Thompson, *The Life of That Most Excellent Citizen and Uncorrupted Member of Parliament Andrew Marvell*, from *The Works of Andrew Marvell* (1776), Vol. III, p439.

2 Kelliher, p20; W.W. Rouse Ball, and J.A. Venn, *Admissions to Trinity College Cambridge* (1913), Vol. II.

3 *The Rehearsal*, p133–4.

4 Thomas Fuller, *The History of the University of Cambridge from the Conquest to the Year 1634* (1655), 1840 edition, p316ff.

5 See David Masson, *The Life of John Milton*, 2nd edition (1875), Vol. I, Chapter IV, p75ff.

6 See L.372n.

7 Pauline Burdon, 'The Second Mrs Marvell', *Notes and Queries*, February 1982, pp33–44. See also her two articles on 'Marvell and his Kindred', *Notes and Queries*, September 1984 and June 1985.

8 J. Kenyon, in *Andrew Marvell Essays on the Tercentenary of his Death* (1979), p7.

9 Kelliher, p22.

10 Ibid.

11 Thomas Cooke, *The Life of Andrew Marvell* (1726; 1772 edition), Vol. I, pp4–5.

12 See both Kelliher, p25, and H.M. Margoliouth, *Modern Languages Review* (1922), XVII, pp353–6.

13 *The Rehearsal*, pp131–2.

14 Kelliher, p26.

Chapter 3: At the Sign of the Pelican

1 Samuel Parker, *A Reproof*, p270.

2 John Milton, Letter to John Bradshaw, Public Record Office, *State Papers Domestic* 18/33, No. 75. Also in Kelliher, p56.

3 L.324

4 The evidence is reviewed by H.M. Margoliouth, *Modern Languages Review*, 1922, XVII, p355–6.

5 William Empson, 'Natural Magic and Populism in Marvell's Poetry', *Using Biography* (1984), p4.

6 A point made by John Kenyon, 'Andrew Marvell: Life and Times', R.L. Brett (ed.), *Andrew Marvell: Essays on the Tercentenary* (1979), p7–8.

7 See Margoliouth, loc. cit., pp356–60.

8 See, for example, L.364n.

9 H.M. Margoliouth, *Review of English Studies* (1926), Vol. 2, No. 5, January, pp96–7.

10 Kelliher, p31.

11 For this speculation as well as a full account of these deeds, see Pauline Burdon, 'Marvell after Cambridge', *British Library Journal*, 1978, Vol. 4, No. 1, pp42–8.

12 Samuel Parker, *A Reproof*, pp274–5.

13 P.274n.

14 P.270n.

15 The speculation about Edward Skinner and Marvell being his tutor in Rome was made by H.M. Margoliouth in a letter to *The Times Literary Supplement*, 5 June 1924, p356. The contrary evidence from Padua was presented by L.N. Wall in *Notes and Queries*, June 1962, p219.

16 Quoted in Augustine Birrell, *Andrew Marvell* (1905), p20.

17 Joseph Gillow, *A Literary and Biographical Dictionary of the English Catholics from the Breach with Rome, in 1534, to the Present Time*, Vol. II (1885), pp293–5.

18 Richard Fleckno, *The Idea of His Highness Oliver, Late Lord Protector etc with Certain Brief Reflexions on His Life* (1659).

19 The theory is Pauline Burdon's in 'Andrew Marvell and Richard Flecknoe in Rome', *Notes and Queries*, January 1972, pp16–18.

20 Burdon, loc. cit.

Chapter 4: The World's Disjointed Axle

1 'Tom May's Death', ll65–6. P.96.

2 The documents are at present in the collection of Hull City Libraries but are reproduced and discussed by Hilton Kelliher, *British Library Journal*, 1978, No. 4, pp122–9.

3 Christopher Hill, 'Society and Andrew Marvell', in *Puritanism and Revolution* (1958).

4 Wood, Vol. III, p.460.

5 Christopher Hill, *God's Englishman: Oliver Cromwell and the English Revolution* (1970; 1972 edition), p117.

6 Ibid., p115.

7 See for example: Pierre Legouis, 'Marvell and the New Critics', *Review of English Studies* (1957), Vol. VIII, No. 32, pp382–9; Frank Kermode, 'Marvell Transprosed', *Encounter*, November 1966, XXVII (5), pp77–84; John Carey, 'Introduction' in *Andrew Marvell: A Critical Anthology* (1969); J.P. Kenyon, 'In pursuit of Marvell', *Times Literary Supplement*, 17 November 1978, pp1341–2; Harold Tolliver, 'The Critical Reprocessing of Andrew Marvell', *English Literary History* (1980), No. 47, pp180–203.

8 John Carey, loc. cit.

9 Matthew Arnold, *Culture and Anarchy* (1869; ed. Dover Wilson, 1960), p163.

10 Samuel Johnson, *Lives of the English Poets* (Oxford edition, 1906), p14.

11 See Christopher Hill, 'Society and Andrew Marvell', loc. cit.

12 P.303n.
13 Wood, quoted in DNB entry on May.
14 Grosart, plxii.

Chapter 5: The Batteries of Alluring Sense

1 Legouis, 1928, p41.
2 Fairfax, *Short Memorials of Some Things to be Cleared During My Command in the Army*, in Edward Arber, *An English Garner* (1896), Vol. VIII, p565.
3 *The Rehearsal*, p135.
4 See Christopher Hill, loc. cit.
5 Fairfax, *Short Memorials*, op. cit.
6 *The Poems of John Milton* (ed. Carey, 1968), p321.
7 *Clarendon: Selections from The History of the Rebellion and Civil Wars and The Life by Himself*, ed. G. Huchns (1955), p314.
8 *Aubrey's Brief Lives*, ed. Oliver Lawson Dick (1949), p104.
9 For Fairfax's life, see Charles Firth's entry in DNB and M.A. Gibb, *The Lord General* (1938), which includes a selection of Fairfax's poems as an appendix.
10 The Fairfax–Alured connection is explored in depth by Pauline Burdon in *Andrew Marvell: Some Biographical Background: Who Recommended Marvell to Fairfax?* (n.d. but based on a paper delivered on 22 May 1975; copy in Local Studies Library, Hull), Polytechnic of Central London, School of Languages.

Chapter 6: Green Thoughts

1 Cited in P.280n.
2 See Richard Wilson, *Times Literary Supplement*, 26 November 1971; John Newman, *TLS*, 28 January 1972; A.A. Tait, *TLS*, 11 February 1972; J.G. Turner, *Notes and Queries*, December 1977, pp547–8; W. McLung, *Notes and Queries*, October 1979, pp433–4; Lee Erickson, *English Literary Renaissance*, 1979, Vol. 9 No. 1, pp158–68. The issue is also discussed by Kelliher, p46, and Dixon-Hunt, pp80–3.
3 For a valuable account of this genre see G.R. Hibbard, 'The Country House Poem of the Seventeenth Century', *Journal of the Warburg and Courtauld Institute*, 1956, XIX, pp159–74.
4 Certain similarities between the work of Marvell and Thomas Stanley are explored by Kelliher, pp33–4, who thinks their relationship has been underestimated.
5 See, for example, Lee Erickson, loc. cit.
6 See John Barnard, 'Marvell and Denton's Cataracts', *Review of English Studies* (1980), 31, pp310–15.

7 L.341.
8 L.356.

Chapter 7: A Gentleman Whose Name is Marvell

1 Samuel Johnson, 'Life of Milton', *Lives of the English Poets* (1906, ed. Arthur Waugh), p85.
2 Public Record Office, *Calendar of State Papers Domestic 1652–1653*, p176. SP 18/33, No. 75.
3 Phillips's *Life* is reproduced in Helen Darbishire, *The Early Lives of Milton* (1932), p74.
4 Aubrey, op. cit., p203.
5 See French, *The Life Records of John Milton* (1958), Vol. V, p278.
6 Cited in French, op. cit., Vol. III, p296.
7 *Historical and Genealogical Memoirs of the Dutton Family, of Sherborne in Gloucestershire, as Represented in the Peerage of England by the Right Hon. the Baron Sherborne* (1899, privately printed), author identified as Blacker Morgan, p120.
8 Dutton, *Memoirs*, p117.
9 L.304–5.
10 DNB quoting John Evans, *Chronological Outline of the History of Bristol* (1824), p192n.
11 P.315n, citing *Calendar of the Clarendon State Papers* (1869), Vol. II, p208.
12 Aubrey, op. cit., p118.
13 *The Rehearsal*, p79.
14 L.305–6.
15 On 3 August 1654 Marvell signed legal documents authenticating two leases at Eton, one to Oxenbridge. See Noel Blakiston, *Times Literary Supplement*, 8 February 1952, p109.

Chapter 8: A Fine and Private Place

1 J. Nickolls (ed.), *Original Letters and Papers of State . . . addressed to Oliver Cromwell*, 1743, pp95–6.
2 Ibid., p99.
3 For the 1653 date, see Roger Sharrock, *The Times Literary Supplement*, 31 October 1958, p625, challenged by Elsie Duncan-Jones, *TLS*, 5 December 1958, who proposes 1646. See also Sharrock's reply, *TLS*, 16 January 1959.
4 See for example my discussion of Matthew Arnold's poems to Marguerite in Nicholas Murray, *A Life of Matthew Arnold* (1996), p80.
5 Philip Larkin, 'The Changing Face of Andrew Marvell', *English Literary Renaissance*, Winter 1979, pp149–57. Reprinted in *Required Writing* (1983).
6 John Crowe Ransom, The New Criticism (1941), p311.
7 M.C. Bradbrook and M.G. Lloyd-Thomas in *Andrew Marvell* (1940), p43n.

8 Dutton was born 'about the year 1641' according to the only extant history of the family by Blacker Morgan, *Historical and Genealogical Memoirs of the Dutton Family* (1899). He had no issue and no portrait of him is known, unless it is 'the portrait hanging near the door of the dining-room at Sherborne House of a young man handsomely attired and with a gold bracelet upon his wrist'. A memorial in the parish church at Sherborne in Gloucestershire indicates that he died on 24 March 1675.

9 The letter is in the Public Record Office (State Papers Domestic, 18/123/40) and this postscript was first highlighted by Elsie Duncan-Jones in *TLS*, 20 June 1958. See also her letters, *TLS*, 2 December 1949 and 31 July 1953, for further details of the Saumur visit.

10 Legouis, 1965, p105.

11 Ibid., pp106–7.

12 Letter dated 15 August 1656 in the British Museum. Add. MS. 15858, f.135. See Duncan-Jones letters cited above.

13 Masson, *Life of Milton*, Vol. V, p367. Also quoted by Duncan-Jones, *TLS*, 31 July 1953.

14 The 1681 Folio of the Poems from the British Library (C.59.i.8), together with some pages from the Bodleian copy, were reprinted in 1969 by the Scolar Press in facsimile.

15 P.329n.

Chapter 9: A Good Man For the State to Make Use Of

1 Samuel Parker, *Bishop Parker's History of His Own Time* (1727; translated from the Latin by Thomas Newlin), p332.

2 See L.380n for some examples of these duties.

3 See Kelliher, 'Some Notes on Andrew Marvell', *British Library Journal* (1978), No. 4, pp129–34, for a very valuable summary of Marvell's work as a civil servant and for a reproduction of his handwriting in this document.

4 Christopher Hill, 'Society and Andrew Marvell', op. cit.

5 Kelliher, loc. cit., lists all the known documents in chronological order.

6 *Calendar of State Papers Colonial, 1574–1660* (1860), p462.

7 Whitelocke quoted in DNB.

8 *The Rehearsal*, Part 2, p203.

9 Wood, p232.

10 Cited in Dryden, *Absalom and Achitophel*, ed. James and Helen Kinsley (1961), p55n.

11 See, for example, R.I.V. Hodge, *Foreshortened Time: Andrew Marvell and Seventeenth Century Revolutions* (1978), who suggests that 'Upon the Hill and Grove at Bill-borow' could have been written in the 1660s.

12 *Life of Milton*, op. cit.

13 J.B. Leishman, *The Art of Marvell's Poetry* (1972 edition), p29.

14 Frank Kermode, 'Two Notes on Marvell', *Notes and Queries*, 29 March 1952, p136.
15 Samuel Parker, *A Free and Impartial Censure of the Platonick Philosophy* (1666), p74.
16 Wood, Vol. III, p1027.
17 Quoted in Christopher Hill, *God's Englishman* (1970; 1973 edition), p184.

Chapter 10: I Saw Him Dead

1 See W. Arthur Turner, 'Milton, Marvell and "Dradon" at Cromwell's Funeral', *Philological Quarterly* (1949), No. 28, pp320–3.
2 French, *The Life Records of John Milton* (1949–58), Vol. IV, p235.
3 L.372n.
4 L.307. I take it to be addressed to Popple because it uses the salutation normal between them: 'affectionate cosin'.
5 *Calendar of State Papers Domestic 1659–60*, p27.
6 French, *The Life Records of Milton*, Vol. IV, pp280–1.
7 L.307.
8 *Brief Lives*, op. cit., p125.
9 See Henning, *History of Parliament 1660–90* (1983) Vol. 1, p476.
10 See, for example, Annabel Patterson, *Andrew Marvell* (1994).

Chapter 11: His Majesties Happy Return

1 Hollis (1720–74) bequeathed the portrait of Marvell painted around 1662, which is now the property of the Hull Museums.
2 G.N. Clark, *The Later Stuarts 1660–1714* (1934), p1.
3 Cited by Mark Kishlansky, *A Monarchy Transformed: Britain 1603–1714* (1997), p222. A present-day historian whose picture of the King's return differs little in essential respects from Clark's.
4 *Journals of the House of Commons*, cited by Pierre Legouis in *Modern Languages Review* (October 1923), p421, who says the proposal to use Marvell came from a 'humorist' in the House.
5 For a full list of these committees see Legouis, ibid.
6 *The Rehearsal*, p44.
7 L.7.
8 L.2.
9 L.6.
10 L.8.
11 L.10.
12 Clarendon, op. cit., p83.
13 L.13.
14 *Parliamentary History of England, Vol. IV 1660–88* (1808), p162.

15 Quoted by French, *Life Records of Milton*, Vol. IV, p350.
16 Latham, p40.
17 R.C. Latham, 'Payment of Parliamentary Wages – the Last Phase', *English Historical Review* (1951), LXVI, 66, pp27–50.
18 Wildridge, *Hull Letters* (1887), p63.
19 Cited by Legouis (1928), p227n. The original anecdote seems to have been told in the *London Journal*, 13 May 1738.

Chapter 12: A Breach of the Peace

1 Anonymous author of *A Reproof to the Rehearsal Transpros'd* (1673), p77.
2 Henning, *History of Parliament*, Vol. III, p25.
3 L.17.
4 L.15.
5 L.18.
6 L.20.
7 L.21.
8 Quoted in DNB.
9 L.22.
10 L.24.
11 L.27.
12 L.26.
13 This account of Trinity House is derived from L.371n.
14 L.247.
15 L.28.
16 L.30.
17 L.33.
18 L.32.
19 L.32.
20 *Journals of the House*, Vol. 8, p389.
21 Quoted by Legouis in a valuable account of the whole incident in *Modern Languages Review* (October 1923), pp420–6.
22 Ibid., 20 March.
23 'Tom May's Death', line 86.

Chapter 13: Beyond Sea

1 Lytton Strachey, 'John Aubrey', *Portraits in Miniature* (1931), p19.
2 Basil Willey, *Seventeenth Century Background* (1950), p101.
3 L.248.
4 L.249.
5 For an account of the Spurn Lights issue see *Victoria County History of England: East Riding* (1969), pp401–2.

6 L.250.
7 L.251.
8 See L.373n for a letter to Edmund Popple announcing Marvell's safe arrival at the Hague.
9 Henning, *History of Parliament 1660–90* (1983), Vol. 1, says that the 'mysterious mission' may have been at the instigation of Sir George Downing who 'may have hoped to use him to trepan some of the English exiles there' (p25).
10 Hull Bench Books, quoted by Legouis (1928), p247n.
11 L.34.
12 L.34.
13 L.35.
14 L.36.
15 Samuel Parker, *A Reproof to the Rehearsal Transpros'd* (1673), p270.
16 Ibid., p245.
17 John Aubrey, *Brief Lives*, op. cit., p196.
18 Samuel Parker, *Bishop Parker's History of His Own Time* (1727), translated from the Latin by Thomas Newlin, pp332–4.
19 Richard Leigh, *The Transproser Rehears'd* (1673), p31.
20 L.37.
21 L.37–8.

Chapter 14: Peasants and Mechanicks

1 Guy Miège, *A Relation of Three Embassies from His Sacred Majesty Charles II to the Great Duke of Muscovie etc* (1669), p113.
2 All details of the voyage are taken from the account of Miège.
3 L.39.
4 L.254.
5 Quoted in Kelliher, p83.

Chapter 15: Sober English Valour

1 L.373n.
2 L.362n.
3 Henning, Vol. III, p25.
4 L.372n.
5 G.A. Aitken, *Satires of Andrew Marvell* (1892), pp124–5.
6 Thomas Cooke, *The Works of Andrew Marvell* (1726), Vol. I, p10.
7 Cooke, op. cit., p13.
8 Aubrey, p196
9 Discussed by Thompson, p471, but the threat is referred to on the title page of *The Rehearsal*, Part 2.

10 L.40.
11 L.362n.
12 L.41.
13 L.41.
14 *The Diary of Samuel Pepys*, ed. G. Gregory Smith (1935). Entry for 2 September 1666, pp412–13.
15 *Journals of the House*, Vol. 8, p629.
16 *The Somers Collection of Tracts* (1812), Vol. 7, pp615–34, 'A True and Faithful Account of the Infornmations Exhibited to the Committee Appointed to Inquire into the Late Burning of the City of London, 1667'.
17 L.42.
18 L.43.
19 L.45.
20 L.44.
21 L.45.
22 L.49.

Chapter 16: An Idol of State

1 L.50.
2 L.50.
3 L.51.
4 L.53.
5 L.55.
6 L.54.
7 L.54.
8 L.310.
9 L.56.
10 John Evelyn, quoted P.341n.
11 Cited in P.341n.
12 Samuel Pepys, *Diary*, 14 June 1667, p508.
13 Mary Tom Osborne, *Advice-to-a-Painter Poems 1633–1856: An annotated finding list* (1949), p12.
14 Samuel Pepys, *Diary*, p448.
15 Marvell's editor George deF. Lord prints them in his 1984 edition (Everyman edition, 1993) and justifies his attribution in 'Two New Poems by Marvell', *Bulletin of the New York Library*, November 1958 and July 1959.
16 Wood, cited P.348n.
17 Aubrey, p196.
18 John Evelyn, 18 September 1683, cited P.351n.
19 P.352n.
20 This is discussed in more detail in Chapter 29.
21 Clarendon, op. cit., p480.

Chapter 17: The Faults and the Person

1 Marvell's speech 14 October 1667 reported in *The Diary of John Milward Esq* (ed. C. Robbins, 1938), p328.
2 See E.E. Duncan-Jones, 'Marvell's Letter to Sir John Trott', *Notes and Queries*, January 1966, pp26–7.
3 L.311–12.
4 Quoted in Grey, *Debates*, Vol. I, p6n.
5 L.57.
6 L.58.
7 Quoted from Add. MSS. 35,865.f.10, 10b by Caroline Robbins, 'A Note on a Hitherto Unprinted Speech by Andrew Marvell', *Modern Languages Review* (1936), p549.
8 Diary of John Milward, p85.
9 *Parliamentary History*, 1667, col. 376–7.
10 Ibid, col. 376–7.
11 L.59.
12 L.59.
13 See Grey, p36; *Parliamentary History*, col. 385; Milward, p116.
14 L.61.
15 L.62.
16 L.63.
17 L.256.
18 Grey, *Debates*, 1668, p70.
19 Milward, p185.
20 Pepys, 17 February 1668, p617.
21 Legouis, 1928, p264n, citing *Arlington's Letters to Sir William Temple* (1701), p226.
22 Milward, p197.
23 L.373n.
24 L.74.
25 L.82.
26 L.68.
27 L.363n.
28 L.67.
29 L.91.
30 L.257.
31 L.258.
32 L.258. I have preferred the reading 'we' to 'he' here.
33 Kelliher, pp85–6.
34 L.87.
35 L.92.

36 L.93.

Chapter 18: Arbitrary Malice

1 L.314.
2 L.96.
3 L.313.
4 L.100.
5 L.104.
6 L.316.
7 L.263.
8 L.265.

Chapter 19: Our Mottly Parliament

1 'Further Advice to a Painter', P.177.
2 L.119.
3 L.113.
4 L.364n cites the brief report in *Grey's Debates* that sheds little further light on the nature of the issue at stake.
5 L.317.
6 L.123.
7 L.319.
8 L.322.
9 L.321.
10 *The Satires of Andrew Marvell* (1892), ed. G.A. Aitken, pp201–3.
11 L.323.
12 L.130.
13 L.130.
14 L.322.
15 L.323.
16 See entry in DNB.
17 P.184–5.
18 Legouis 1965, p143, and Legouis 1928, p271n.
19 See E.E. Duncan-Jones, 'Marvell's "Friend in Persia"', *Notes and Queries*, November 1957, pp466–7.
20 L.326.

Chapter 20: A Gracious Declaration

1 *The Rehearsal*, p73.
2 Quoted by Legouis (1928), p107n, from a letter by the Reverend Robert Banks dated 14 April 1708 in *Letters of eminent men addressed to Ralph Thoresby*,

1832, Vol. II, p102.
3 Halifax, *Complete Works*, ed. J.P. Kenyon (1969), pp255–6.
4 L.328.
5 L.273.
6 L.276.
7 Jonathan Swift, from the 'Apology' to the fifth edition of *A Tale of a Tub* (1710).
8 See entry in DNB.
9 Ibid.
10 Ibid.
11 *The Rehearsal*, p28.
12 Ibid., p182.
13 Burnet, cited in entry on Parker in DNB.
14 Ibid.
15 Wood, Vol. IV p231.
16 These excerpts cited by Smith in his introduction to *The Rehearsal*, p xi.
17 Samuel Parker, *A Discourse . . .* (1670), Preface, pxxv.

Chapter 21: Animadversions

1 *The Rehearsal*, p163.
2 Henry Morley, introduction to *Burlesque Plays and Poems* (1885), p6.
3 Ibid., p80. Also quoted in *The Rehearsal*, introduction, pxii.
4 Sir John Reresby, *Memoirs*, ed. Browning 1936, p84. Also quoted by D.I.B. Smith in his introduction to *The Rehearsal*, to which I am greatly indebted for the background to this controversy.
5 Gilbert Burnet, *History of my Own Time* (ed. Airy, 1897), Vol. I, p555.
6 *Reliquiae Baxterianae*, Part 1, p39.
7 Burnet, *A Supplement to the History of My Own Time* (ed. Foxcroft, 1902), p216.
8 All quotations in this chapter are from *The Rehearsal*, ed. Smith; individual page references, for the most part, are not given.
9 *The Rehearsal*, Part Two, p165.
10 Ibid., p238.
11 Ibid., p107.
12 Ibid., p357n.

Chapter 22: Rosemary and Bays

1 Samuel Parker, *A Reproof to the Rehearsal Transprosed, in a Discourse to its Author by the Author of the Ecclesiastical Politie* (1673), p212.
2 Aubrey, p196.
3 Thompson's evidence for this 'faithfully transcribed' anecdote (pp473–5) is

a letter from the dissenting minister Caleb Fleming written on 5 May 1671 to Thomas Hollis. Fleming claims to have been told the story 'thirty years ago [i.e. fifty-three years after Marvell's death] in the north'. He insisted: 'I am conscious of not having contrived one circumstance.'

4 Wood, cited in DNB entry.
5 Henry Stubbe, *Rosemary & Bayes etc.* (1672), p1.
6 From the papers of Sir Heneage Finch, Attorney-General (167–73) at the Leicestershire Record Office: Finch MSS. Cited in full by Kelliher, p108.
7 Ibid.
8 Cited by Smith, introduction to *The Rehearsal*, pxxiii.
9 Samuel Parker, *A Reproof to the Rehearsal Transprosed* (1673), 'To the Reader'.
10 Ibid., p77.
11 Ibid., p526.
12 *Bishop Parker's History of His Own Time* (1727), trans. Thomas Newlin, p331.
13 Ibid., p334.
14 Richard Leigh, *The Transproser Rehears'd* (1673), p135.
15 *S'Too Him Bayes* (Oxford, 1673), p107.
16 Edmund Hickeringill, *Gregory, Father-Greybeard* (1673), p164.
17 *A Common Place-Book Out of the Rehearsal Transpros'd* (1673), p18.

Chapter 23: A Shoulder of Mutton

1 L.328.
2 Ibid.
3 Ibid.
4 Grosart, pxlix.
5 Grosart, loc. cit.; Thompson, pp460–4; Cooke, pp11–13; Legouis 1928, pp226–7; Legouis 1965, pp120–1; Dove, pp34–7.
6 Thompson, p463.
7 Also cited by Legouis, p227n.
8 See title page to *The Rehearsal Transpros'd: The Second Part* (1673).
9 *The Rehearsal*, p146.
10 *The Rehearsal*, pp159–69.
11 Wood, pp230–1.

Chapter 24: Tinkling Rhyme

1 K.H.D. Haley, *William of Orange and the English Opposition 1672–4* (1953), p52.
2 Ibid., p57, citing Williamson's unpublished journal in the Public Record Office.

3 Cooke, p9. See also L.N. Wall, 'Marvell and the Third Dutch War', *Notes and Queries*, July 1957, pp296–7.
4 Henning, Vol. III, p26.
5 L.282.
6 *The Rehearsal*, p311.
7 *The Poems of John Milton* (ed. Carey and Fowler, 1968), pp456–7.
8 L.283.
9 L.333.
10 L.332.
11 L.334.
12 L.339.
13 L.144.

Chapter 25: The Late Embezzlements

1 *A Dialogue between the Two Horses*, Vol. II, pp159–60.
2 Thompson, Vol. 1, p432.
3 L.144.
4 L.146.
5 L.150.
6 Quoted from CSPD 1678, p85, L.N. Wall, 'Marvell's Friends in the City', *Notes and Queries*, June 1959, pp204–7.
7 L.160.
8 Unpublished letter of John Aubrey (Bodleian MS.), quoted by French, *Life Records of John Milton*, Vol. 5 (1958), p234.
9 L.341.
10 L.166.
11 L.169.
12 L.344.
13 L.391n.
14 Cooke, p10.
15 Thompson, p464.

Chapter 26: Divines in Mode

1 *A Short Historical Essay touching General Councils etc* (1676), Grosart, p134.
2 Burnet, cited in DNB.
3 Wood, cited in DNB.
4 Text used is Grosart, Vol. IV, pp1–162.
5 Grosart, Vol. IV, p11.
6 Ibid., p15.
7 Ibid., p60.
8 Ibid., pp91–162.

9 Ibid., p148.
10 Croft's letter is reproduced in Marvell's letter to Will Popple dated 15 July. L.347.
11 L.344.
12 L.346.
13 Letter quoted in L.394n from *Hatton Correspondence*, I, 128.

Chapter 27: This Sickly Time

1 *Parliamentary History* (1677), Col. 857. Speech by Andrew Marvell.
2 L.287.
3 L.285.
4 L.349.
5 L.287.
6 L.375n.
7 L.176.
8 L.177.
9 L.178.
10 L.179.
11 L.189.
12 *Parliamentary History* (1677), Col. 854–7.
13 Henning, Vol. III, p26.
14 *Parliamentary History* (1677), Col. 858–9.
15 L.356.
16 L.205.
17 L.368n.
18 Legouis 1965, p158, raises what he calls a 'mere conjecture' of some ulterior motive in these visits.
19 L.208.
20 L.209.

Chapter 28: No Popery

1 *An Account of the Growth of Popery, and Arbitrary Government in England* (1677), Grosart, Vol. IV, p250.
2 L.296.
3 L.375n.
4 L.376n.
5 L.296.
6 L.298.
7 L.220.
8 L.221.
9 Ibid.

10 L.226.
11 L.227.
12 Ibid.
13 L.230.
14 L.244.
15 L.357.
16 Cooke, p31.
17 Thompson, p478.
18 All quotations are from Grosart, Vol. IV, pp245–414.
19 Ibid., p252.
20 Ibid., p261.
21 Ibid., p248.
22 *London Gazette,* 21–25 March 1678. The advertisement is reproduced in Kelliher, p113.

Chapter 29: A Death in Bloomsbury

1 Aubrey, p196.
2 William Empson, 'Natural Magic and Populism in Marvell's Poetry', *Andrew Marvell: Essays on the Tercentenary* (1979), ed. R.L. Brett, p48.
3 Elsie Duncan-Jones, 'Marvell: A Great Master of Words', Warton Lecture on English Poetry, *Proceedings of the British Academy,* 61 (1975), p277.
4 William Empson, 'The Marriage of Marvell', *Using Biography* (1984), p80.
5 Ibid., p79.
6 L.245.
7 L.369n, citing Bench Books for 29 July 1678.
8 L.369n.
9 See Legouis 1928, p298.
10 For a detailed account, see L.N. Wall, 'Marvell's Friends in the City', *Notes and Queries,* June 1959, pp204–7.
11 For the fullest account of the business and the role of Mary Palmer, the definitive account, based on an examination of depositions in the Public Record Office, see F.S. Tupper 'Mary Palmer, Alias Mrs Andrew Marvell', *PMLA* (1938), Vol. 53, pp367–92. Tupper's interpretation of events, however, is challenged by William Empson in *Using Biography* (loc. cit.).
12 Tupper, loc. cit., p374.
13 Andrew Clark (ed.), *Wood's Life and Times,* Vol. II, p414.
14 L.376n.

Chapter 30: The Island's Watchful Sentinel

1 Anonymous verses 'On his Excellent Friend Mr Andrew Marvell', from *Poems on Affairs of State,* ed. George deF. Lord (1963), Vol. I, pp436–7.

2 Frank Kermode (ed.), *Andrew Marvell* (1994), Oxford Poetry Library, 'Introduction', p xiv.
3 Grosart, Vol. IV, p168.
4 Ibid., p242.
5 *The Poems of John Dryden*, ed. John Sargeaunt (1948), p98.
6 But see also Denis Davison, 'A Marvell Allusion in Ward's Diary', *Notes and Queries*, January 1955, pp22–3, which quotes a rare allusion to Marvell by a contemporary, the Reverend John Ward, on the Parker controversy.
7 Cooke, Vol. I, Preface.
8 Thompson, Preface, plvi.
9 Charles Lamb, 'The Old Benchers of the Inner Temple', *London Magazine*, September 1821, *The Works*, II, pp83–4.
10 William Hazlitt, *Select Poets of Great Britain* (1825), cited by Elizabeth Story Donno, *Andrew Marvell: The Critical Heritage* (1978), p134.
11 Augustine Birrell, *Andrew Marvell* (1905), p2.

Acknowledgements

I should like to express particular gratitude to the British Library Centre for the Book for the award of the first Gladys Krieble Delmas Fellowship in 1997, which greatly facilitated access to and use of the British Library's collections. The Local Studies Library at Kingston-upon-Hull Central Library has a special collection relating to Marvell, containing some unique items, which was of exceptional value. I am also grateful to staff of the London Library, the Bodleian Library, and Llyfrgell Genedlaethol Cymru (the National Library of Wales). Mrs Pat Dyson of Greenland Farm, Patrington, kindly opened up for me the Parish Church at Winestead-in-Holderness. In writing this book I have found myself repeatedly in debt to the work of a number of twentieth-century Marvell scholars and historians who have greatly added to biographical knowledge about the poet: Pauline Burdon, Elsie Duncan-Jones, Hilton Kelliher, J.P. Kenyon, Pierre Legouis, H.M. Margoliouth, D.I.B. Smith and L.N. Wall are among the most prominent.

Index